THE
KABUL
PEACE
HOUSE

'Told with his trademark empathy, Mark Isaacs cuts through cruel politicising and empty rhetoric to show our common humanity – and a story of individuals at their very best.'

DEBRA ADELAIDE

'As someone who was born in war and grew up in war, I know that peace cannot be achieved without the people of the land. The so-called peace projects of the superpowers have always ignored the people. Mark Isaacs' book focuses on one project established by young people of Afghanistan – a project where young Afghans grow ties across communities as they themselves reach toward peace in their homeland.'

BEHROUZ BOOCHANI

Author of *No Friend but the Mountains: Writing from Manus Prison*, winner of the Victorian Premier's Prize for Literature and Nonfiction and the ABIA General Nonfiction Book of the Year

A portion of the proceeds from this book will be donated to the Edmund Rice Centre's 'Afghan Project' in support of the community in Afghanistan.

THE
KABUL
PEACE
HOUSE

MARK ISAACS

Hardie Grant

BOOKS

Published in 2019 by Hardie Grant Books,
an imprint of Hardie Grant Publishing

Hardie Grant Books (Melbourne)
Building 1, 658 Church Street
Richmond, Victoria 3121

Hardie Grant Books (London)
5th & 6th Floors
52–54 Southwark Street
London SE1 1UN

hardiegrantbooks.com

Copyright text © Mark Isaacs 2019
Excerpt on page 233 from *I Am the Beggar of the World*, translated by Eliza Griswold,
photographs by Seamus Murphy. Text copyright © 2014 Eliza Griswold.
Reprinted with permission of Farrar, Straus and Giroux.
Excerpt on page 234 from *Poetry of the Taliban*, edited by Alex Strick van Linschoten
and Felix Kuehn. Text copyright © 2012 Alex Strick van Linschoten and Felix
Kuehn. Reprinted with permission of Hurst Publishers.

A catalogue record for this
book is available from the
National Library of Australia

The Kabul Peace House
ISBN 978 1 74379 315 2

10 9 8 7 6 5 4 3 2 1

Cover design by Josh Durham, Design by Committee
Typeset in 11/15 pt Minion Pro by Cannon Typesetting
Cover images courtesy of Getty Images/Roberto Schmidt; Wikimedia/Masoud Akbari
Printed by McPherson's Printing Group, Maryborough, Victoria

CONTENTS

FOREWORD

WHAT KIND OF human beings are we becoming, when 65 million people do not have a safe place in their home countries? What kind of a world are we nurturing and accepting? The scale of today's global human tragedy is hard to comprehend and the causes complex, but we must try to come to grips with it: to understand, to tolerate, to empathise, to love.

At the Kabul Peace House, we follow a simple path of love. Without love, we and the universe are but empty atoms. Our community came about in response to forty years of war – both from within and beyond our borders – but it was also forged to bring about change, to foster new ways of thinking, to counter a fear of *otherness*.

The world has fixated on otherness, yet in every cell of ours, we share 99.9 per cent of the same human genome as those different from us: as humans we share a staggering sameness. When we hurt one another, even in the name of defence, we are hurting none other than ourselves. When we enrich and empower ourselves in the name of progress and ignore others, we may make some material gains, but we lose the most powerful force we have as sentient creatures: love.

'What would you like the people of the world to do?' I asked one of the members of our community, Taqi, recently.

'To know one another,' Taqi replied. 'We should reach out to understand each other as members of one family, instead of believing what the media or a few books portray. Does the rest of the world see us as human beings?'

Sadly, governments rely on the narrative that many people are 'bad, ignorant and pugnacious', and should be guided and controlled by elites who are presumably 'good, intelligent and peace-loving'. For too long, people have blindly accepted this black and white assessment. I too used to believe that the policies of our elites were reasonable, like when US President George W Bush launched the war on terror in 2001, triumphantly unloading bombs on an already devastated Afghanistan. The reality is that terrorism has increased five-fold since that time and is now worldwide.

What I saw unfold around me in Afghanistan shook my beliefs, including my philosophical or spiritual beliefs, and more importantly, my way of reasoning and feeling. I could no longer ignore my blind spots.

I faced the ugly possibility that many of us are unknowing accomplices in the promotion of terrorism, either as left or right or centrist supporters, or as Christian, Muslim or other dogmatic believers. We have watched on as local and foreign governments made life untenable in Afghanistan. Corporations and despots finance the elites, wrecking the earth with minimal account-ability. The masses accept the status quo because current systems allow us to chase the very same things the elite are fighting over: money and power. We become them, the people we detest. The violence and inequality persist.

Unless, like at the Kabul Peace House, we begin wondering if we have been misled. Unless we learn how to question everything. To sceptics who may doubt us, come and live in Afghanistan. Perhaps only then will you know or believe that we all deserve to live in peace, with love, on a healthy planet.

Our community dreams that, without being intrusive, technology can be used compassionately to connect us with the seven billion other human beings on earth, and with our natural environment, if only to acknowledge their presence and to wish them well.

We sound idealistic? No, we refuse to believe that love is idealistic. Relationships are revolutionary and love their most powerful energy.

War separates us, often forever. And so too does migration, which is a fraught move for those who consider it. The prospects for a safe and secure migration, to a future with work, security and a semblance of welcome, have never been less assured. For Afghans now, is their fate better here or there – or anywhere? Becoming refugees or asylum seekers may yet be the lonely outcome for some of our community.

'Insaan' in Dari means 'human'. I chose it as my pseudonym because that's who I am and what I am – that's who we all are. I like to believe we can evolve from *Homo sapiens* to *Homo relationis*: beings who are *connected* to each other. Taqi is wise: in order to know ourselves, we need to know others. In that future place of peace and connection we may be able to stand in solidarity with you and feel free enough and safe enough to tell you our real names.

With love,
Insaan

Kabul 2019

INTRODUCTION

THE GENESIS OF this book was a trip I made to Afghanistan in 2016 as part of a small team of volunteer researchers, sent by the Edmund Rice Centre (ERC) to report on the safety of rejected asylum seekers returned to the country by the Australian government. The ERC works in research, education programs, advocacy and direct service, primarily with indigenous people, with refugees and asylum seekers, and with people from the Pacific struggling with climate change.

Since 2002 the ERC has been documenting the fate of rejected asylum seekers returned to their countries of origin by the Australian government.

A portion of the proceeds from this book will be donated to the ERC's 'Afghan Project' in support of the community in Afghanistan.[1]

As part of the preparations, I was excited but slightly anxious to be told, 'You'll be going in the winter, which is safer. The fighting usually stops because of the snow.' News reports suggested attacks in Kabul were on the rise and kidnapping of Westerners was a serious threat.

As part of our assignment we spent time with a group of volunteers, a multi-ethnic community living in a share house, creators of a peace park, a community centre and progressive community projects. At its heart is a manifesto, a group of young people and their mentor – somehow, I had stumbled upon a peace movement in Afghanistan.

In answer to what can seem like never-ending violence in Afghanistan, the group formed to bring about change, to try to achieve peace where so many others had failed. Their ideology of equality, their compelling personal stories and the practical steps the group are making prompted me to make a second trip in 2017, to document how they have lived with war but have become a viable movement for peace.

AUTHOR'S NOTE

I T IS IMPORTANT to understand that in a country as complex as Afghanistan it is impossible to accurately reflect the plethora of different views, experiences, opinions and histories of the country and its people. This is the story of the community, based on their experiences of Afghanistan.

This is a fully authorised work of creative nonfiction, based on hours of interviews and transcripts. While all the stories in this book are true, not surprisingly, names of individuals, places and identifying details have been changed to maintain the anonymity of the people involved. I refer to the group – the collective, if you will – as 'the community' throughout.

The risks the members face from full transparency are many. There are internal risks from within the community, and risks from members of wider society who may have unfounded suspicions about their philosophy. One of their greatest threats, particularly for women, comes from conservative members of their own families. Having a foreigner publish their story increases the danger and opens them up to being criticised for being influenced or manipulated by Western ideology.

After much discussion, the community confirmed their commitment to the project. 'We want you to tell our story. We are scared, but we are also excited because we feel that our story is important. It's affirming to know that we have done some good in the world and we hope the group can be an example to the rest of the world.'

To tell a story such as this, in a country as volatile as Afghanistan, is a courageous act. Speaking out – suggesting an alternative way – embodies the philosophy of nonviolence. This book is a nonviolent attempt to negotiate an end to the violence of war. Despite the risk of retribution, armed with a pen, the community are continuing their struggle for peace. I'm fortunate to be their messenger.

We are a land whose people are its greatest treasure.
We are at the edges of empires at war with each other.
We are a fractured land in the claws of the Hindu Kush mountains,
scorched by the fiery eyes of the northern desert.
Black rubble earth against ice peaks –
we are Ariana, the land of the noble.

– The Breadwinner
(from the animated film adaptation of Deborah Ellis' novel of the same name)

PROLOGUE

Stumbling Upon a
Peace Movement

The plane skimmed over the snowy peaks of the Hindu Kush before the mountains dropped away to a dusty, flat plain on which the sparse infrastructure of Kabul was sprinkled. The vast expanse of arid land met the base of the mountain range like a poorly laid brown carpet that crawled up the wall instead of edging neatly against it.

In the weeks prior to our departure, my colleague Martin Reusch bombarded me with articles about the current situation in Afghanistan. Despite fifteen years of foreign occupation by US and NATO–led forces, Afghanistan remained a violent and unstable country. A UN report released in February 2016 stated that more civilians had been killed in 2015 than in any of the previous fifteen years.[1] The Afghan government and military were unreliable and depended on foreign finances and support; the Taliban movement was increasing in power and influence; warlords in various provinces were gathering forces; a branch of the militant Islamic State of Iraq and the Levant (commonly referred to as ISIL, ISIS, the Islamic State, and the Arabic acronym, Daesh) had established itself in the country; and neighbouring nations such as Pakistan, India, Iran, Saudi Arabia and China continued to play influential roles in the country's future. Most commentators I read felt certain that Afghanistan and its citizens still had many hard years ahead of them.

When the plane touched down in Kabul, it felt like I had crossed a frontier of safety and comfort. Any fears I harboured were overwhelmed by the fascination of being in a country that could be described as an epicentre of world politics.

The history of Afghanistan is one of invasion and occupation. Its geopolitical position, wedged between empires stretched across the Eurasian steppe, made it a place of great political importance. Control of Afghanistan had passed between great civilisations: Persian empires, Turkic nomadic empires, the Greeks and Alexander the Great, the Arabs and the Mongols, and the British. When Afghanistan was not being invaded by foreign forces, the country remained politically divided. Afghanistan had welcomed traders on the Silk Road, passing from east to west and west to east; it was a region where the ancient religions of Buddhism, Zoroastrianism, Manichaeism, and, later, Islam found their feet. It had been a centre of arts and culture, of poetry, agriculture and architecture, all of which had been destroyed and rebuilt time and time again. When the Soviet Union and the United States became involved in Afghanistan, they were just the next formidable empires to try to use the nation for strategic influence. Both their disastrous invasions were pivotal moments in the history of the superpowers and of the world. Despite captivating the world's attention for so many centuries, it seemed Afghanistan was still an enigma to those who wanted to control it.[2]

Martin and I were met at the airport by Muslimyor, an Afghan teenager. He wore a grey blazer over a T-shirt, and his hair was neatly combed with some rugged-on-purpose messiness at the back. He hugged me and kissed me on the cheek in greeting and offered to carry my luggage to the taxi.

Our accommodation for the first few days would be a communal home shared by young adults. Muslimyor was a member of this community. Martin had not elaborated on who these people were or why they lived together; however, I understood that for a conservative country like Afghanistan, where it was against culture and tradition to live with people other than family, this was an unusual arrangement. Add two international guests to the equation and it was potentially dangerous.

The taxi took the ring road around Kabul, bypassing the centre of the city and the main security zone called the 'Ring of Steel', which consisted of twenty-five Afghan National Police checkpoints that protected the international embassies, the government ministries and the city centre. A cavalcade of soldiers nursing large guns thundered past; one, two, three, four trucks, and then I lost count. I was half mesmerised, half fearful. I'd never seen such an intimidating display of military power. The streets were, for the most part, well paved and free of debris. There were few buildings taller than three storeys in the low-rise outskirts of Kabul. Many of the buildings were new or were being built.

'I was expecting more buildings,' I remarked.

'I was expecting fewer,' Martin said. 'Just a few years ago the city was reduced to rubble.'

For all the action on the street, my eyes were drawn to the sky, which was a spectacular blue.

Our taxi stopped outside an unnumbered house on a dirt road. A rickety steel gate protected a dusty yard, inside of which a sorry-looking swing hung off one rope attached to a rusted frame, alongside leafless trees. On the corner of the street there was a hut full of Afghan soldiers in army fatigues shouldering rifles. Children in scruffy shoes played football and cricket in alleyways; bearded men in traditional Afghan attire – long, loose shirts and baggy pants, embellished with a waistcoat, scarf or turban – sat on street corners chatting to each other; young women wearing colourful headscarves held hands as they walked down the street. The white Hindu Kush mountains sparkled in the daylight, the air pollution not yet creating haze. Muslimyor apologised for the smog and explained that many people didn't have money for firewood in Kabul, so they burned plastic instead.

'Sometimes the pollution can be so bad you can't see more than twenty metres in front of you,' he said.

He spoke some English, which was a relief for me as I did not speak any of the numerous languages spoken in Afghanistan and was relying on Martin's interpreting skills to communicate. Afghanistan has two official languages: Pashto, spoken by Pashtuns, living in the south and east of the country; and Dari, spoken by most of the other ethnic groups. However, each ethnic group has their own dialect or language. Martin spoke Farsi, the language of Iran, and broadly synonymous with Dari.[3]

We were met at the front door by Insaan. He was wearing a blue flannelette shirt over a maroon cardigan, plain blue pants and characterless shoes. His wide, bunched-up smile and hearty laugh were instantly welcoming.

'Welcome, welcome,' he said, and ushered us inside.

We entered a cold, dusty vestibule. Directly ahead of us, through the cloudy glass panes of a door, I could see a sparse garden and a makeshift greenhouse. Insaan showed us a cramped squat toilet to the left of the garage. We took off our shoes, added them to a disorganised pile of assorted footwear and changed into slippers. Then Insaan led us to the right, into a small antechamber that connected the kitchen, a bedroom, a bathroom, and what my mother would call a 'family room'.

This room was clearly the centre of the household's activity. At one end there was a small bookshelf of writings on social justice and nonviolence; at the other, there was a plastic chair and a small school desk on which school books rested. Posters of snowy mountain ranges and green valleys plastered the walls. In the middle of the room there was a metal stove called a *bukhari,* in which wood was being burned to heat the house; smoke funnelled from the house via a pipe. Mattresses, duvets and cushions were rolled up and stacked in the corners of the room. A wall of windows lit the space. During the day, the community of young people socialised, ate meals and drank tea in this space, but in the evenings, the bedding was prepared and the room became a dormitory for the community members. Insaan called this humble dwelling the Peace House.

Martin and I joined the community members at a plastic mat on the floor for a simple meal of tea, thick bread and kidney-bean broth. The stove crackled and popped, warming the otherwise icy room. I was introduced to the other teenagers in the house. Horse had dark, weather-worn skin. He wore shorts over trackpants and a Barcelona football jersey. Hafizullah had a broad face with big cheeks, and a gravelly voice. He cracked his neck by moving it side to side, a little tic. Rosy-cheeked Asghar had nervous mannerisms. He had an unsteady, high-pitched laugh and he stole glances at me out of the corner of his eyes. Nadir, on the other hand, was silent, disengaged to the point of indifference. They were all very attentive to my needs as a guest, ensuring I always had a full glass of tea, not commenting on my obvious discomfort with sitting on the floor for an extended time, and allowing me to eat more than my share of the food.

After the meal, Hafizullah swept up the crumbs on the dinner mat with a rectangular piece of foam and then folded the mat away. Then the young men either curled up on cushions to do their homework or retired to the other room; every so often, an eruption of giggles could be heard. Martin and I lounged on large red cushions on the carpeted floor. The kettle was kept bubbling on the stove so we could drink tea and we were offered mandarins as dessert.

'Yesterday we had our monthly Skype conversation, in which we speak with people from different parts of the world,' Insaan said. 'A young student from the States asked the community a question: "Is it possible there will be a tangible world in which people will not be judged by where they are born?" All the community members in the room answered, "Yes." I use that anecdote to describe the community because most of their peers would say, "This is not possible."'

Insaan's voice resonated in the small room, swelling to embellish a point and dropping to a whisper during more serious moments. His face was expressive, almost like a caricature: bright and merry at one moment, but quick to turn into a frown if his mind swung to darker, more painful thoughts.

'We first came together in a unique way, to live intentionally across ethnic groups for the practice of nonviolence,' Insaan said. From the beginning, we have faced problems from Afghanistan's conservative society. But, again and again, I have found that human beings are much more resilient than we imagine ourselves to be, though we never know this until we are almost breaking down.

'After forty years of war, most of the Afghan people have never lived peace,' Insaan said. 'They haven't got any transactions of peace in their culture anymore because of this never-ending war. The social fabric of the country has been destroyed; culture and traditions have been destroyed. The infrastructure, the education system, law and order – everything has been destroyed. So, it makes it even more extraordinary that a group of young people can say: "We don't care, we're going to give it a try." Working for peace is one of the biggest concepts the community could tackle. But it's the only one that matters because the fighting won't stop until someone says *enough*.'

'Do you think these goals of yours are unrealistic?' I asked Insaan.

'No, I don't think the desire for peace is unrealistic,' he replied. 'I'll tell you what is unrealistic: the idea that fighting wars will achieve peace; the idea that building militaries and stockpiling nuclear weapons will make us safer. No, I think we are the realists. We believe you can only reconcile with the Taliban if you see the Taliban as fellow human beings who have had legitimate grievances, who have basic human needs which must be met. We believe the Taliban need to be loved and perhaps then they will not want to fight with us.'

I went to bed that night, on my mat on the floor, listening to the snores of Martin and the community members. I couldn't stop thinking of what these people were trying to achieve. My first reaction had been to admire their ambitious endeavour, and yet the more I thought about the impossibility of what they faced the more I doubted them. After all, what could these few young people dare to achieve in a country as hopeless as Afghanistan?

IN THE MORNING, the mattresses were rolled up, and bedding folded and placed to one side. Hafizullah laid down a plastic mat, and breakfast was served: fresh bread from the bakery with jam and tea. I could see the dry, leaf-covered garden outside, enclosed by a high wall. Dead-looking plants, bare trees and a block of melting ice and snow in the corner showed that winter was almost over. Plants in pots, tyres, and garden beds that had died off over winter looked ready to thrive again with the coming spring.

After breakfast, Insaan invited Martin and I to visit the group's community centre.

'The mission of our group is to build a critical mass of nonviolent relationships and practices for a green, equal and nonviolent world without war,' Insaan said. 'The youth have arranged a diverse program of activities and projects based on these three themes. The Community Centre is a safe space where the community members can work together, interact, become friends, hold meetings and take action in teams. We don't want to draw any unwanted attention to the group and our activities.'

It was only a short walk to the centre, but Insaan preferred me to wear long sleeves and a scarf so I would blend in more with the locals. He was worried that I looked too Western in jeans and a T-shirt. Interestingly, my red hair and white skin weren't the issue. According to Martin, I looked Nuristani, an ethnicity from eastern Afghanistan. He repeated the joke often to anyone who would listen.

'Don't spend too much time on the street,' Insaan said, frowning at me despite my change of clothes. 'And don't take too many photos, especially don't take any of women or of the military.'

Our route took us past a group of young men playing cricket in the street on our left and a military checkpoint on our right, and we crossed a busy road shared by cars, taxis, motorbikes and wooden rickshaws. A group of men sat on a street corner playing *carrom*, a board game involving flicking small discs into holes.

We turned onto a quiet, tree-lined street; the gravel surface crumbled into putrid gutters. The houses on the street varied in condition. Some were freshly painted, proud boxes that represented wealthy and fortunate families; others desperately needed repairs. Shards of glass and barbed wire topped the walls to prevent intruders.

Insaan approached the graffitied front wall of one cracked and unpainted building. In front of this a small sliver of dirt, littered with rubbish, separated the unnumbered building from the street. The face of the building was just as shabby, with its clouded glass windows and cluttered balcony. Insaan pushed open the yellow metal gate and motioned me to enter.

Inside the yard, young men and women were talking with each other. On the right, a wall bordered the property and its garden, with a painted mural of a mountain and a river, similar to the posters in the Peace House. On the left was the community centre building, which was also decorated with art. A picture of a child balancing bricks on their head was crossed out by red paint and 'enough' was written on the child's chest. It seemed to be a comment on child labour. There was another painting of an Afghan girl carrying two buckets of water. The bucket on her left had three words written in it: peace, nonviolence, love. The one on her right had another three words written: green, equal and nonviolent.

A large patio edged the back of the Community Centre, overlooking the yard. The garden at the back of the compound lacked vegetation and looked like it had suffered through the winter. It appeared to be one large experiment, littered with tossed-up dirt, limp plants, assembled tyres and a greenhouse. There was a DIY solar water heater.

The moment I walked into the compound, young people greeted me with enthusiasm. The young men shook my hand vigorously and kissed me on the cheek. The women bowed their heads respectfully and I placed my hand on my heart in greeting. I was struck by how different they all looked: a mixture of ethnicities and races created by thousands of years of migration, warfare and blended communities. There were people with green eyes and dark hair, red hair and brown eyes, there were dark-skinned and white-skinned people, some who looked Chinese and some who looked Turkish.

There are four major ethnic groups in Afghanistan, traditionally divided geographically by the Hindu Kush mountain range, which cuts the country in half from north-east to west. The Pashtuns, who make up roughly 40 per cent of the population, are concentrated in the southern and eastern parts of Afghanistan. The second largest ethnic group are the Tajiks, generally located in the north-east, north and west. The Hazaras are mainly settled in the central and southern highlands and the fourth largest ethnic group, the Uzbeks, are in the north. Pashtuns, Tajiks and Uzbeks are largely Sunni Muslims, while Hazaras are predominantly Shia. There are many other ethnic groups including Nuristanis, Aimaks, Turkmens, Brahuis and Baluchs. Traditionally, the Pashtun majority has controlled the country's politics. However, since the Soviet invasion in 1979, continuing war in Afghanistan has vastly changed the balance of power among the ethnic groups.[4]

'Our community strives for diversity,' Insaan said. 'The diversity of our members must reflect the diversity of society, so every type of person is represented. But this is challenging in Afghanistan. Decades of war have established division and suspicion between ethnic groups. One of the first steps to peace needs to be ethnic cooperation.'

While there was diversity in the community, I could also feel the pull of fitting in with their peers for these young people. The men were all acutely aware of their fashion. Their hair was perfectly styled, short on the back and sides, combed over and fixed with hair product. Any loose strands of hair were casually flicked out of their eyes with a hand or a head toss. More than a few of them sported tight pants and leather jackets. The women were dressed conservatively in loose-fitting clothes that would not reveal any skin, their hair covered in headscarves of varying quality and print, from black to lavender, floral to paisley.

We took off our shoes and left them at the front door with a pile of other shoes before entering the centre. We made our way to a large room full of teenagers sitting on the floor in front of two elderly Americans who were holding a meditation and breathing exercise. The students swivelled to stare at me. Some wouldn't look away until I stared back at them and then they dropped their eyes to the floor. The young male students gathered at the back, while the young women sat closely together at the front, adopting an ingrained gender segregation.

During a break in the session I took the opportunity to speak with a few of the group. Malvina was an enthusiastic sixteen-year-old student, who learned about the community through a friend and had been a member for four years. She joined the group because she cared about women's rights but after becoming familiar with the organisation she began to participate in the classes and learn about unfamiliar concepts such as nonviolence. She joined the permaculture class because she was interested in solving Afghanistan's pollution issues; she wanted to teach others what she learned. She was currently studying English and Pashto with the community. She wanted to study at university, but she couldn't decide between psychology or journalism.

'There is a hope growing in my heart for the future of Afghanistan,' she said.

'And how are you going to play a part?' I asked.

'We should start from ourselves and then go to family and then to the community and then to society and then all the world.'

I was amazed by Malvina's drive and maturity at such a young age. But I soon learned that her attitude was not unique in this group of students: most of the young volunteers were at university, many studying psychology, archaeology, law, journalism and graphic design. I was not sure why I was surprised by this; I guess I thought that universities wouldn't function while the country was in turmoil. If these students were the next generation of Afghanistan, perhaps the future was not so bleak.

We left the meditation session to go upstairs and see the rest of the centre. There were six rooms upstairs: one toilet, two classrooms, an office, a library, and a room for the centre's resident security guard and his toddler son.

Everyone in the community was a volunteer. New volunteers were recruited through word of mouth recommendations amongst friends and family of existing members, slowly spreading awareness and making contacts from their central group. They attracted new members through their events and activities and communicated amongst themselves and mobilised volunteers for events via phone calls and social media.

Insaan opened the door to one of the rooms, interrupting the chatter of a group of women sewing jackets and coats. He apologised, before closing the door.

'That's our tailoring collective, who are currently sewing coats for the street kids who attend our school.'

In the next room we found a group of teenagers and university students engaging in lively discussion.

'This is Team EarthGEN,' Insaan said. 'The team evolved out of learning circles we organised for new volunteers to learn about the three crises: climate change, inequality and war. The volunteers started to describe themselves as the generation that doesn't want any of these things anymore. They are the Earth generation.'

A young woman, who was clearly a nervous public speaker, softly addressed the group from behind her shawl. Her hands twitched, and she spoke quickly to try and cover up her trembling voice. But when she realised she wasn't being listened to she became indignant and stared at the transgressors with a jutted jaw.

'They work through relational learning circles in Kabul to educate other young Afghans in the practice of nonviolence and to connect with other groups in other countries,' Insaan said. 'Their aim is to build a critical mass of relationships. This is the very slow person-to-person work of changing minds about war.'

It was hard for me to grasp exactly what I was witnessing. After all the warnings of terrorism and warfare, bombings and kidnappings, somehow there existed a community of young people fighting back against the attrition of a nation, a community that was fuelled by an optimistic energy. Even so, the goal of achieving a green, equal and nonviolent world seemed overly ambitious to me. I asked Insaan why they didn't focus on one of the three goals.

'People in the developed world with no knowledge of Afghanistan think that the reason the country is in trouble is because of terrorism or the Taliban or the Islamic State,' Insaan said. 'But this impression is simplistic. In Afghanistan you will see millions of people suffering because of an international intervention in the name of bringing peace, prosperity and liberty to the country. You will see that war perpetuates poverty. You will see war perpetuates agricultural destruction. In the developed world, people don't feel responsible for global wealth inequality, but in Afghanistan you will see that inequality, warfare and environmental destruction are intrinsically linked to the actions of wealthy countries. Every issue is related to another. We can't address one area without addressing the others.'

A FEW DAYS later, Martin and I relocated to a guesthouse in the city centre. The architecture on the cross-town drive was a museum of warfare and invasion. We passed favela-like hillsides of boxed mudbrick houses, Soviet silos and barbed wire military compounds; roundabouts that moved in any and every direction; and eventually reached the 'Ring of Steel' checkpoints manned by police in army fatigues holding AK-47s. High above the Hindu Kush mountains hovered a white blimp.

'Government eyes looking down upon the citizens of Kabul,' Martin said.

The blimps, called aerostats, were US military surveillance balloons that had been monitoring Kabul day and night since they were introduced to Afghanistan in 2007.[5]

Tall buildings began to emerge and the streets became busier, full of beeping Toyota Corollas. It was rumoured that Osama bin Laden once donated 1000 Corollas to the Afghan people. Every so often we saw military leaders drive through the streets in armoured cars with entourages of militia. Ahmad Shah Massoud's face was plastered on billboards all over the city. The Tajik warlord from the Panjshir Valley, known as the Lion of Panjshir, was one of the most infamous commanders of the Northern Alliance. He was declared a national hero after he was assassinated on 9 September 2001 by two al-Qaeda suicide bombers disguised as Tunisian cameramen.[6] It was rumoured the assassination was arranged by bin Laden to secure his protection by the Taliban.

Police in a pillbox guarded a rusty boom gate at the entrance to our street. Martin said that the security was tightened after the Indian con-sulate was bombed in 2008 and in 2009, killing and wounding more than one hundred people in the two attacks.[7] We were staying in a comfortable guesthouse, thankful to have electricity after the intermittent connection encountered elsewhere. In the previous few weeks, Kabul's power grid had been crippled by conflict in Baghlan province in the north-east of the country. With 60 per cent of the power to the city cut, citizens, local businesses and government departments suffered.[8] At the best of times, Afghanistan had one of the lowest rates of electricity usage in the world, with only about 38 per cent of its population connected to the grid.[9]

During the next few weeks, we moved about the city with a surprising amount of freedom. We walked the streets unencumbered by security entourages, hailing taxis off the street when we needed. Some called this approach to travelling around Kabul risky and unwise, but I was following Martin's better judgement. He'd visited Afghanistan almost every year since 2004 and was my modern-day dragoman, a guide and interpreter who arranged our schedule and interviews.[10]

Six days after we arrived in Kabul, on 28 February 2016, a suicide bomber killed twelve people in front of the defence ministry building in central Kabul, just a kilometre or two from where we were staying.[11] I jumped online to assure my loved ones I was safe and unhurt, but no-one had even heard of it. As far as the rest of the world was concerned, it was just another bomb.

When we walked the streets, we didn't see any foreigners. Men sat in the main squares waiting for work. A young man and a woman walked past us holding hands, causing Martin to raise his eyebrows. Street kids followed us, relentlessly demanding money. In a park, children played cricket alongside drug addicts who smoked pipes amongst the rubbish. We squeezed into an antiques and rug shop and drank tea with a man named Jaffar.

'There is no business. Everyone wants to go to Germany. My son, he is sixteen, he tells me he wants to go.' Jaffar mimes a smack and laughs. 'We only go together. As a family.'

Near Jaffar's shop was Chicken Street: a block of shops selling antiques, handicrafts, jewellery and precious stones. There was a sense of desperation in the air as we passed through. We were the only ones browsing. Less than two years later, in January 2018, that street was bombed by Taliban operatives, killing 95 people.[12]

Talk of leaving Afghanistan was on everyone's lips. A Pashtun friend of Martin's found his children playing a game in his living room.

'What are you doing?' he asked them.

'We are immigrating,' his ten-year-old daughter said.

'Where are you going?' he asked.

'I think to Australia,' she replied.

Then, his other daughter, who was five years old, said: 'Not Australia. It is too far. Let's go to Canada.'

Every taxi driver we spoke to mentioned the insecurity. Babur was a twenty-nine-year-old photojournalist living in Kabul. After four o'clock, he worked as a taxi driver to supplement his income and support his wife and child.

'When we go to the office or to work, we don't know if we will return home to our loved ones,' Babur said.

Most of Babur's relatives fled Afghanistan during the Taliban regime and they now lived abroad in Australia, Germany, the United States and Canada. They were the lucky few to be resettled from Pakistan by the UNHCR. He wanted to join them, but he didn't think it would be possible. Nobody was accepting Afghan refugees anymore.

Martin and I spent the next weeks speaking with experts from different NGOs about the security situation in Afghanistan. Within the embassy district, we passed what looked like maximum security prisons: thick blast walls, hurricane wire fences, armed soldiers with face masks. These were the international NGO compounds, the embassies, the government ministries, the expat hotels. The international embassy and NGO staff worked from within compounds, which they weren't allowed to leave because of targeted kidnappings and murders of foreigners, including journalists. Most foreign workers were escorted from the airport to their compound and to the airport again. We waited outside the UNHCR compound for ten minutes for security to let us in; soldiers with rocket launchers, guns and grenades stood beside us and I started feeling uneasy. A man holding a briefcase passed by and I found myself wondering if it was a bomb; I was starting to see how this anxiety could affect a person's daily life.

When the number of people fleeing to Europe surged in 2014 due to the conflict in Syria, many European governments claimed they were being overwhelmed by refugees. They called it a 'migrant crisis'. Many European governments, and the Australian government, deemed it possible to deport rejected asylum seekers to Afghanistan safely. Through our discussions and investigations, it very quickly became obvious that it would be impossible for any government to guarantee the safety of people deported to Afghanistan.

Afghanistan was beset with problems. It had been at war since 1979, when the Soviet Union invaded and occupied the nation. When the Soviet troops withdrew a decade later, the tribal warlords and militia who opposed them turned on one another and engaged in civil war. Out of this turmoil emerged the Taliban, who ruled the country until 2001, when the United States and NATO invaded. Fifteen years later, there was widespread, intensifying violence in thirty-one of Afghanistan's thirty-four provinces, which was causing mass displacement of the population; the Taliban controlled or influenced more than a third of the country (the strongest they had been since 2001); and a branch of the Islamic State known as the Islamic State Khorasan Province (IS-KP) had established itself in the country and increased its influence in numerous provinces.[13] In 2015, the year before our visit, there were 249 significant attacks in Kabul, a supposed 'safe zone'.[14]

The political and economic situation of the country was unstable and heavily reliant on international support, which was waning. Since 2005 foreign aid had averaged 76 per cent of the country's GDP.[15] The 'intervention' economy was centred around the military presence of the international coalition, and the international organisations and humanitarian organisations that invested money in the country. However, the deterioration of the security situation had hampered international development and relief agencies from fulfilling their project obligations. The perception that Afghanistan was in a never-ending state of war, combined with NGOs relocating their efforts to the new conflict in Syria, was diverting humanitarian funds away from Afghanistan. With the international community scaling down operations in the country, the experts we interviewed were worried the country's economy was failing further.[16]

The National Unity Government of Afghanistan (NUG) had been a fragile political arrangement ever since its controversial and unconstitutional formation. When the validity of the 2014 Afghan presidential election was challenged by accusations of fraud, the former US Secretary of State John Kerry brokered a power-sharing deal and created the NUG. Ashraf Ghani became president, while runner-up Abdullah Abdullah was appointed as the Chief Executive Officer of the government, with powers similar to those of prime minister. The CEO position was not in the constitution but had been deemed a necessary creation to ensure political stability.[17]

However, the deal was seen as a major setback in Afghanistan's democratic transition. The power-sharing agreement had failed, with inaction and division rendering the government ineffective over time.[18] The government didn't deliver basic services to citizens across the country with hospitals, schools and basic amenities losing funding, and it hadn't made significant gains in achieving human rights reforms because it had been unable to restrain abusive militias, reduce corruption, improve good governance, promote women's rights and reform the judicial system.[19] Afghan citizens rated the judiciary as the most corrupt institution in the country, and in 2016 Afghanistan ranked 169 out of 176 countries in Transparency International's Corruption Perceptions Index.[20]

The Afghan people had lost confidence in their government and were losing hope that peace and stability could be restored in their country. The possible collapse of the government would lead to further conflict and potentially another period of divided warlord rule. The people lived in a state of uncertainty, waiting for society to fall apart. All this was leading to people leaving the country in their hundreds of thousands.

These were grim findings and I couldn't help but think of Insaan and the community and their ambition for a peaceful Afghanistan. The group had made a powerful impression on me. I asked Martin what he first made of them when he met them in 2010.

'I thought they were all dreamers. They wanted something which was so unrealistic, which would never be. They were thinking of nonviolence? In Afghanistan? Absolutely impossible. I still think that to a certain extent. But they have proved me wrong. Not only are they still around after so many years, they are growing. If you want to change something, you have to try different methods. Afghanistan has used violence for such a long time, why not try nonviolence?'

I could easily have dismissed these people as dreamers, like Martin did all those years ago, but that would have been too easy, too pessimistic. I wanted to believe they were creating something special in the most unlikely of places. I wanted to believe they were rebuilding hope among those who had long forsaken it.

Part 1

LOVE IS HOW WE WILL
ASK FOR PEACE

Don't say what is the use
Of me alone being peaceful
When everyone is fighting.
You're not one
You're a thousand
Just light your lantern.

– Rumi

Chapter 1

Genesis in the Mountains

I lined up at immigration in the Hamid Karzai Airport in Kabul, alongside Afghans in suits, burqas and traditional robes, feeling very conspicuous. The small number of foreigners present were most likely on diplomatic business. Insaan and Muslimyor had arranged to meet me at the airport, but I was nervous in case the plan fell through; I didn't feel confident taking a taxi across Kabul by myself and without any language skills. The long walk out of the airport, past numerous security checkpoints, was made to feel even longer due to my anxiety. I reached the crowd at the last gate, conscious of the looks I was receiving, trying to remain calm. The mob spread to allow me through and in the gap appeared Insaan's smiling face. Relief swept through me.

It had been a year since I was last in Afghanistan and in that time the violence had intensified further still. On 19 April 2016, a Taliban bomb blast near government offices in Kabul killed thirty people and wounded 327.[1] On 25 May, eleven people were killed when a Taliban suicide bomber targeted rush-hour traffic in Kabul, including a bus full of judiciary department employees.[2] A twin bombing on 23 July targeted thousands of Hazaras who were peacefully protesting a discriminatory political decision to divert a new electricity supply line away from their provinces in the central region. Over eighty people were killed and more than 230 were injured in the attack.[3]

In April 2016, armed men in military-style uniforms abducted Kerry Wilson, an Australian aid worker, in Jalalabad.[4] In June 2016, an Indian aid worker, Judith D'Souza, was snatched in Kabul.[5] Two months later, academics at the American University of Afghanistan, American Kevin King and Australian Timothy Weeks, were kidnapped.[6] Wilson was released four months after her capture, and D'Souza was rescued one month after being taken. King and Weeks are yet to be released.[7]

With this in mind, Martin advised that I should travel in February, before the spring offensive normally started – one of the blessings of Afghanistan was the arrival of winter snows, which impeded military operations.

Returning to the Peace House felt like coming home in a strange way: my safe haven in an unpredictable country. When I arrived, Horse was playing an instrument called a *dambura*, which looked like a squashed guitar, and he sang with a breaking, adolescent voice. Muslimyor was studying at a desk, headphones in, singing along quietly to a tune from the Disney movie *Frozen*. Hafizullah sat on the cushions reading a book about Gandhi. Nadir had left the community and returned to the mountains, and Asghar was studying abroad in Mongolia. The house felt quieter and slightly empty without them. I sensed hurt in Insaan's forced smile.

That evening we gathered at the Community Centre. We were joined by a young woman Insaan introduced to me as Hojar, one of the two community managers, the only paid roles in the entire community.

'Hojar pioneered the female live-in community,' Insaan said.

Hojar bent her head in greeting. Her resting expression was solemn, but her face softened and brightened the moment Insaan introduced us. When she spoke English, she screwed up her face in concentration.

'The first time I met Insaan was the first time I heard the word peace,' she said. 'But I didn't understand what it meant. Through Insaan I learned about Martin Luther King Jr, Gandhi, Mother Teresa and others who talked about peace, and that motivated me to believe it was possible.'

We knelt on the floor, warming ourselves by the *bukhari*, drinking tea and eating a dinner of black tomatoes, rice and bread. All the young volunteers present were Hazaras, the third largest ethnic group in Afghanistan and a historically persecuted group. When the British Empire first invaded Afghanistan in the 19th century, the British supported the Pashtun King Amir Abdur Rahman Khan, who ruthlessly suppressed the Hazara, Tajik and Uzbek tribes of northern Afghanistan. When the independent Hazara tribes revolted against

King Abdur in the late 19th century, he waged war against them, killing thousands, destroying their villages, confiscating land, displacing entire populations and enslaving thousands of survivors. Since then, the Hazara ethnic group have continued to endure discriminatory government policies.[8]

'I'd like to know what this community means to you,' I asked the young volunteers.

Their English skills were limited, so Insaan translated where necessary.

'The community is about working with people from other countries and ethnicities, and learning that we are all human,' Muslimyor said.

'Living and working with the community can be very hard. We have faced many challenges, but we are family,' Hafizullah said.

'Working with community has allowed me to pursue my own goals and dreams. If I lived at home in the rural areas I must fulfil the duties of a woman. I must get married and remain in the house,' Hojar said.

Horse enjoyed the centre as a safe space where he could socialise with his friends without trouble. 'With the community I can laugh and enjoy life.'

Horse described an excursion the group went on, to a park and a river. The boys played football, the girls sat around talking, some of them played in the river. They cooked chicken wings on a barbecue.

'We were so comfortable with one another. It seemed that for those few hours we were together, we were there as friends and we could leave behind the worries of war. I didn't have to think about school or my family problems. I was just there to be with friends,' Horse said.

Horse explained that feeling uncomfortable in social situations was normal in Afghanistan. It was brave of the women to willingly sit in a public place with young men and face the judgement of passers-by. Even a group of young men sitting together in a public place could give rise to antagonism from other men. As he spoke, Horse would occasionally touch a red scar on his right cheek self-consciously.

'Do you have girlfriends?' I asked the young men and they laughed uproariously.

All three of them were eighteen years old and their immaturity regarding relationships would have been strange in Australia, but this was Afghanistan and I gathered it was quite daring of me to ask something like this. Despite it being a taboo topic, Muslimyor was happy to talk about his love life.

'My ex-girlfriend is very beautiful. She loves me like the sky,' he said in English, and then he laughed wildly – I wondered if something had been lost in translation.

Muslimyor had flared nostrils, a straight pointed nose, slightly arched eyebrows and a strong jaw. He was good-looking and he knew it. He smiled and joked often, and I guessed he was the kind of person who made friends easily. He was heartbroken when his relationship with his ex-girlfriend ended.

Hafizullah half-scowled, half-smiled, but was not comfortable talking about this topic.

'It is not like in countries like Australia,' Hafizullah said. 'Society does not allow us to have girlfriends. If we do, we must keep it secret. We can't be seen in public with them. It would be very shameful for the woman. We must ask our family for permission to marry.'

'I have a girlfriend,' Horse said, not to be beaten by Muslimyor, and they all laughed again. 'But I don't want to marry her. She is not my life partner. I am happy working hard in Kabul, looking for a wife. I am the right age for love, but I am an honest man. I told a woman I like, "I have no house, no money. Take me for what I am."'

'What happened?' I asked.

'She did not take me.'

I looked at these teenagers, who joked about girlfriends, and wondered how they ever became involved in a group with such radical philosophies and action.

'This group here are my stalwarts. They have been with me since the beginning,' Insaan said.

THE MOUNTAINS, 2009

Getting up was the hardest part of the day for Hafizullah. Winter mornings were bitterly cold and leaving the house before the sun had risen was torture. In the warmer seasons, the seventeen members of the family, which included the wife of one of his brothers and their children, spread themselves out over four rooms, but it was so cold during the winter that they crammed themselves into two rooms, heated by a metal oven called a *tandoor*. He removed himself from the warmth of the family pile with much difficulty. There was no point in feeling sorry for himself. All the family started their day at about this time. There was work to be done in the potato fields and someone had to feed the cows. But this wasn't the work Hafizullah was dreading. Eleven-year-old Hafizullah knew the family was in financial trouble, after they had once again spent all their savings on one of their son's weddings. The henna paint on the ends of Hafizullah's nails was a wedding tradition, but instead it reminded him of their dire circumstances. The first concern of Hafizullah and his family was how to put food on the table; if he could play a part, he would.

Hafizullah put his falling-apart leather shoes on his bare feet and stomped on the ground to get the circulation flowing. The moment he stepped out of the house the snow wet his feet and the cold began to spread. He walked across the muddy courtyard, squawking chickens dancing out of his way, and he pushed open the metal front door. His house squatted on a wind-shredded hillside, in a narrow valley that was home to around 500 other families; Grandfather Mountain peered down at them from its immense height. Hafizullah's family lived at the bottom of the valley, near the river, where the ground was more fertile and where people could plant fields of potato and wheat.

Hafizullah's grandfather lived the farthest up the valley, the closest to the mountain, which in Hafizullah's eyes meant he was the king of the valley. But now he was too old to move from his throne, isolated in the high snows. When Hafizullah was young he thought the mountain was named after his grandfather. His skin was almost black in colour, he leaned heavily on a staff, and his earlobes drooped like dried black apricots. It was hard to imagine this kindly, frail old man killing anyone, but Hafizullah had concluded a long time ago that he must have.

Hafizullah knew his father had spent his whole life at war, and so he reasoned that his grandfather must have too. For years they fought the Taliban during the civil war, and before that they fought the Russians, but neither of the men ever talked about war. If they did, they spoke in general terms.

'Yes, I had a weapon. Yes, I fired the weapon, but I'm not sure where the bullets went.'

Hafizullah had learned that most people who were involved in wars or fighting never talked about their experiences.

Hafizullah was too young to remember any stories of violence and conflict. The little he did know was one story told by his mother and older siblings, about the time his father was beaten senseless by the Taliban and left for dead in the street. He was unconscious for hours but eventually dragged himself back to the house. To this day, Hafizullah's father feels that his back pain, his body aches and his fragile mind are related to that incident. His father and grandfather were lucky to have survived. Many of their friends and relatives were killed during the wars.

Hafizullah's family had to flee their village several times to avoid raids by the Taliban. They placed their household possessions on donkeys, and the family crossed the mountains and hills on foot to escape, heading towards Ghazni or Kabul, grazing the sheep, goats and cows on the way. By the time Hafizullah was old enough to form memories, the Taliban had been defeated and driven out of the mountains. The worst violence he had seen was fisticuffs between neighbours. When his uncle's cow had grazed on the field of another farmer, the farmer aggressively confronted his uncle; his uncle hit him with a shovel. The only gunfire Hafizullah had heard as a child was from hunters.

There were times when Hafizullah could look out across his valley home and appreciate its beauty. Sometimes the snowy mountains looked like delicious *mantu* dumplings. Today was not one of those days – today the valley looked like a frosted pile of dung. He stacked the frozen discs of cow manure, which they would later use as fuel. Next he would walk into town, to earn a pittance selling knick-knacks on the streets.

When he went inside, some of his brothers were eating breakfast.

'Will today be the day you are going to learn to read?' Ali Jan said to him and his other brothers laughed.

He scowled at them, but he had nothing to say in reply. He was eleven years old and he still couldn't read. Maybe they were right, maybe there was something wrong with him. He wasn't in the mood to pretend their ridicule didn't hurt him. He gulped his tea, swiped some bread, checked his stock – cigarettes, pens, nail clippers and pulverised tobacco – and stepped outside into the blistering wind. At least their teasing had motivated him to leave the house.

In summer the walk was pleasant. The sun would be warm and the hills green and full of flowers. But in winter there were times when the snow was so deep it came up to his knees. Thankfully the worst of the winter had passed, and it was almost spring. It wasn't so bad once he got moving, he reasoned. But it was more than an hour's walk to town and now his brothers had him thinking about reading again.

Hafizullah really had tried to learn, but he couldn't understand what the other children were doing that he wasn't. He thought it would come naturally, from the alphabet itself. If he followed the alphabet with his eyes, something about that following would give him the sounds to pronounce the letters. But it didn't work. When he saw other students reading, they shifted their eyes and head, so he mimicked their actions, hoping the sounds would be heard in his mind. But that didn't work either. The alphabet and the strokes of the characters were just blurry lines that didn't make any sense to him.

Last semester he had to take his written exam even though he was illiterate and couldn't read the questions. Even if a classmate had told him the answer, he couldn't write it down. For his answers, he rewrote the words in the questions backwards, so the last word of the question would become the first word of the answer and so on. He did not want to submit a blank exam paper. But none of the teachers cared whether the students knew the work or not, they passed anyway; there were forty-five students in his class and, even though he couldn't read or write, he was always ranked thirty-second.

The teachers who couldn't accept his illiteracy would punish him. They would verbally abuse him, call him an idiot, hit his hand with a wooden stick, twist his ears, hit him on the head. They tried harder at disciplining him than they did at teaching him – not one teacher had ever encouraged him. So Hafizullah learned creative ways to avoid punishment.

Last year Hafizullah had a Dari teacher who was particularly fierce. The teacher would ask them to write stories for homework, read their story out in front of the class and submit their written work for marking. Hafizullah would copy a paragraph straight from a Dari book even though he couldn't read it. The more literate students would sit in the front rows and read aloud first. Hafizullah would sit in the fifth bench of the class and he would memorise the story of one of his classmates who spoke before him. When his turn came, he would pick up his piece of paper, point at the words he had copied, and from his memory he would recite the other student's story. When he finished, the class would clap and congratulate him.

Hafizullah's mother was also illiterate, so she couldn't help him. His father was literate and tried to teach him the Quran and the Arabic alphabet, but he was so busy working that he didn't have the time or the energy to sit down with his son every evening.

Hafizullah trudged along, deep in his own thoughts, oblivious to the pomegranate-red cliffs either side of him. He followed the stream, running swiftly thanks to snowmelt from the Grandfather Mountain. Black-and-white swallows darted across his path. At the end of the valley he took a shortcut through a farmer's field. He was pleased to see the little mounds of earth which meant preparations for potato-planting season were underway. Soon the potato storage sheds, sunk into the ground with their different coloured doors, would be full. Hafizullah almost put his foot through a small, frozen-over stream. The ice was thin, and parts had cracked like glass to reveal fresh running water underneath. All around him there were signs of the coming spring.

This was exciting and demoralising. The snow would be gone and the warm weather would return, but it also meant school would be starting again. If he was caught out still not being able to read, which was a certainty, he would have to face the teachers' punishments for another year. The thought of it left a knot in his stomach. Why should he go to school anyway? He felt guilty at the thought. When the Taliban were in power, schools were shut down and no-one was allowed to study. He should give up his work and make the effort to learn.

Hafizullah first started working on the street when he was nine years old. During the school term, he went to school in the morning and then after school he worked until the evening, selling knick-knacks from his wooden tray. In winter, when school was off, Hafizullah worked from eight in the morning until it got dark. When he worked the hotels, he wouldn't finish until nearly midnight and he would sleep the night at his older brother's shop. He hated the hotel shifts because some of the hotel owners would insult him and kick him off their premises. On a good day he could earn 150–200 Afghanis profit (US$3–4), sometimes he even made 250 Afghanis (US$5). He knew his work was important for his family, but it was exhausting.

When the stream hit the river, he headed towards town. Women walked home from the water pump with jars on their heads, the wind whipping the bottoms of their burqas around their legs in a mad dance; children threw rocks at each other from behind an abandoned Soviet tank. Men led donkeys down well-trodden paths, past lonely graves marked with green martyr flags.

The ancient city on the hilltop slowly came into view. The crumbling ruins leant into the mountains, defeated, except for one old watchtower that proudly exposed itself to the town. Hafizullah had never walked to the top of the Ruins of Slaughter. The name was enough to scare him, but he had also been warned about unseen landmines that dotted the hillside.

To the north stretched an immense sandstone cliff face, high enough to disappear into low-hanging clouds. The orange cliffs overlooked the valley and were dotted with caves, some inhabited by people. When Hafizullah passed his school, he kept his head down and didn't look at it. Likewise, he kept his gaze averted from the dog-fighting pits, which were silent in the morning. He had been to one dog fight and would never go again; the sight of one dog ripping out the throat of the other dog had horrified him.

Hafizullah passed tradesmen who had set up shop in empty shipping containers alongside the river and were making elaborate metal gates for houses. He weaved in and out of the fruit and vegetable bazaar, eyeing apples and oranges and greyish grapes. He tried to avoid the men fanning kebabs on the side of the street. It was an unnecessary temptation when he knew all he would get to eat for lunch was bread. Hafizullah was feeling lazy today, so he decided to ply his trade on the two roads that marked the town centre. The town spilled out chaotically from there, like ants swarming on a piece of meat.

As he worked his patch on the street, underneath one of the rickety two-storey shops, and daydreamed of ways to take revenge on his brothers, a strange man approached him and asked if he could take a photograph of him. Hafizullah was immediately wary of this stranger, with his silver digital camera. No-one had ever asked him for a photograph before and he didn't know why this man wanted one. Plus, he had a strange accent that made Hafizullah think he wasn't a local. But there was some kind of warmth that emanated from him, and his enthusiastic smile put Hafizullah at ease.

'You know, there is a chip shop on this street that is looking for shop assistants. I can introduce you to the manager there if you like,' he offered.

Hafizullah wasn't sure what to make of this proposal, but he followed The Stranger to a little shop selling French fries and crisps where he was introduced to Nadir, a stocky little teenager. After speaking with Nadir, Hafizullah calculated that he'd earn more money with his current street job than the new role, but the shop assistant position would be a more stable form of income. The work seemed genuine, he thought.

'You could work half days at the shop, so you can study at school in the afternoon,' The Stranger said.

On his way home that afternoon Hafizullah considered The Stranger and the new job offer. It would be nice to stay off the street, to avoid the hassle of angry shopkeepers. When he worked on the street he felt like a vagabond. There was legitimacy to working in a shop and he liked the look of Nadir and The Stranger. They seemed friendly and honest. If he worked at the shop in the mornings, maybe he could learn how to read at school in the afternoons. Maybe he would take the job.

THE MOUNTAINS, 2009

Horse was a mountain boy. He had taut, skinny calf muscles, strengthened by climbing the loose gravel slopes of his province with his beloved donkey. He had been a shepherd, a labourer, a shop-hand, a farmer, a forager and a school student all by the age of ten. He was an avid player of *buzkashi*, or 'goat-pull', which was the favourite sport of the mountain tribes in his region. In the game, two teams of horse-riders attempted to drag a goat carcass into a goal, although Horse rode a donkey instead. He loved the game because it demanded aggression, strength and horsemanship, all characteristics to which he aspired.

Horse looked ahead at his partner in crime, Muslimyor. Even now, when they were alone in the scrub leading donkeys up a mountain, Muslimyor walked with a purposeful slouch. He was wearing his favourite grey suit jacket and he had a scarf wrapped around his head. His 'gangster style' he called it.

Horse got to know Muslimyor when he was about nine years old and his family moved from their rural village into the main provincial town. The family was struggling financially, and their farmland wasn't profitable. Even though Horse and Muslimyor's mothers were cousins, Horse didn't know Muslimyor well before the move. Now they were in the same class at school together, they played soccer together, they went for walks together. They became inseparable. Today they were heading high into the mountains to collect thornbushes for their families to use as fuel.

Muslimyor stopped suddenly and pulled out his slingshot from his pocket.

'Shhhh,' he hissed at Horse, who almost walked straight into him.

Muslimyor had spotted a swallow perched in some scrub just ahead. The bird cocked its head at the pair and its long tail twitched. Muslimyor placed a stone in his slingshot pouch and drew back the band slowly. He closed one eye, took aim and fired off a stone that flew miles above the target. Horse whooped with laughter and the bird swooped off into the distance.

'Ah, shut your mouth,' said Muslimyor, scowling at him, and resumed his lazy swagger up the mountainside.

Muslimyor and Horse had left their homes at two that morning, well before the sun had risen. They had a long way to walk to find the tufts of thornbushes that were best for burning. Once they found the greener slopes, they would uproot the bushes with a pick, bag them and secure them on the donkeys. By the time they were finished, the boys would have filled the bags to twice their own size and the sun would be close to setting; then they would have to walk home.

If they passed through some areas of the mountains that had been marked out as territories of different villages and tribes, Horse would be burdened by apprehension. Although the war against the Taliban was over, resources were scarce and there was still suspicion and rivalry between tribes. If they were caught collecting fuel from those areas the other villagers might attack them. In those areas, he and Muslimyor would be on edge, watching out for potential enemies. But once they crossed the territorial line marked by a small stream on their way home, they would start singing with relief.

Horse had spent his whole life in these dry, rocky mountains. As a shepherd he had traversed these peaks by himself. It could be lonely work, but for the most part he enjoyed the company of the long-haired sheep. When he grazed the animals, he could play his wooden recorder without disturbing any of his family members or neighbours. Sometimes he would ride the fatter sheep like a donkey. There was a freedom to walking amongst the mountain passes, cooking his own food and sleeping under the stars. Plus, it paid well.

He earned 250 Afghanis (US$5) per sheep for one whole year of grazing. He looked after between 150 and 200 sheep, so his annual income could be as much as 40,000 Afghanis (US$750–1000). But there were eight people to feed in his family: his mother, four brothers and two sisters. His father had left some years ago after a number of failed business attempts had mired the family in debt. As the oldest male, Horse became the man of the house. Throughout his childhood, it seemed as if Horse's family couldn't shake the cloud of poverty that engulfed them.

'Let's eat now,' Muslimyor announced. 'I'm starving.'

They found a pleasant stream to sit by, set their donkeys to grazing and pulled their lunch supplies out of the saddlebags. If Muslimyor's older brother Qasim was here, he would've caught them fish from the stream and they would have cooked it on an open fire. Instead they dug a hole in the ground and baked potatoes in it. Muslimyor had also scrounged some leftover bread from his home. They propped themselves up against sun-warmed rocks with a cup of tea and ate.

'You know I have a story about Paristu,' Horse said.

Muslimyor grunted. 'I thought you liked Kala.'

That was true, he did like Kala. He would snatch looks at her during class, but he would never speak to her. Horse couldn't speak to girls the way Muslimyor could.

'Paristu asked me to help her cheat in the exam the other day,' he said.

'I hope you said no,' Muslimyor said.

'Of course,' Horse said. He was an honest boy and he had immediately refused to help her, but now he was regretting the decision. He thought she was a good Muslim girl, but maybe she was a little simple and she needed his help. They could have been friends.

'We have to do well in class, we have to get good grades,' Muslimyor said. 'You don't want to be known as a cheat.'

Horse knew Muslimyor was right, but he couldn't help wondering what would have happened if he had helped Paristu.

'What do you think of Marvana?' Muslimyor asked Horse.

'Ahh, you think she is pretty?' Horse teased.

Muslimyor laughed like a dog barking. 'No, I just wanted to know if you think she is pretty.'

'You like her,' Horse sang and Muslimyor jumped on him, wrestling him to the ground. He was much too strong for Horse and he easily pinned him.

'Take it back,' Muslimyor said and pushed Horse's face into the grass. 'Take it back.'

'Okay, okay,' Horse laughed. 'I'm sorry.'

Muslimyor released him and they laughed together.

'You know how I started work at a confectionery shop?' Muslimyor said.

'Do you get to eat the food?' Horse asked.

Muslimyor laughed. 'Sometimes,' he said. 'But that's not my point. A strange man came into the shop one day and began talking to me about a group of young people in the area who are working for peace. It seemed interesting so I think I might join them. You should come.'

Horse didn't understand what Muslimyor was saying. He'd never heard of anyone 'working for peace' before. But if Muslimyor thought it was a good idea, Horse was sure he'd like it.

'Okay, I will,' Horse said.

THE MOUNTAINS, 2009

Muslimyor approached The Stranger and a group of fifteen young people sitting on the grass. It was lunchtime and the group were eating French fries together. Muslimyor was filled with suspicion and anxiety. He didn't know any of these people, and he could see a Tajik person in the group. Until now, he had been taught to distrust Tajiks, Pashtuns, anyone who was not a family member, really. And The Stranger was clearly not from their province. If Muslimyor joined the group, this would be the first time in his life he would socialise with a person who was not Hazara. He hesitated, but then The Stranger spotted him and waved him over with great enthusiasm. Muslimyor couldn't turn away now. Despite all his instincts telling him this was a bad idea, a dangerous idea, he sat with the group.

Muslimyor had lived a rough childhood. Life in his village was hard. People were mainly concerned with surviving – they worked so they could eat. There were ten people in Muslimyor's family: him, his parents, four brothers and three sisters. They lived on a small plot of land on a hill, which his father farmed for a living, just outside of the region's main town. When Muslimyor was young, his oldest brother moved to Iran for work, his second oldest brother joined the Afghan army and his third oldest brother worked as a farmer. That left Muslimyor and his younger brother to help around the house and earn extra income for the family. Muslimyor started working when he was ten years old. Before school, he used his two donkeys to fetch water for other families for a fee. Aged twelve he was already accustomed to working in the fields and shepherding livestock.

As a young boy he'd picked up some tough-guy manners and social skills that could have been described as antisocial. He swore profusely and was rude about women. He presumed that's why he was cast as a Talib in a film produced in the local area. He didn't understand what a healthy society was like. Most members of his community were traumatised by decades of war. He had never thought about his purpose in life or the significance of being alive. He lived to work and worked to live.

It was his need to work that eventually led him to The Stranger and the group. One of the households to which he brought water opened a confectionery shop in the city. They offered him a job working from eight in the morning until noon every day. After that he went to school until four in the afternoon. One morning a stranger came and spoke to him at the shop.

'Did you know there is a group of young people in the area organising social activities? Would you be interested in joining their programs?' The Stranger asked.

Muslimyor was curious but he didn't join the group. Strangers were rarely trusted in these small mountain communities. The second time The Stranger visited the confectionery shop he mentioned that the young people were working for peace and this piqued Muslimyor's interest. Muslimyor had heard radio programs talking about the need to work for peace in the country and he was keen to learn what that meant. He had seen his older brother go north with the army to the fighting in Kunar province, taking his mother's mind with him.

His mother had started a bakery to supplement the family income, even though it was unusual for women in the rural districts of Afghanistan to work outside of the home. After his brother left for Kunar, she became anxious and so distracted she sometimes burned herself while cooking. When she started fainting the family decided she had to stop working at the bakery. Motivated by a determination for a better future for them all, Muslimyor decided to visit the group to see if peace was possible.

This impetus didn't make his introduction to the group any easier. Gripped with discomfort, he sat down and observed The Stranger lead their discussion.

'How can Afghanistan become peaceful?' The Stranger asked the group.

Muslimyor wasn't used to being asked questions. He was usually lectured by his teachers, his parents, his religious elders. He was rarely asked his own opinion. He looked around at the other members of the group and saw that they were all thinking hard, eager to respond.

'We should stop fighting with each other,' one of the Tajik members of the group called Arif said.

'That's important,' The Stranger said. 'We are all here because we are tired of violence, because we want peace. The natural answer is to not use violence, to not fight.'

'Why are people fighting each other in Afghanistan?' The Stranger asked.

'People are fighting each other because of their ethnicity or religion. They have stopped trusting each other,' Arif said.

'So how can we help people learn to trust each other again?' The Stranger asked.

'We should act truthfully and not lie or cheat,' a young Hazara boy called Asghar said. He looked to be about Muslimyor's age.

'It is important to act responsibly on an individual level,' The Stranger said. 'But what can we do as a group to convince other people to stop fighting? How can we convince other people to act truthfully?'

The group remained silent, thinking, and Muslimyor found himself thinking too. But his brain felt like a rusty wheel on a bike trying to change gears. How could he solve this problem?

'What emotions do you feel when you act violently?' The Stranger asked.

Muslimyor thought about all the times he had been in fights or his family had suffered violence and he was amazed to hear his feelings reflected in the others' comments, even those of the Tajiks.

'I feel angry.'

'I feel hatred for my enemy.'

'I become like a wild beast and I can't control myself.'

'I get scared,' a young man called Nadir said.

Muslimyor carefully observed The Stranger out of the corner of his eye. The Stranger sat cross-legged in the grass. There was no malice in his voice or body language. In fact, his eyes were kind and he used his smile to encourage the young men to speak. It was very unusual behaviour, but it made Muslimyor feel more comfortable in this unfamiliar environment.

'And what emotion do you feel when you *suffer* violence?' The Stranger asked.

'Fear,' they all agreed.

'Afterwards I am angry, and I feel hatred for my attacker.'

'I become like a wild beast trying to defend myself.'

Muslimyor was shocked by the similarities between the feeling of being attacked and that of being violent, but he agreed with everything the group said.

'There was a man called Martin Luther King Jr who once said, "Violence is immoral because it seeks to humiliate the opponent rather than win his understanding; it thrives on hatred rather than love. It destroys community and makes brotherhood impossible. Violence creates bitterness in the survivors and brutality in the destroyers."[9]

When The Stranger finished speaking the group sat in silence, processing the eloquence of the words spoken.

'What are the opposite emotions to those you just mentioned?' The Stranger asked.

'Love.'

'Safety.'

'Happiness.'

'So perhaps one way to build peace in Afghanistan is to instil these emotions into our communities,' The Stranger said.

Muslimyor was finding this whole experience very strange. His instinct was to distrust this stranger and his odd way of speaking and asking questions, but so much of what he said appealed to Muslimyor.

'We should be an example of peace to Afghanistan,' Arif said.

'And how would you do that?' The Stranger asked.

'Perhaps the people of the world don't believe that we understand love,' Asghar said. 'Maybe if they see that among our families and our friends we wish for love, that will help bring peace.'

'We should demonstrate our understanding of love to the world,' Arif said.

'Love is how we'll ask for peace,' Muslimyor said.

Chapter 2

To Serve Humanity

It didn't take me long to blend into the daily routine of the house. I ate meals and drank tea with Insaan and the Stalwarts. I showered from a bucket and used a squat toilet. The meals were cooked in pots on a gas cooker attached to the top of a gas cylinder in the middle of the kitchen. They didn't own a refrigerator so the community members bought fresh produce from the market for meals every day. We usually ate vegetarian dishes, sometimes served with rice, but we always had bread. Every so often the community indulged in a meat dish. Meals were served with fresh lettuce, shallots and sliced cucumber with salt. I could never get completely comfortable sitting at the dinner mat and found myself constantly switching between awkward positions and angles, usually ending up with my knees around my ears. The Stalwarts who lived in the Peace House never ate in restaurants, and Insaan preferred if I didn't offer to pay for meals or give presents. He did not want my presence to foster any jealousy within the community. The most I could offer was a donation to the community fund.

Each morning, Insaan and I performed our exercises in the dusty basement. Prayers were said in private. I watched the young men leave for school and then come home to study and perform their responsibilities with the community. Some days, Horse woke up earlier to take his mother to her work on his bicycle. Most days of the week, we welcomed visitors to the Peace House and sat around the heater drinking tea and telling stories.

I caught glimpses of community life through random incidents like when the kitchen erupted into screams and screeches and Muslimyor

finally emerged holding a dead mouse. Over time, I observed the community members, their interactions, their squabbles, and came to understand
that the house dynamic resembled that of a family.

Living in community was a peaceful existence, interrupted by a
suburban soundtrack: shouting neighbours, the occasional helicopter, the
tinny happy birthday ditty of street vendors on repeat, or the screeching
of alley cats. But as long as it wasn't gunfire and bombs I was happy. In
the short time I stayed in Kabul, there were two major attacks in the city.[1]
Insecurity could shut down parts of the city without warning, causing
city-wide traffic jams and ruining carefully made plans.

I visited the Community Centre each day, but even this involved
some risk.

'Kidnappings occur when you assume a routine. If we are going to visit
the centre, we should do so at different times each day, so our movements
are unpredictable,' Insaan advised me.

I never felt scared while in Afghanistan; I imagined that was because
I was never directly threatened. Being kidnapped or attacked felt like an
abstract threat. Certainly, I felt self-conscious, apprehensive, but never
frightened. It was only once I left the country that I realised just how
exhausting that state of alertness was. Pent-up stress and pressure flowed
out of me the instant my plane left the ground: a deep, relieved, whole-
body sigh.

Through my visits to the centre, I met the other volunteers and learned
their stories. There were around forty active members and another forty
irregular members in the community, almost half of whom were women;
only a few members lived in the house. Among the volunteers was Tara,
the nervous public speaker from my first visit; and Taqi, who had lived
in Pakistan most of his life, after his family fled the war; Mikha, the Tajik
freestyle rapper who told me that Afghanistan was a graveyard for stories;
and Yani, the comedian from Maidan Wardak province. Every volunteer
had a personal tale of tragedy and violence; few would be heard outside
of Kabul.

Insaan warned me of the phenomenon of 'changing narratives' in
cultures at war.

'Anthropologists have recorded observations about how the many
stresses of war caused the evolution of stories in oral tradition societies,'

Insaan said. 'The stories changed as was needed for survival, for comfort, for saving face, for honour. In community we experience these things as well and that creates stress for everybody. I appeal to them to stick as close to the truth as possible, but often my appeals don't work. I soon realised it was I who needed to accept the reality of changing narratives.'

There were twenty-two teams in the community, working on different projects. Their projects varied from a mediation and conflict resolution team, which tried to reach out to young people who they knew had leanings towards extreme ideologies; to a psychological care team, which conducted trauma healing workshops to help them cope with their mental health challenges. Each team elected a project coordinator who would represent their views at the coordinator meetings. In an effort to share responsibility, and leadership, and to work cooperatively, the community tried to make all decisions by consensus. But this was a difficult task given that the number of volunteers was continually growing and the commitment levels of each volunteer varied. The nature of volunteerism meant that people came and went, but the core philosophy and vision of the community remained. Many of the volunteers didn't think a consensual decision-making system would be possible considering most people were accustomed to the tribal, top-down approach of Afghan society. Insaan admitted it was a longer process and it was not perfect, but he believed it strengthened the community.

Every few days the yard of the Community Centre would be occupied by a group of young men, who danced in a circle around another volunteer who beat a drum. Step, kick, sway hands, spin; step, kick, sway hands, spin faster. This was the multi-ethnic dance group, consisting of only male dancers. They were learning the *attan*, a traditional Pashtun dance, which they hoped to perform at the community's official ceremonies. They also planned to host their own dance festival.

Each Thursday the community went to an indoor sports centre to play football. We walked in a group to the venue. Horse was a fan of Barcelona and Lionel Messi, although he'd seen neither the player nor the team play a football match – not even on television. Most of the community members weren't great football players, but they tried hard and enjoyed themselves. Even Insaan joined in with his duck-footed run down the sideline.

'This soccer team helps to build our multi-ethnic relationships and promotes healthy exerting of energy,' Insaan said. 'We also run a weekly exercise day for women at the centre. On this day, the men are not permitted to enter.'

I ended each day in conversation with Insaan and the Stalwarts. Our talk usually centred around their stories, but we also grappled with philosophical discussions as well.

When I asked Insaan what he thought of the concept of war crimes, he answered in a fashion I was beginning to understand and admire.

'Ironically, the Geneva Conventions further formalise the idea that wars are "conventional" and "legal". For combatants, war is execution without trial. For civilians, who have always suffered the greatest in any war, war is an aberration. What are war crimes? War itself is the crime.'

I found these exchanges of ideas refreshing. The Stalwarts were open to new ideas without betraying their cultures and traditions, and they didn't dislike or judge me for thinking differently to them, even though the differences could be immense at times.

One day at the Community Centre I asked them, 'Do you think that peace is possible in Afghanistan?'

The young volunteers looked at each other, at first cautious, and then Hojar spoke.

'We will not achieve peace during our generation. We are simply laying the foundations for a better future,' Hojar said. 'We will encourage every Afghan to bring change within themselves because personal change becomes a solid foundational change.'

I was surprised by that response. I had always thought of the community as ambitious, but that seemed quite conservative to me.

'Why won't it come during your generation?' I asked.

'Afghanistan is not an independent country. It has become a field of war where foreigners come and fight,' Muslimyor answered authoritatively. 'Foreign nations have their own agendas in Afghanistan. They interfere in our politics, sell weapons, use drones, to continue their wars. The exit of foreign powers will make peace possible in Afghanistan. But we are still divided by ethnicity and religion. It will take a sustained national campaign to demand an end to the war. But the people are too poor to engage in such immaterial issues. While they are preoccupied with meeting their basic human needs it will be almost impossible for them to maintain a peace movement. Right now, the people are not self-reliant. They don't have financial autonomy. So foreign powers have a hook that they can use in providing financial aid and therefore fulfilling their own foreign agendas.'

The other volunteers nodded in agreement.

'Women have not been included in the general affairs of Afghan society and this has weakened the peace movement,' Hojar added. 'Including women in community decision-making will double the strength of the movement. Right now, this is not possible, but perhaps by the next generation, society will be ready for this change.'

I could see their point, but I wanted to believe that they would see their work come to fruition.

'A lot can happen in a generation. Afghanistan was at peace forty years ago. Don't you think in another forty years there could be peace again?' I asked.

'Well, the average lifespan in Afghanistan is much shorter than the world's average life span. Perhaps we won't be alive in forty years' time,' Hojar said, and they all laughed.

'The average lifespan in Afghanistan used to be around forty-five,' Insaan explained. 'The community members joke with me that I'm already dead.'[2]

Insaan laughed loudly and freely. He smiled with his whole face.

'Perhaps we should invite Miss Universe to visit the community as a delegate because she is always saying she wants world peace,' Insaan said.

The thought of a bikini-clad supermodel visiting Afghanistan had me laughing, but I was determined to press my point nonetheless.

'Other nonviolent movements, like those led by Martin Luther King and Gandhi, achieved a significant amount of change in a forty-year period,' I said.

'Both Martin Luther King and Gandhi were assassinated and didn't see the final outcomes of their movement,' Muslimyor said. 'So, we have learned to adjust our expectations of what we can achieve within *our* lifetime.'

I was stunned by Muslimyor's response. But I thought their recognition that working for peace challenged authority and could be dangerous indicated maturity and bravery. Insaan remained the great mystery of the group: a philosopher trying to make sense of the world and its chaos. He shaped the conversations and prompted the young people to respond. From where did he spring, this strange man and his unusual theories?

INSAAN'S MEDICAL CLINIC, 2002

Insaan finished treating an elderly female patient and saw her out, her thanks echoing in the hallway. He tidied up and returned to his leather chair and his dark wooden table. After seven years practising as a medical officer and a family physician in government hospitals and then in a private family medical clinic, he had achieved a certain level of comfort, but it had not been an easy road. Both his parents came from humble, frugal immigrant backgrounds and Insaan had paid for his own university education.

Sitting there in his clinic, surrounded by symbols of success and achievement, he didn't feel satisfied. He felt restless. Not a physical restlessness, but a spiritual one: a yearning in his chest for a higher calling. When he was a teenager, Insaan had wanted to change the world – more of a naive and grandiose dream, rather than an actual understanding of what it meant to dedicate one's life to helping others. Nevertheless, that idealism helped motivate him to become a doctor, even as that same idealism was curbed by the actual experience of working as a student doctor. It was in hospitals that he learned about the real world, and saw, first-hand, crippling illness and death among young and old. Exposed to misfortune and injustice, his idealism was replaced with what he considered realism or pragmatism.

When he graduated he still had a strong desire to serve humanity, in particular to practise abroad. However, every day he worked in family medicine the desire seemed to diminish, until eventually it became almost fanciful. It was easy to settle when life was so comfortable. But today, when he looked at the chair, the table, his clinic, the yearning for something *more* returned so strongly he felt nauseous.

The last patient of the day entered Insaan's office and sat down, interrupting his existential crisis. Insaan followed the same procedure he'd been doing since he qualified: he listened to the patient, helped the man as much as he could and referred him to a specialist as necessary. At the end of the consult, the patient made to leave, but then turned back to Insaan, almost as an afterthought, and said:

'You know, I've been doing some work with a retired general and his daughter on the border of Pakistan and Afghanistan, in the city of Quetta. Five million refugees who fled Afghanistan over the past century have ended up in Pakistan. The situation there is horrendous. You could be of great service over there.'

The patient placed a photo on Insaan's table. 'Think about it. They really need people there.'

In Insaan's current state of mind, the meeting felt like destiny's call. The mention of Pakistan had struck a chord inside him. Insaan had been to the valleys of the North-West Frontier Province of Pakistan, where he had met the Pashtun tribes of the Hunza Valley. They were a people who used the tribal council, the *jirga*, for the enforcement of disputes and local decision-making. Insaan learned of the *Pashtunwali*, the Pashtun code of honour, comprised of the principles of hospitality, revenge, refuge, justice, loyalty, righteousness, faith, respect, pride and courage. Within this code, men were expected to protect their women, gold and land. Once the Pashtun gave you refuge, they would protect you with their life.[3] The patient's mention of the refugee crisis in Pakistan appealed to that long-suppressed desire Insaan had to be at the service of humanity. It was April 2002; just six months earlier, in October 2001, the United States and its allies had invaded Afghanistan.

Insaan looked down at the photograph, of a man dressed in a tan-coloured Afghan *perahan tunban*, with a young girl in a light-blue dress. She stared straight at the camera with a tentative expression. He allowed his imagination to transport himself away from his desk and the clinic to the refugee camps of Quetta, where humanity most needed him. He could use his skills to help those who really needed help, rather than prescribing cold and flu tablets to the wealthy elderly.

Insaan had always been interested in the mechanisms of war and poverty. When he saw injustices, he wondered why the systems weren't working and he wanted to fix them. When he dwelled upon these injustices, Insaan realised his motivation to relocate to Pakistan was more personal than just a desire to serve humanity; there was an emotional and historical connection to his grandparents, who had suffered through poverty and war. Insaan's maternal grandmother was a refugee, who raised three kids on her own after her husband was killed in war. To earn a meagre living, she put her children under a wooden cart and pushed the cart through the streets all day selling leftover bread. Though she suffered greatly, she never complained of hardship or life's unfairness. She kept a framed photo of Insaan's grandfather in her living room until her own death.

When Insaan asked her about the story of his grandfather, she'd narrate the tale in a matter-of-fact tone, even though she'd lived with the traumatic scene in her mind for decades. He had been caught up in the madness of war and was killed in a random massacre. Invading soldiers were given instructions to kill those men who were seen as threats to the foreign military regime. The captured men were put in two lines, and the line her husband was in was loaded onto a truck and driven away. Insaan's grandfather was made to dig his own grave. He was then made to squat in front of that open grave and he was shot from behind. Insaan often imagined himself digging that grave instead of his grandfather. He thought he would have given up or broken down. He thinks his grandfather must have been strong. Maybe to the last moment he was hoping something different might happen.

In contemplating the photograph of the general and his daughter, Insaan realised somehow that patient had sensed his restless spirit. A look had passed between them, a look that said, 'I know what you're looking for and I have the answer.' He was mentally and emotionally prepared to leave; he was thirty-two years old, with no wife or dependants. If he left his clinic there would be another doctor ready to sit in his comfortable leather chair.

Insaan put the photo in his drawer, absentmindedly drumming his fingers on the desk.

A few months later, he sold his share in the practice and moved to Quetta.

THE MOUNTAINS, 2004–07

Insaan sat on a cushion, on the floor of a little hut in the mountains of Afghanistan, contemplating humanity's relationship with war. His young housemate, Nadir, sat opposite him, lost in his own thoughts. When Insaan thought of their unlikely companionship, he couldn't help but laugh. It had come about with much sacrifice and some resistance, but here they were.

They lived with one 150 families in a village of simple, spartan mud houses. There was no electricity in the village and there was no furniture in the houses, just cushions and mattresses. Most of the families lived together in one or two rooms. They cooked their meals and baked their bread in metal or brick *tandoors*. Some of the houses had an air passage running from the oven into a space below the room, to heat the floor. This was an essential method of survival in the mountain winters, which were so cold that when Insaan filled up a pot of water from the spring, by the time he returned to his house it had frozen.

Around the houses the villagers grew wheat and potatoes, with simple channels to capture the runoff. Behind Insaan's house there was a plateau of farmland, and in front the land dropped away steeply to the stream. If Insaan followed this downstream it would lead him out of the valley and into town. Upstream took him to the source of the water, the Grandfather Mountain range.

The seasons were pronounced in the mountains. During spring, Insaan would wake to glistening dew on fresh green grass and walk amongst golden apple orchards. In the winter, the valley would turn a brilliant white and the snow would sparkle like diamonds. Either way, whether the leaves were falling in autumn or the stream was full in summer, he breathed fresh mountain air every morning and thought, *I am in heaven.*

Insaan worked with Afghan refugees in Pakistan for two and a half years from June 2002 to August 2004. During that time US and NATO forces had invaded Afghanistan and dismantled the Taliban regime. The first contingent of foreign peacekeepers, the NATO-led International Security Assistance Force (ISAF), had been deployed in the country and the international community was pouring in funds, trying to rebuild a nation on the verge of collapse. By 2004, three years after the United States had invaded Afghanistan, the Afghan people felt like the country might finally return to peace.

Insaan watched the families he had come to know as friends pack up their meagre personal possessions and begin the hopeful return journey to Afghanistan. Watching his new life walk away from him, Insaan felt the pang of heartache. He realised that he had grown to love these polite, resilient, hospitable people. He decided to follow them home.

Insaan road-tripped across the border from Quetta into Afghanistan, hopping on trucks and hitching lifts all the way to Kabul. Afghans didn't recognise Afghanistan as a bordered nation. They didn't see themselves belonging to a physical space. They belonged to tribes and communities that crisscrossed the imaginary boundaries of the artificially created nation states of Central Asia. The modern borders of Afghanistan were formally drawn up by the British and Russian empires during the late 19th century and were not designed to promote cultural and ethnic harmony in the region. The Durand Line, for example, was a tactical border created in 1893 by the British to divide and weaken the Pashtun tribes between British India and Afghanistan. The border still caused trouble between Afghanistan and Pakistan, since Afghanistan refused to recognise the Durand Line as the international border between the two countries. As Insaan crossed those arbitrary boundaries, in the company of millions of refugees, whilst yet another great empire attempted to invade Afghanistan, he wondered if humanity ever learned from its past.

Insaan was deployed to a mountainous region of central Afghanistan, where he worked in public health education for an international NGO. He stayed in a hotel for several weeks while he explored the regional parts of the province, investigating the work he was about to commence. In that time, he came to know Zee – a restaurant owner who wore a dirty apron, smoked cigarettes while he cooked and cut meat on an unhygienic table. Zee was used to drifters like Insaan and took a liking to him. He often invited Insaan to smoke marijuana with him behind his restaurant. Insaan would always decline the offer to smoke, but he would chat with Zee while Zee got high. Insaan quickly learned that Zee was not a normal Afghan.

Zee grew flowers, which were seen as a luxury in Afghanistan, and Insaan would bring him seeds for his garden. Zee had adopted a crippled black crow who hopped around his restaurant on one leg. He used to feed the bird scraps, and he told Insaan the crow was his best customer. One evening Insaan noticed the crow had disappeared and Zee, who was quite upset, told Insaan that the crow had hopped into the kitchen and then into the *tandoor* and had incinerated itself.

Zee was also fond of dogs, which was strange in Afghan society as dogs were traditionally considered unclean animals. Insaan told him that in other countries people liked dogs, gave them names and kept them as pets. After several days Zee came back to Insaan with a stray black puppy that usually lazed under an apple tree near his restaurant.

'Let's give this dog a name,' he said. 'I want this dog to be fast and quick and be a good watch dog. Maybe we can use him for dog fights when he is older. Let's call him Electricity.'

Zee had brought Electricity to his powerless village. Despite Zee's great ambitions, the dog didn't move from under the apple tree. After a month or two, Zee came back to Insaan and said, 'I don't think Electricity is a suitable name. I'm going to give him away.'

When Zee learned Insaan was staying in a hotel, he was outraged.

'I will take you in as my family. Come and stay with me in my village,' he said.

Insaan was surprised by the invitation but he was also aware of just how significant the offer was. Only family members were allowed in these rural villages. The only way Insaan could enter as a stranger was by invitation. Zee's offer of refuge, and his invitation to become part of his family, touched Insaan's heart. He accepted.

When Insaan joined Zee in the village he immediately regretted his decision. He had not realised it, but Zee expected Insaan to live in his house with his mother, two wives and six children. Insaan tried to politely decline the offer but Zee was quick to negotiate.

'I'll build a separate room for you,' Zee said.

Unwilling to cause offence to Zee and his family, Insaan agreed to this arrangement.

Understandably the villagers were suspicious of Insaan, the newcomer. They knew nothing about him except for Zee's assurances of his character, assurances established during a three-week acquaintance. Insaan built trust in the village community by not making eye contact with any of the women in the village for an entire year. If women passed him in the village, he would look down at the ground and step aside on the path, acting against his own nature which was to address, greet and look people in the face. He found the experience very dehumanising, but, with time, people began to trust him enough to use him as a doctor. They brought their loved ones to see him, which fostered more goodwill and a growing relationship with the community.

Insaan moved into the new room under the impression that he was going to live alone. But Zee and Zee's mother had other plans.

'Why would you want to live alone?' Zee said. 'It is strange. No, you cannot live on your own. You are family, you will have a family member live with you.'

Insaan asked if they could respect his desire to live alone and they refused.

'You mean you don't like your family members? You don't want us to live with you?' Zee responded.

Insaan blustered and argued. He wanted privacy, he wanted solitude, he wanted his own space. They told him they would start knocking before entering his room, but they still didn't think he should lock his door. Insaan thought of the Afghan author Tamim Ansary, who wrote that Afghans could have a space of solitude by being with another person, that the Afghan sense of group was just as real as their sense of self, perhaps more so. When Insaan first read that, he thought, *if that is true, Afghans don't understand solitude.*

After much argument, Insaan finally relented, realising he would never be allowed to live alone in the village.

'If there has to be someone, just make sure he doesn't talk,' he told Zee.

They sent him fifteen-year-old Nadir. From this point on, Insaan's life was turned upside down. Nadir arrived at Insaan's door looking sheepish, devastated, lost. *Maybe this will work*, Insaan thought. Not only did Nadir not talk, he could not talk. He was vacant. He was immersed in his own world. They would exchange greetings and that was it. One day Insaan asked Nadir, 'There are theories that say there are seven heavens on earth and we are currently in one of those heavens. Which one do you think we are in?'

Nadir contemplated the question and then said: 'The fourth one because then there are heavens below us and heavens above us.'

Insaan warmed to this humble, unassuming character. He perceived a great wisdom in this closed book.

Nights in the house together were particularly quiet. Insaan would contemplate the calamity of war and scribble in his notebook, while Nadir stared into space. The only sound would be the crackling of the fire, or the elements outside, a whistling wind from the Grandfather Mountain or the *rum dum drum* of a downpour. Nadir's slow opening up to Insaan was unexpected and beautiful. Perhaps it was Afghan culture to reveal one's deepest emotions and feelings at night, a trait belonging to their ancient oral culture. Perhaps in this closed society, where people so often couldn't speak their mind, people felt protected by the cover of darkness and encouraged by the warmth of a fire.

'My mind is just gone,' Nadir broke the silence.

His voice quavered. Insaan's breath stopped in his mouth and he looked over at Nadir, who was staring at the roof, grief-stricken.

'How can I help? Why are you so sad?' Insaan asked. But Nadir did not say any more that night.

Insaan used to think he could only know himself by possessing his own space. Now he was not so sure. Maybe knowing oneself involved recognising other people's spaces as well and allowing those spaces to merge. Before entering this village and meeting Nadir, he feared he would lose himself by losing his privacy. Maybe that fear wasn't so well founded, because he hadn't lost himself in this mountain community. Maybe his understanding of society, science, communication, of being, was just his version and he needed to learn from Nadir. He needed to learn what Nadir was going through, what was going on in his mind.

In the beginning, Nadir's stories only came out when that shared space, with the tea and the fire and the dead of night, morphed into a space where Nadir felt safe enough to say, 'I'm in a cage and I don't know how to get out of it.'

Insaan wondered if this was clinical depression. Does he need medication? Insaan asked himself. The answer was no. Nadir was hurting. He lost his father during the war, killed by the Taliban. He was trying to make sense of a world that stole his father from him when he was twelve.

These thoughts on shared space, shared healing and relational learning were the embryonic stages of a philosophy that was forming in Insaan's mind. An Afghan solution to Afghan questions of war, peace and healing.

Insaan continued working in health education with remote villages in the area. During his visits, he learned that lack of clean water was one of the major killers of Afghan children in the region, but he also concluded that every Afghan family in the region needed more than just medical assistance. They needed safety, they needed to be emotionally and mentally healthy, they needed to process feelings of anger and revenge, they needed to be educated, and they needed to know how to work with the land. He talked to families decimated by war, who would do anything for the killing to stop.

No-one was exempt from war. Every family had a story of losing someone.

A seven-year-old Afghan boy told him, 'Without peace it is impossible to live.'

Insaan began to see that the best way to address these families' problems was to address the problem of war, to understand and challenge the world's capacity for violence. In that way, his transition from public health professional to peace activist was not purposeful, it was gradual and subconscious, a reaction to the environment around him.

During the day, Insaan would often walk far from the village, high into the mountains with the village, the valley and the river spread out below him. The snowy tops of the peaks fanned out around him. He truly felt like he was looking across the roof of Afghanistan.

We are at war with everything, Insaan thought. *We are at war with countries. We are at war with our neighbours, with our fellow human beings. We are at war with religion, with ideologies, with cultures. We are at war with terror, we are at war with drugs, we are at war with our climate. We are at war with fat, with sugar, with our own minds. Our world is not healthy. So why this obsession with violence? Why do we hurt ourselves and others so much? What can I do?*

Each evening, Insaan returned to his room to read and write and contemplate in the company of Nadir. Insaan had painted the room orange and red and he called it the Room of Revolution. When Zee built the room for Insaan, he accidentally mixed the mud with wheat grain, so by the first spring wheat had sprouted in the walls.

'What am I supposed to do with this wheat in my walls?' Insaan asked Zee.

'Harvest it,' Zee replied casually.

It was in this wheat-filled house that revolutionary ideas began to take seed, grow and sprout. Insaan read widely and thoroughly; he discovered

Thoreau and Tolstoy, and Gandhi and King and Mandela, and he became convinced of the power of love.

If war was the problem, peace was the answer. If violence was the disease, love was the cure. Tolstoy talked about turning the other cheek and not retaliating, about the need to resist evil with love rather than violence.[4] He learned of Gandhi's 'Satyagraha', the force which was born of truth and love, and his philosophy of Ahimsa, the desire for peace, justice, order, freedom and personal dignity. Where violence degraded and corrupted, nonviolence healed and restored a basic law of being.[5]

Insaan came to understand that there were universal values that most people understood to be true to life, that were common throughout all religions. Treat others as you would want them to treat you, love thy neighbour, thou shalt not kill. So, why was it that most human beings acknowledged these universal values, but they were not public practices? Why did human beings denounce murder and immortalise the conqueror? Why was killing illegal, but warfare glorified?

Almost by accident, Insaan had stumbled upon the core philosophies of nonviolence, teachings that originated thousands of years ago and had spread all over the world. This was not a passive movement; it was a movement of positive action, the true expression of which was compassion.

Through the work of Martin Luther King Jr, Insaan learned that non-violence sought more than just an end to violence. The goal of nonviolence was to use love to liberate humanity from discrimination, prejudice and hatred. Real freedom liberated both the oppressor and the oppressed.

This was not a futile and ineffective idealism. Gandhi and King had taken on two of the greatest modern empires in their struggles for independence and civil rights – and won.

'Nonviolence is a powerful and just weapon,' said King. 'It is a weapon unique in history, which cuts without wounding and ennobles the man who wields it. It is a sword that heals.'[6]

Nonviolence didn't just appeal to Insaan's idealistic nature, it was as imperative to his being as breathing. Somehow Insaan had to make those universal personal values into public practices; an integral part of the public consciousness. If that seemed a formidable task, Insaan found comfort in his books. He was not alone in this endeavour, even if he was just one man in a small mud hut in Afghanistan. He was joining a historical, philosophical movement of thinkers and activists who had proven the effectiveness of nonviolence. It was a truly revolutionary idea, even if it was as ancient as the first religions. It was an idea that sought to completely change the nature of society, it was a threat to the established order, and for that reason it was something profoundly dangerous.[7]

As Insaan's ideas flourished, so did the wheat in the walls. By the time he emerged from the metaphorical woods, the surfaces had cracked so much that the walls were caving in and the structure was about to collapse.

In order to build a peaceful economy and a peaceful environment, Insaan theorised that the people of Afghanistan had to develop nonviolent relationships and practices. He wanted to be on that journey with them, but he wasn't sure how he could achieve such a monumental task. He drew strength from a phrase he came across in his readings, a phrase attributed to American anthropologist Margaret Mead:

Never doubt that a small group of thoughtful, committed citizens can change the world; indeed, it's the only thing that ever has.

It was time to take action.

Chapter 3

Chips and Duvets: Tackling Intergenerational Poverty

I left the Peace House, trailing an anxious-looking Muslimyor. We had a busy day of work with the community's duvet project ahead of us and he wanted to get home in time to study. First, we needed to distribute the wool and duvet covers to the seamstresses so they could make the next quota of duvets. Then, in the afternoon, we were delivering finished duvets to families in the outskirts of Kabul. Muslimyor said we had enough time, but in Kabul nothing ever seemed to go as planned.

The warehouse where the community stored the wool and duvet covers was only two blocks from the Peace House. We walked past the guardhouse on the corner of the street, fortified with bunkers of sand and surrounded by razor wire. A guard stared down the street at nothing, bored out of his mind. Another guard was asleep on a bunk bed inside the shipping container that acted as their barracks.

We crossed a bridge over a filthy river, avoiding men on bicycles riding to work. Women in hijabs and burqas walked toddlers to the shop. Old men without work slept in wheelbarrows. A girl in a purple velvet dress and cowboy-style gumboots ordered around a tribe of youngsters alongside the river. Kids flew plastic-bag kites, dodging carts and cars on the dirt road. A four-wheel drive boasted a slogan on its back window, 'Better to die standing than to live on your knees'.

Muslimyor had been coordinating the duvet project since its inception five years ago. He enjoyed the work, even the difficult and emotional parts. He and the other volunteers conducted surveys of families to assess their finances and their situation. They inspected their houses and asked them questions about their earnings, how many people were in their house, and their daily expenditure. Then they assessed whether they should receive duvets or not. Those who were eligible were usually widows, the visually impaired and the disabled. To sew the duvets, they paid twenty Tajik, twenty Pashtun and twenty Hazara women from destitute families. The intention was to employ and empower Afghan women to make important survival items for other Afghans.

The project was financially supported by an organisation from the United Kingdom, run by a woman named Mary Smith. Muslimyor liked the project because it wasn't just a handout from foreigners; rather it encouraged Afghans to work for Afghans.

Muslimyor found the work hard at first. He was a young man assessing people's wealth, and this process seemed almost disrespectful. It was dangerous to go out and inspect the houses. He risked being attacked or robbed. Female volunteers couldn't go alone. The trade-off for taking these risks was being able to help the most vulnerable. He was easily moved by their suffering and he wanted to help everyone, but, now he was more experienced, he had strengthened his heart and he was better at his job.

When we arrived at the warehouse a number of the seamstresses were waiting for us.

'They're already hassling me, and I haven't even opened the door,' Muslimyor said.

The woman who was first in line began wringing her hands and pleading with Muslimyor.

'Gruta is always first in line, and every week she asks about enrolling her children in the community's school,' Muslimyor explained.

He rattled open the roller door to the warehouse and the sorting began. Each woman was given thread and ten duvet covers. Amidst clouds of dust, bales of wool held tight by wires were cut open with pliers. The seamstresses filled one duvet cover with wool and then weighed it on a giant hook connected to a scale. Each bag should hold four kilograms, but this didn't stop some women trying to get more.

'Stop lifting the bag up, woman,' Muslimyor had to chide one seamstress.

One woman returned leftover wool from her last batch. 'Honesty is important,' she said.

We were joined by two volunteers from the community, Musa and Malvina, and some bored street kids who were more hindrance than help. The women wearing burqas lifted their veils over their heads so they could see properly and breathe easier. One woman hoicked loudly and spat on the ground after she inhaled too much dust. Little children lost themselves in the skirts of their mothers and grandmothers. Once the sorting had been completed, the women picked up their loads of wool and took them away in cars and taxis.

We collected finished duvets from another warehouse and loaded them into the back of a pick-up truck. This was the last batch to be delivered for the winter. It would take the total number of duvets donated that winter to 3000. Muslimyor and I hopped into the front seat of the truck and peered out at dusty Kabul from behind a cracked windscreen.

On our way to the delivery point, we drove past the skeleton of the Darul Aman Palace. The neoclassical building, with its distressed and fragmented facade, was originally built in the 1920s and was intended to be the future parliament, yet it never served its original purpose. Instead, it had been a home for government industries, housed a medical school, been a warehouse and acted as a displaced persons' camp. It had been set on fire in 1968 and again in 1978 during the communist coup. Then it was destroyed by heavy shelling by the Mujahedin in the 1990s and was the target of an attack by the Taliban in 2012.[1] It now stood as a sad reminder of fratricide. Opposite the palace was another unfortunate edifice: the grey-stoned National Museum of Afghanistan. The vast majority of the museum's exhibits were looted during the civil war and, in 2000, the Taliban destroyed over 2000 ancient works of art that offended their concept of God.[2]

Hundreds of plastic bags were caught on the barbed wire fences around the palace. Bobcats shovelled away rubbish, to be relocated to another part of the country. The government was spending $20 million on refurbishing the palace.[3] Meanwhile Muslimyor was handing out free duvets to desperately poor families.

The site of the duvet distribution was a sandy courtyard amongst stone streets. When we arrived, the local neighbourhood swarmed the truck.

Delighted families took their duvets and left, walking clouds of pink and blue on a sky of orange dirt. Children stared shyly at my camera and an old war veteran on crutches proudly posed for a photo, shifting his robes to reveal the space where his right leg used to be. The crowd was predominantly made up of those who were registered with the project, waiting to collect their duvets. But word got around the neighbourhood, and the crowd grew as opportunists arrived hoping for some luck.

'Please sir, please,' they cried.

'Why are they being helped and not us?' one woman asked.

'You must register with us in the next round of assessments,' Muslimyor shouted over the throng.

The desperation in the street was palpable. Muslimyor didn't blame the people for their behaviour. All of them needed a little bit extra, but there was only enough for those who had registered.

Since its inception, the duvet project had donated winter bedding to some 9000 destitute families in Kabul and had offered a winter income to 360 seamstresses. Yet the community heard a persistent plea from seamstresses who, while appreciative of the seasonal project, expressed their acute need for an income throughout the year.

Muslimyor had been involved in several different projects with the community over the years. He participated in the theatre group and the dance group, he worked with two other volunteers in the accounts team, and he also taught the street kids nonviolence for three years. The next year, the community planned to form a seamstresses' cooperative that would manufacture clothing year-round for inexpensive local sale.

Muslimyor tried to take lessons from each of the projects. He loved the theatre group because he liked to use laughter and humour in his productions, to explore important issues in a simple way. He thought that although theatre was not so well-developed or valued in Afghanistan, it could be an important tool for educating Afghans because it was understood by the literate and the illiterate alike.

The duvet project taught him what it meant to be appreciated by society for helping people. But he was also realistic about the goals of the project and he knew it was not sustainable. It didn't solve any of the major issues that afflicted the Afghan people; it was a humanitarian response only made possible by the financial support of international friends.

Muslimyor thought emergency responses such as this were necessary, but they didn't deal with the root causes of the problem. He believed the community had to think of strategies to fight the outward pressures of society on the individual. His long-term goal was sustainability and autonomy for the community.

When all the duvets were distributed, we returned home, dusty and exhausted. Night had fallen and Muslimyor still needed to study for class the next day.

THE MOUNTAINS, 2007–08

Insaan and Nadir lived together for two years, until one morning during Ramadan, when Nadir came to Insaan's house looking very pale.

'Insaan, the sky has collapsed into the earth.'

One of Nadir's uncles had decided that Nadir would no longer be able to stay at Insaan's house. The reason the uncle gave was that Insaan was a stranger to the province and Nadir should live with a family member. To Insaan, the uncle's decision smelled of jealousy. It was a cruel blow to a young man who had finally learned to trust again.

Nadir began to cry, and he apologised for leaving.

'Don't be sorry,' Insaan said. 'You have been a good protector and a good friend. You have to listen to your uncle, or you will lose your community.'

Zee's family would not allow Insaan to live alone, so they found another housemate to replace Nadir. Insaan's new protector was Asghar: a younger, smaller version of Nadir. Twelve-year-old Asghar was not as quiet as Nadir, but he was as sensitive and insecure. He'd been Insaan's neighbour for the past few years and he had badgered Insaan incessantly to teach him English. Every Friday for the previous year, Asghar had come to the Room of Revolution to learn.

When Asghar first moved in, Insaan noticed he did the housework, which was unusual for Afghan males. Asghar expected some standard of cleanliness in the house, which suited Insaan just fine.

Insaan owned a small digital camera, which he often lent to his housemate. The camera quickly became Asghar's first love, and most days he would go out into nature and take pictures of the trees, valleys and rivers in the area. Asghar used photography to escape from the pressures of a life that was usually centred around surviving. Whenever he felt sad or angry, he would go out and talk with people and ask them about their lives. He wanted to know about their likes, their wishes, their dreams; what they hoped for and what they lived for; and then when he heard their stories, when he took pictures, this encouraged him to be strong.

Nadir's family was one of the first beneficiaries of Insaan's experiments in peace. Grappling with ideas of peace and justice, Insaan had come to the conclusion that one of the root issues was economic inequality. The global economic system of capitalism was not and had not been working for millions of people worldwide.[4] In these mountain areas there were certain necessities for life that were never fully satisfied: education, health-care, food, water and employment. Insaan had seen how Afghan families couldn't maintain a healthy diet; their children died from drinking unclean water; their education system was poor; they struggled to earn an income from farming or to find other meaningful employment. All this meant that many families relied on their children to work and some people were even forced to join the militia to earn wages. Insaan wanted to approach the issue of economic peace on a micro level by assisting an individual Afghan family in the village to overcome economic hardship and rise above the economic restrictions the global system placed upon them.

Insaan assessed Nadir's family finances and saw that this family of six children and one widowed mother were stuck in the lowest strata of the global economic system and there was no way they could pull themselves out of this financial rut without assistance. So Insaan devised some experiments to help them. Insaan asked his colleague who was an agriculturalist for advice on how to improve the yield of their crops. They tried different worm farms and different composts to fertilise the soil, but Insaan soon realised that it didn't matter how productive their crops were because the family did not own enough land to make a subsistence living from farming.

Acquiring more land in the area was not simple. They did not have money to buy land, but within the village there was land seen as 'common areas', with no private owners. Insaan noticed that other villagers had begun to build houses on this land without permission, so he advised the family to secure some of it for farming. Nadir's family did so, acknowledging that if they left it to the village council to make allocations, they may not receive any land as they were a 'fatherless family'. Being a vulnerable family without a man as their head, they didn't have the authority to demand a fairer deal. But even with this extra land they couldn't produce enough to yield a sustainable living.

Insaan turned to the only other source of income for the uneducated rural Afghan family: run a shop, sell goods, trade wares, like many millions of people all over the world. But how could they earn enough capital to start their own business? Nobody was going to give them capital, that's not how the system worked. If the system lent them money, they would be charged interest, which would eat into their profits and increase their financial debt. In Afghan society, interest was considered *haram* and was not allowed, according to Islamic law. However, the reality was that organisations charged interest on loans; they just called it by another name, so it would be religiously legitimate. Taking a loan with interest was not going to work for Nadir's impoverished family, so Insaan arranged an interest-free micro-loan through friends of his. Using this loan, the family made a metal shed from which they ran a store selling household provisions. Nadir and his brother travelled into town every week to buy oil and other necessary items and brought them back to the village to sell on the side of the road. Nadir and his brother ran the shop with so much success that they paid the loan back in full. They didn't get rich from the earnings, they didn't make any savings, but it helped them to get by a little better than before.

Insaan drew hope from this success. Perhaps if he could teach Nadir creativity in business and problem solving, Nadir could raise his family out of economic misery. Potatoes were the prized crop of the region – they were reputed to be the best potatoes in Afghanistan, maybe in the world, or so the locals said. There was no shop making packeted potato crisps in the entire province, so Insaan encouraged Nadir to try it. Nadir rented a shop in town and started making French fries and crisps. He and Insaan hired local youth in the area as shop assistants, choosing working children on the street to offer a safe job with a stable income. Hafizullah, Arif and Muslimyor all joined Nadir as employees.

Nadir made a successful business selling his homemade produce, but he was fighting an uphill battle. His sole competitor was Lay's chips, a multinational corporation that monopolised the market, selling to every store in the province. Against this giant of industry, this symbol of globalised capitalism, Nadir and his staff of young boys were only ever going to earn modest gains from their chip shop. The venture would never lift Nadir out of poverty; it wouldn't earn enough funds for him to buy land for his family, or fund future investments or business ideas. It was just another survival mechanism.

Through these experiments Insaan realised that the impoverished family of rural Afghanistan was destined to live a life of hardship. Success in this global system was based on possessing capital, but these families couldn't churn out something from nothing. Their only hope to rise from the bottom economic rung was to study at university and find work in an urbanised city centre, paying rent to live in homes they would never be able to afford to buy. However, they spent their childhood working to survive, barely learning within an education system that failed to teach children how to read. What chance did they have to enrol in and graduate from university? For Nadir's family and for many of the families in the area, capitalism would never work.

It became clear in Insaan's mind that they lived in a system of economic warfare that exploited large masses of people for the profit of a few. This modern-day feudalism in itself was damaging when it denied people the basic human needs of food, water, shelter, healthcare, education and healthy relationships. Insaan reasoned that most of the profiteering elite probably did not think about their business methods being directly or indirectly harmful or violent to others, but he witnessed the poverty maintained by such a system and believed it was one of the root causes of 'terrorism' in this region. This was economic violence. The global economic system was broken. If he was going to challenge the violence of war, it was important to address the violence of economics as well.

Rather than demoralise Insaan, his understanding of economic violence motivated him to continue his experiments in peace. He refused to accept that the unjust system would shape the Afghan destiny. The unexpected reward from these experiments was the creation of a small community of like-minded youth, who first gathered together in Nadir's chip shop under the care and attention of Insaan.

For Insaan, his experiments in peace had only just begun. His next step was to approach the local university with a unique proposal.

GRUTA ARRIVED AT the warehouse early that morning. She wanted to pick out the prettiest duvet covers, even though she was paid per duvet produced, no matter how nice they looked. Maybe making beautiful duvets was a matter of self-respect, of pride in her craft. *Her craft?* She laughed to herself. When she started the project just a few months ago she had never sewed a duvet in her life. But it was a craft of sorts. She had been sewing and mending richer families' clothes for years. And it was better than washing other people's dirty laundry to earn money.

The other seamstresses lined up behind Gruta, all waiting for Muslimyor to arrive. Waiting, lining up, persistent in their need for help: these were their survival tactics. Gruta had applied many times to be enrolled in the duvet project before Muslimyor finally visited her house to conduct an eligibility survey. She was excited and ashamed when he came to inspect her household.

She displayed her poverty like a museum exhibit, hoping she would be destitute enough to be eligible for assistance. The survey didn't take long. She lived in one room, three metres by three metres, with her four daughters and one son. Adjacent to that one room was a small corridor that she used for cooking. It was a miserable room that never caught sunlight and seemed eternally gloomy. But it was cheap rent at 2000 Afghanis per month (approximately US$28) and she had chosen it because her brother lived next door. One of their neighbours was a shopkeeper whose financial situation was much better than her family's. Sometimes he would give them second-hand clothes or leftover food for lunch. Acceptance of this charity was tinged with feelings of gratitude and shame, her constant internal struggle.

Gruta was the only breadwinner in the family. Her husband was in prison, after killing a pedestrian in a car accident, and her children were too young to work. Sometimes she had been unable to prepare a meal for her children and she was terrified at the prospect of the oncoming winter. All her thoughts were occupied with finding enough food and money to help her children survive. She desperately needed this work.

The day she learned that she was being accepted into the program she was so happy she felt as if she was going to faint. For every duvet she sewed she received 150 Afghanis. It took her a week to sew a batch of ten duvets and she was asked to produce five batches over the winter. At the end of the project she would also receive two duvets for her own family.

But there was more value to the work than just money. Sewing these duvets returned to her some kind of self-worth. She was helping other families in need by sewing duvets, not just her own family. If people were doing good deeds for other people in a country as hopeless as Afghanistan, there was hope for all humanity.

Standing in line with the other women, waiting for the materials to make her fifth and final batch of duvets, she acknowledged the enormous help this program had been for her. She recognised how lucky she was to be involved in such a program when so many had no assistance. But she was also acutely aware of the fragility of her survival status and she saw in the other women the same fear, the same desperation that she felt. What would happen to them when this program ended? Where would they get their next Afghani?

She hoped that if there was a duvet project next year she would be given the opportunity to be involved in the project again, even though she knew the rules – Muslimyor hired different seamstresses every year, in order to spread the work out equally. But that didn't stop her from being hopeful. Maybe that's why she wanted to produce beautiful duvets. As if that might make people think she deserved to be picked again.

She did have another plan. She had been trying to enrol her children in the street kids school. She wanted her children to be educated, but she also wanted the food donations that the students of the school received. She had asked Muslimyor every time she had seen him. His answer was always the same.

'The school is full.'

But she knew that often the loudest cry would get the most attention, so she persisted. One day she had sent her daughter to the food cooperative to ask for rice and oil but because she was not part of the school, they couldn't help her. The poor girl had to walk home in the snow in her torn shoes and was depressed and withdrawn for days afterwards. Gruta wouldn't make that mistake again. From now on, she would do the begging in this family. She would pray to God her children would be enrolled in the school. She would pray to God for Muslimyor and the other volunteers.

HORSE APPROACHED THE house, trying to repress the shame inside of him. He knew how valuable his work for the community was, but it didn't make it any easier to knock on strangers' doors and ask them for donations. A man with a beard opened the door, looking down at Horse with suspicion in his eyes. Horse smiled and began his explanation of what a food cooperative was, but halfway through his speech the man interrupted him.

'Why is a young man like you asking for food?' he said bluntly. 'Get a job.' Then he slammed the door in Horse's face. Horse sighed and resumed his trudge through the hillside neighbourhood.

Horse's responsibility with the community was to coordinate the food cooperative. He had previously been involved in the networking team, the accounts team, and had even worked on skills training for women, but his most recent role was by far the most stressful.

The cooperative provided monthly food gifts to the impoverished families of the one hundred children who studied at the street kids school. The community calculated that it would cost US$430 per street kid to provide their family with rice and oil for one full year, as well as to provide school materials and winter clothing. The initiative was only six months old, launched in September 2016 on the International Day of Peace, so there were still many challenges for Horse to overcome in establishing the program. One of the main duties of coordinating the food cooperative was to raise donations. Rather than seek assistance from the international aid sector, the community wanted to encourage Afghans to help their fellow Afghans by donating to the cooperative. The volunteers themselves all donated to the scheme, but most of the donations were made through door-to-door house requests for rice and oil. Horse hated this part of his role. When 54 per cent of the population in Afghanistan lived below the poverty line, and unemployment sat at 40 per cent, it was not easy talking to people about the idea of a cooperative.[5] Convincing them to give up any of the little they had was a hard ask. Distrust had become entrenched in Afghan society, after years of international, governmental and societal corruption. There were two common reactions to his request: he could be praised and thanked for doing the work and he might get a donation; or the more frequent reaction was suspicion, ridicule and hostility.

People thought Horse wanted the food for himself. Some people thought he was trying to steal from them. Sometimes Horse was confused for a beggar or perhaps they thought he was a drug addict or mentally unwell. One time, Horse was attacked by a group of seven men, who tried to rob him of his phone. One man punched him in the face, giving him a black eye and a swollen cheek. Horse was still frightened about something like that happening again. He also had to negotiate the cultural barriers that made door-to-door requests awkward, such as the restrictions on a woman answering the door to a man.

People didn't believe Horse was volunteering his time and energy for the benefit of other people. Decades of war and poverty had meant that very few people in Afghanistan acted without some kind of personal benefit. There was no culture of volunteerism. Horse was constantly accused of being a cheat and a liar, and he was discouraged by the negative comments from the public. He tried to motivate himself by thinking of the families he was helping. He focused on the purpose of the work: to be in the service of other people. However, the people's low opinion of his work caused the teenager to wrestle with the task ahead. Afghan society didn't respect or value his struggle for peace; worse, they called him crazy for even trying it. The more ambitious young people in Afghan society saw volunteer work as a stepping stone to becoming a doctor or a lawyer or a politician; peace activism was purely an achievement to place in their resume.

This frustrated Horse. All Afghans understood the benefits of peace, so why didn't they choose to struggle for peace like he did? He reasoned that for poor Afghans, who were preoccupied with meeting their basic survival needs, it was almost impossible to sustain a long campaign to demand an end to the war. How could they afford to pay rent or buy food if they sacrificed any of their valuable time by volunteering? But the richer members of society, those with the most power, weren't interested in helping lift Afghanistan up. They were purely motivated by their own desire for success and status.

When Horse visited his family home after a long day working without pay, society's disrespect for his work and his feeling of inadequacy ate away at him. He left behind the modern two- and three-storey buildings near the Community Centre and entered the narrow mudbrick alleys of his family's suburb. He pushed open a gate and walked into a filthy courtyard, a smelly outhouse crumbled into itself in the corner. The house was a long, single-storey building, with broken windows covered in plastic to stop the rain and retain the heat. His three younger brothers, his sister and his mother shared the house with three other families. Each family lived in one room. His mother worked as a housemaid, earning a pittance. She didn't want her children to work because she was so worried about militant attacks, but this put extra pressure on her to be the breadwinner. While Horse's family's focus was survival, while they struggled to meet basic human needs, he found it difficult to imagine choosing the immaterial benefits of being a peace activist over a career that would reward him and his family financially. He was on the verge of graduating from high school and he felt burdened by the need to choose a life path.

Even though Horse had been working with the community for more than five years, his struggle with the perceptions of his volunteer work and the desire to support his family was ever present in his mind. Horse balanced those negative feelings by talking with his team and other volunteers, who supported him through his concerns. When he talked to Insaan about the ridicule, Insaan quoted Gandhi.

'First they ignore you, then they ridicule you, then they oppose you and then you win.'

Horse realised that rather than waiting for society to value his work, he needed to change something within himself to value the work and not feel ashamed.

Once a month, directly after the street kids school finished, the volunteers stacked the donated tins of oil and sacks of rice in the yard of the centre to be collected by the beneficiaries of the food cooperative project: the families of the street kids.

Children ran around the garden, screaming and laughing, pushing and pulling each other, playing tag, riding bicycles, crashing bicycles. Some parents stood to one side, slightly embarrassed behind burqas and scarves and thick coats, waiting for their ration to be distributed. Other parents waited outside, away from the hubbub. Horse began the distribution process, standing on the elevated patio above a clutch of children, calling out names from a clipboard registry. Underfed and undernourished children shouldered bags of rice as big as them and staggered off to their parents. The last of the winter duvets were distributed. Some children sat on their family's hoard, against the wall, until the crowd had dispersed and then their parents entered with a wheelbarrow to take their goods away. Passers-by observed this charity and wanted to receive help too. The program was explained to them as 'giving to the needy, starting with the street kids'. This resolved some of the observers' curiosity, but others were not satisfied with being turned away and never would be. There were very few families in Afghanistan who didn't need an extra blanket or bag of rice.

It was during the madness of one such food distribution that Horse found clarity of thought. Amongst this distribution of goodwill and restoration of hope, Horse realised that the people who valued his work the most were the people he was helping. The ridicule of the ignorant was meaningless next to the gratitude of these families.

From that moment on Horse became determined to improve the process of asking for donations. When they approached houses to make an appeal, they brought brochures explaining that they were part of an organisation and what the group was doing. This acted as their armour against suspicion. They asked those who distrusted their motives to come to the centre and see the good work they did. In an attempt to break away from performing the dreaded door-to-door appeals, they started approaching businesses and mosques to try to establish regular donors. They refused to ask the government or agencies for assistance.

'Don't go to the thieves,' Insaan had said.

Despite the challenges, the food cooperative team managed to secure help from a few local sources. Horse started to develop more self-belief and he worked out that the cooperative was about rebuilding a sense of community among the people. It was about reminding people how to give rather than just take and gave them an opportunity to be generous. By doing all that, it offered people hope that they could help each other out of their poverty and teach each other how to be good people again. They didn't need the international community to do this or the government. They could do it themselves. And it was this type of work that would build the foundations towards future peace in Afghanistan.

Chapter 4

Radical Thinking

Insaan stood before a class of university students and delivered his final address.

'Einstein said when talking about war, "We cannot solve our problems with the same thinking we used when we created them. We shall require a substantially new manner of thinking if mankind is to survive." War is the same old, tragic story. It will never be that new manner of thinking required for our survival, for our freedom from fear and our search for meaning.'[1]

Insaan had been living in the mountains of central Afghanistan for more than three years, and he resolved that something needed to be done about the disease of warfare. He had approached the local university with an idea to run a peace workshop. He didn't have a grand plan behind the workshop; he just wanted to start the conversation. The university approved the idea and fifty undergraduates at the university agreed to meet on a weekly basis over a three-month period to discuss whether it was possible to build peace in Afghanistan. Today was the last class of the workshop and Insaan wanted to pose a final question to the students.

'Martin Luther King spoke of a revolution of values, which will lay hands on the world order and say of war: "This way of settling differences is not just." Attend to the means by which peace is pursued, Gandhi said, and the ends will look after themselves. There is a blueprint here for a path to peace. Do you think peace is possible in Afghanistan?'[2]

The culmination of the workshop was that the majority of participants felt peace was impossible in Afghanistan. Insaan understood why the students reached such a conclusion: their experiences over the past few decades left little hope for reconciliation. But he was also slightly stunned by the response. Throughout the workshop, Insaan had tried to open doors in the students' minds; he had tried to guide them towards different ways of thinking; he had introduced them to different thinkers and activists; all tactics to drive them towards alternatives to warfare, towards methods of peace. The students' conclusion left the group with the dilemma of endless war. How were they supposed to continue to live with war and this impossibility of peace? Insaan couldn't accept that. He had to do something. By that time, it had become clear to Insaan that one contributing factor to conflict in Afghanistan was ethnic division. Perhaps it was time Afghans addressed this.

'Thank you very much,' Insaan said. 'It's been a valuable three months for me. I respect the conclusion of the majority that peace is impossible in Afghanistan. But what are we going to do about this impossibility?'

Insaan looked out across a silent audience who stared back at him, half-fearful, half-expectant. *What could they do about an impossibility?* They sat on the edge of their seats, holding their breath, waiting for him to offer some ideas.

'Martin Luther King grew up in a segregated society, where black people drank from different water fountains to white people. Is this what you want for Afghan society? Separate toilets for Hazaras and Tajiks and Pashtuns? There is no segregation by law in Afghanistan as there was in the United States when Martin Luther King was alive, but there is segregation in the workplace. There is social segregation. There is mental segregation. Perhaps segregation begins primarily in the mind. Perhaps that is where we can begin. Would any of you consider living together in a multi-ethnic community for one semester? Think of it as an experiment in peace, an attempt to mend the ethnic disharmony that prevents Afghans from seeing each other as human. If we can create a microcosm of a peaceful multi-ethnic community here in this town, perhaps we can act as an example to the rest of Afghanistan. Perhaps we can be the leaders in a more peaceful future.'

Afghanistan used to be a country connected by interrelated networks of tribes, clans and families. Within these communities, people built and strengthened social networks. That cohesion had been damaged by decades of fighting; Insaan theorised that in order to achieve peace and restore society, Afghans needed to regain that sense of community.

It was a radical idea, a dangerous experiment in a country as divided as Afghanistan. Participants had many people to fear: the religious elite, warlords, the Taliban, their government, their own communities and their own families. And yet, at the end of the class that day, Insaan was surprised to be approached by sixteen male students, from seven different ethnic groups, who wanted to participate in the project. They agreed to live together in one house for one semester.

The first multi-ethnic live-in community consisted of a mixture of Pashtuns, Hazaras, Uzbeks, Turkmen, Tajiks, Sayyids and Pashai. The students moved into a building of four rooms. Insaan chose not to live with the group but instead urged them to make their own observations and draw their own conclusions from the experience, which they communicated to him. Not one member of the group had ever lived with another ethnic group before, let alone six others. This was an opportunity for them to talk about the different ways they ate, prayed and thought. There were personality clashes as expected, but they told Insaan they found the experience to be a positive one overall.

Before starting the project all the students signed an agreement to say that they were willing participants. Many of the students were concerned that the local people and religious leaders would misunderstand the purpose of the exercise, but in the end they decided they were willing to take the risk. It turned out the students' concerns were not unfounded. They were denied permission to rent a home after telling the owners about the project. In rural towns like the one they lived in, the mosques were intimately involved in the social and political affairs of the area. With that in mind, a few of the students approached the mullah of the local mosque to inform him of the project. Although the mullah never said he was against the idea, it was clear he felt uneasy about mixed ethnic groups of Sunni and Shia Muslims sharing an apartment.

Even though the exercise was run by the university, the local community began to question the students' involvement in the experiment. Through his work as a doctor in the local area, Insaan had established enough trust in the community to enable him to initiate the university workshop. But the live-in community had the potential to damage his reputation. The local community couldn't understand why the students would stay together like this in one house and they questioned the purpose of the project. The students were worried about upsetting the very delicate balance of peace in the area.

Despite these fears, the positive experience of the experiment made such an impact on the students that it gave them the courage to carry on with their peace work after the live-in trial ended.

'The International Day of Peace is coming and we want to celebrate it,' the students told Insaan.

Insaan had already begun thinking that this group of young people could hold the key to the dilemma of war. If he could recruit young people to this group, a group that conversed with fellow Afghans, discussed basic principles of peace, morality and law, they could build a community that would work together for a better Afghanistan. They would need to place the universal values of peace in the public consciousness, and to do that they would need to take action.

Insaan encouraged the group to involve other young people in the area: their friends, their family members, other students from the university; whoever they could muster. While Insaan wanted this movement to be theirs, he treated their budding sense of social justice like a careful gardener, prompting them with encouragement and suggestions. He connected them with other youth organisations and the local youth directorate of the province.

The community and Insaan went from village to village, visiting the local youth councils. They talked about their wish for peace and they asked young people to register their displeasure against war. Initially not many people responded to their call to action. Insaan put that down to a mistrust of the concept of volunteerism. But through the visits, and other circles and contacts, Insaan and the new activists slowly broadened their sphere of influence. The group of sixteen organised a seminar at the university for the International Day of Peace and they invited the contacts they had made. The young people wore uniformed traditional Afghan dress and addressed the seminar with a short testimony about peace. They then sang the national anthem, with its inclusive line, 'This is the country of every tribe', to deliver their message of ethnic unity.

The director of the youth directorate was impressed by the ambitions of the youth and he was in support of the live-in community experiment. He offered his assistance in recruiting more young people and expanding the movement.

At this point the community and Insaan began to start their own local projects. The group's first demonstration was an international peace trek, in which 150 Afghans walked for peace. They were joined by more than thirty-five internationals from various countries, including staff from more than twenty embassies. They trekked for peace amidst the Hindu Kush mountain ranges, finishing at a pristine alpine lake, 4200 metres above sea level. The youth delivered a speech before their countrymen and the guests, a dignified call for harmony.

Through Insaan's work in primary health care, he had been exploring a range of ways to help improve living standards in the district and he encouraged the youth to become involved in the local environment movement. They arranged the district's first 'clean and green' campaign to clean up the local township. This campaign paved the way for their first major development project in the area, the building of a peace park.

THE PEACE HOUSE walls were decorated with photos of friends and guests of the community. I plucked a photo off one of the walls and examined the group of people shown. They were dressed in colourful woven scarves and looked like they might be indigenous to Central America. Part of the message on the back of the photo read, 'To our sisters and brothers whose dignity is the same … We keep you in our prayers to give you strength, love and courage to transform your history of pain into a story that is saving, liberating, integrating and dignifying. May your efforts and the unity of all help join our voices for a better world …'

'These are our brothers and sisters in Guatemala,' Insaan said. 'It's important for the community to understand that all around the world there are examples of peaceful, sustainable lifestyles.'

Insaan had taught the students about peaceful communities all over the world, both contemporary and historical. From the Jewish Kibbutzniks to the Quakers in the United States, he tried to demonstrate the breadth and diversity of peace workers globally. One source of inspiration for the community was the Peace Community of San Jose de Apartado in Colombia. This collective of more than 1000 peasant farmers resisted widespread conflict in Colombia by establishing a peaceful community. The community faced threats, stigmatisation and violence because of its members' choice to resist displacement and declare themselves neutral in the middle of a civil war. Since its formation in 1997, more than 200 members of the community had been murdered.[3]

Insaan wanted the community to be in contact with other indigenous communities because they shared similar histories of invasion, conquest, extermination and colonisation. Indigenous Afghan tribal communities shared a sense of community with other indigenous people; they related as a community more than they related as individuals.

In reaching out to these indigenous peace communities, Insaan and the group were introduced to models they wanted to replicate. Those communities helped their Imagination Team design their own utopian concept. The team had weekly meetings where they put together a vision of a community fifteen years into the future. They imagined a multi-ethnic community that would include families. They would live on a private piece of land that would be border free. They would embody the principles and practices of nonviolence. They would engage in farming and keep livestock and would be self-sustainable.

'It's all described in the concept paper, which will remain a document with the community until they feel ready to focus on it,' Insaan said.

These were admirable philosophies, but I feared their unusual living arrangements would obscure their message and only serve to antagonise the conservative sections of Afghan society. I decided to share my concerns with Insaan, to understand why he was so interested in this idea of community.

Insaan's eyes sparkled and he folded his legs beneath himself, saying, 'If we want radical change, perhaps we need to think radically.

'Modern society is not as advanced as we think. There are eight individuals who own as much wealth as half of the human race.[4] Humanity could end global poverty if the world's priorities shifted.[5] That's what individualism, materialism, consumerism and capitalism have done. It doesn't matter what the names are, it's the principles and practices which have led to this. If we thought more as communities and less as individuals we would meet the basic needs of all our people.'

I did not disagree with him, but I wondered if he was ignoring the clear, if uneven, advances in systemic issues such as global poverty, education and health, thanks to programs of global cooperation. While Afghanistan was mired in conflict, most of the rest of the world was living in the most peaceful time in human history.

Insaan shook his head and then smiled at me with creased eyes. It was the closest he had come to openly disagreeing with me.

'My medical exposure makes me inclined to rely on science and its related technologies to assist life and human beings, but it hasn't helped Mother Earth. Our purpose and practice seem to consist predominantly of love for self, rather than a love for all of life. At the individual level, we live for ourselves; further our personal wellbeing; earn more money; spend it in unlimited consumption; and console ourselves that science and material things have made the planet look physically better. Our inner worlds, however, are not very healthy. For all this talk of "progress", the evidence is pointing in the other direction.'

In the past century, the systems of governance human societies had adopted were hurling us along the road to 'mutually assured destruction'. Indeed, while we spoke there were more than 60 million people displaced worldwide due to conflict and persecution. Trump was threatening nuclear war with North Korea. Putin was bragging about his nuclear arsenal and China's navy was on conspicuous display in the South China Sea. Noam Chomsky called the US Republican Party 'the most dangerous organisation in human history' because their policies on climate change and nuclear war were threatening to destroy the prospects for human existence.[6] The United States was spending over US$600 billion per year on maintaining military hegemony over the world. That amounted to more than a third of the annual global military expenditure.[7] As our planet's essential resources diminished our world leaders would have more reason to go to war.

'The world is currently governed by psychopaths,' Insaan said. 'You know what we need to do? Bring all the world leaders to a camp where they can learn good psychological practices.'

Insaan joked, but I bet if he was given the chance he would happily sit down with Putin and Trump and discuss their emotions.

'We need to understand who we are as a human race. We need to broaden our understanding of community. We need to look after the human family, not just our own family. Each and every attempt to understand this is progress, even if there are mistakes or flaws in our attempts. That's how science discovers new things. It experiments. This community is my experiment. If we can learn to live together, to eat together, to work together, why can't the rest of Afghanistan? Why can't the rest of the world?'

At the heart of this work was relationship-building. That's why Insaan was nurturing nonviolent skills: to listen, to relate, to communicate, to empathise and to compromise. He believed relationships could change the world.

'When atoms fuse together, even though we can't see this process, they release a power which is huge. The power of relationships can be atomic, even though we can't necessarily see the effects of their fusion. If we can learn to relate to people from all over Afghanistan, even those we would consider as extreme in their views like the Taliban, it will lead to peace. If we can recognise all people's humanity – regardless of nationality, skin colour, religion – we can abolish war. Why would we fight against a fellow human being, a person who wants the same things we do: food, water, shelter, love, connection, intimacy? This type of action would enrich the life and knowledge and understanding of every person. It would give a larger meaning to life and work. That's what we all want, isn't it?'

Within three years Insaan had started to see the community members learn to relate to each other. He had seen how people's narrow, conservative, village view of life changed into a world view. Within three years, the youth had learned his relational model. Now they could sit down with an international visitor or a person from another ethnic group or religious group and have a meal.

'If this could happen with everyone else in the world we would take concrete steps toward global peace.'

THE MOUNTAINS, 2009

In working for peace and ethnic equality in a conservative area of Afghanistan, Insaan understood that trouble was likely. What was difficult to predict though, was how trouble would manifest itself. Insaan expected the worst, but that still didn't prepare him for receiving a direct threat.

When the first experimental community of sixteen was established through the local university, certain sectors of society had been immediately opposed to the idea of a stranger teaching new ideas to their young people. He had thought the opposition might have created positive controversies, that the multi-ethnic community could have started people questioning their own ethnic prejudices. Instead, Insaan received an anonymous letter that said: 'Leave the mountains or we will hurt you.'

From that moment, Zee and Nadir and their families never left him alone. When he travelled between the village and the city on his motorbike, he was accompanied by someone from one of their families. Sometimes he had two family members act as bodyguards; he even had a guard at night. Insaan understood that he could be kidnapped or killed at any time and he wondered if he was prepared to have his life end there. He couldn't even be sure why he was being threatened.

At the urging of his employer and friends, Insaan agreed to leave temporarily. He went to his parents' home, but the intimidation followed him there too, when his mother received a terrifying anonymous call that Insaan had been kidnapped and hurt. The hoax had clearly been intended to scare Insaan and his family, but in fact Insaan felt his conviction for the cause growing and strengthening. He believed his departure encouraged aggressive behaviour and weakened his approach to developing non-violent relationships in the community. If he was going to run away at every sign of trouble, he would never achieve any positive progress. After a month away, he returned to the mountains.

When Insaan returned, he wanted to use peace philosophy to treat the root of the problem. This was the true sense of the word 'radical' – to affect the fundamental nature of something – and a method he theorised could help resolve issues of war and terrorism. He believed that the main motive behind the threats made to him was money rather than ideology, acknowledging that in a country as desperate as Afghanistan the opportunistic desire for money always had the power to corrupt thought and deed. He spread a message among the local community saying that he would like to engage in talks with those who threatened him. While he was ready to meet his antagonists, it did not appear that they were ready to meet him. He never received a response to his offer of peace.

Chapter 5

When We Destroy Nature, We Destroy Ourselves

Near the Peace House, alongside the polluted Kabul River, the community established what Insaan called a peace park. Three rows of scrawny trees grew between a dirt road and a stone wall that bordered the waterway. The trees closest to the road were strangled by a roll of hurricane wire: the securitisation of Afghanistan even included their flora. Grass grew sporadically out of the rock-hard clay. One metre from the stone wall ran a gutter of filth. A homeless man wrapped in a blanket slept at the base of one of the trees. The river water next to the garden was filled with sewage and trash. At the far end of the garden, a vagabond investigated a rubbish tip. Each gust of wind picked up rubbish from the pile and flipped it towards the garden or the river. On the riverbank, a drug addict cooked his lunch on a plastic-fuelled fire.

The peace park, like the Community Centre, was a short distance from the Peace House. We walked on disintegrating footpaths alongside a chaotic main road full of beeping, swerving traffic. Buildings barged up to the edge of the road so there was little space to manoeuvre on the narrow sidewalks. The supermarkets were protected by armed private security. We passed young men, some dressed in traditional Afghan robes, others in Western dress, all with neatly styled hair. We didn't say much as we walked; Insaan preferred it if we didn't speak English on the street. We turned a corner and entered a bustling market. Street vendors sold kebabs and French fries; men pushed carts of apples, oranges and bananas between neat stands of eggplant and radishes; meat stalls displayed confronting sections of beef. Life for the everyday Afghan citizen carried on as normal.

'A core part of the community's philosophy is to combat the environmental violence that is polluting the country and destroying their land,' Insaan said. 'The community understands that without a habitable world, all their other activities would be fruitless.'

Indeed, the challenges they faced were great. Afghanistan was a member of the V20 group, a partnership of the twenty countries most vulnerable to the catastrophes of climate change.[1] In Afghanistan there was pollution of every imaginable type, evident in every aspect of their life, which threatened health and life. Inefficient sewerage, drainage and waste management systems allowed plastic and rubbish to litter the city, filling the drains and dumps and clogging the gutters. The Kabul River had been reduced to a fetid sewer, the fish and waterfowl long gone. The waste of close to five million people and their livestock ran untreated in open ditches into the river. In many areas of the country the water wasn't safe to drink or wash with. The number of internally displaced people still fleeing fighting, seeking security in Kabul, was overcrowding the city and draining the water table.[2] Every year the wells were dug deeper.[3] Meanwhile the glaciers and snow pack in the surrounding mountains that previously fed the Kabul River were diminishing due to global warming. Drops in rainfall and snowfall had caused drought in twenty-one of the provinces.[4] There was much wisdom to the Afghan saying, 'May Kabul be without gold rather than without snow'. As an agricultural nation, decreasing snowfall threatened the livelihoods of the majority of its people.

Overcrowded traffic in an overcrowded city kicked up dust and coughed up harmful gases. Malodorous garbage was burned on the sides of the roads and paths. Trees were cut down for firewood so people could survive the harsh winters. When there were no trees to cut down and when people didn't have enough money to buy firewood, they burned plastic instead. While Kabul was losing its trees, the rest of the country was being deforested by business and war. The World Health Organization estimated that air pollution caused more than 11,000 deaths annually in Afghanistan.[5] The environmental degradation of war was becoming as deadly as the blast of missiles and bombs.

When I looked at this collection of emaciated trees, it was almost laughable to think of the community battling the environmental challenges Afghanistan faced. I could understand the practical, environmental purpose to the garden: the community were planting and growing trees to clean the air. And I could see the aesthetic, community-driven purpose: they planned to add seats and paths to the garden, they wanted to erect a sign commemorating peace, and they wanted to plant more flowers. They wanted to make what was ugly, beautiful; to do their little bit to make the world a better, cleaner place. Even so, I once again found myself admiring the community's ambition but doubting their efficacy.

The day the community marched onto this dry, infertile space was a demonstration against war, an act of advocacy, a moment where the community members decided to plant trees instead of reacting in anger.

It happened in response to a bombing in 2013, before the Community Centre was opened. Insaan and the community members heard and felt a loud explosion near their house one afternoon. For the rest of that night they waited anxiously for the sound of rocket fire and bullets to stop. The tension manifested through rage, tears, anger and grief.

It was reported that a ten-year-old girl and four assailants were killed. It took the community a few days to decide upon an appropriate response to the violence perpetrated by the Taliban, the militia groups, the Afghan government, and the US–NATO coalition.

Members of the community decided to adopt an area near the attack site and plant saplings of evergreen trees. It was a simple philosophy. When people take life, replenish the planet with new life. When people destroy the present, build for a better future. When people offer hatred, return that hatred with love.

Not far from that burnt-out, rocket-damaged house, twenty-five members of the community began their work. They started by cleaning the area of litter, that poisonous trickle-down from human consumption.

'Why bother? It'll be even dirtier tomorrow,' remarked an onlooker.

'You're wasting your time,' shouted another man.

Trying not to feel foolish, the community members ignored the cynical swipes. Armed with shovels and picks and goodwill, they attacked the hard ground. Students and street kids, men and women, side by side, chose life over death. They were joined by officials from the city municipality in their black shoes and suits. Then, passing students not connected with the action asked if they could help plant a tree in the dust. Finally, a woman came, stoically holding a sapling. She did not say a word, but with steady hands used to making bread, she planted roots for all of humanity.

They planted sixty trees that day. But they were not just trying to grow trees, they were trying to change attitudes towards the environment. They used water from the neighbouring houses to irrigate the garden; they couldn't use the river water because it was too polluted. Over time the people in the neighbourhood came to protect the garden and stopped others cutting down the trees for fuel. These neighbours even watered the trees for the volunteers. The community was reminding people to care about the environment again.

I started to see the garden in a different light. Insaan's story imbued it with life and character and meaning. It was not a beautiful garden, but it perfectly symbolised the mentality of the community. Those motley trees growing out of dry soil were acts of defiance, just as the community was defiant in the face of war. It was a miracle that the trees could survive in such conditions; it was a miracle that anyone planted them at all.

'This is our second park dedicated to peace,' Insaan said, standing proudly before his urban forest. 'Our dream is to have a peace park in every province of the country.'

THE GARDEN OF the Peace House was full of half-finished projects, scraps of wood, and crumbling concrete. A broken tap and a sink stood against the wall of the garden; the unwashed concrete garden walls that used to be yellow were zebra-striped with grime. At one end there was an abandoned swing-set frame without the swings, and a table. Old clothes had been dragged off the clothesline by the wind and left to fade and crust in the sun. The house rented by the community was the ground floor of a three-storey building that was shared with three families. Every so often you could hear the shouting of the neighbours who lived on the floor above. In this chaotic environment the community's permaculture team built a greenhouse. The flourishing cactuses and herbs had been a small success in a particularly harsh winter.

While I was in Kabul, the community had been hosting permaculture classes with an expert in sustainable gardening, invited by Insaan. Ro was a friend of Martin's from the Blue Mountains, just outside of Sydney. She was more than 70 years of age, but that hadn't tempered her boundless energy and enthusiasm. For several weeks she cut a swashbuckling figure in the centre, teaching the community members about permaculture techniques.

Insaan believed permaculture could be an important tool in addressing the extreme vulnerability of food and water in Afghanistan. Close to one third of Afghans were lacking reliable access to sufficient affordable, nutritious food. Around 40 per cent of children under the age of five had stunted growth, while 10 per cent were acutely malnourished.[6] Even though the majority of the population lived in rural areas and worked as farmers, only 12 per cent of the land was cultivable.[7] Ongoing drought, warfare and human displacement was reducing the already diminished possibilities for agricultural and livestock production. As a result, Afghanistan was forced to import a large proportion of its food from Pakistan and Central Asia, an insecure food network that was dependent on potentially volatile political relationships.[8]

Afghanistan's food vulnerability was an extreme example of a global crisis. Ro taught that it was time to return to local, subsistence farming, appropriate to the environment. The permaculture classes concentrated on small-scale, high-yielding urban gardens, and water recycling and saving.

Under Ro's guidance, the community had begun two 'learning gardens' in the Community Centre and the Peace House. The community had arranged to start another garden on a plot at the Kabul University. They hoped that through this program they could spread their learnings to other students.

'Cuba's agricultural industry was in turmoil after the fall of the Soviet Union in the 1990s,' Ro explained. 'Without Soviet oil the country couldn't transport food from their farms to their cities. The country utilised vacant urban spaces to grow more than ten thousand urban farms, feeding the nation and creating jobs.'[9] She reasoned that if the Afghan people could be encouraged to grow healthy, sustainable urban gardens, the country could resolve its own food crisis and alleviate economic stress on families all over the country.

THE MOUNTAINS, 2009

Insaan joined the local governor of the province in examining a small plot of arid government land covered in pebbles, stones and boulders. The site was edged on one side by buildings and on the other side by the main river and a path heading into town. The governor turned to Insaan with an incredulous look.

'You want to turn this site into a green space?' she asked him.

'Yes,' he replied with an encouraging nod and smile.

'Do you have access to funds?'

'No.'

'You just have a group of teenagers?'

'Yes.'

The governor shook her head at him and gave him a look that made it apparent she worried for his sanity.

'I'm sorry, but you have insufficient resources to complete the job and I don't think it will work,' she said to Insaan.

Insaan regarded this as a temporary setback only: he and the volunteers were going to have to find other supporters.

In the months since the end of the peace workshop, the group had recruited a number of teenagers and university students to their cause, including Arif, Nadir, Asghar and Muslimyor. They were organising more and more activities and their latest idea was to nurture a peace park, stemming from Insaan's growing belief that when we destroy nature, we destroy ourselves.

Insaan was raised in a city. As a child his relationship with nature was academic: he read about jungles in books and he had only ever seen mountains on television. When he moved to this region of Afghanistan, his relationship with nature grew into something real. He came to understand the indigenous Afghan communities' connection with Mother Nature.

Early humans believed in interconnectedness. They understood our place in the universe and our dependence on the natural world. They believed in a responsibility to protect, preserve and live in harmony with the planet. They understood that the world belonged to future generations, not just the current generation.

Nowadays, we speak of nature as separate from ourselves. We mistakenly believe we have evolved beyond the need for nature. We are consuming more resources than ever before, and it isn't sustainable. We dispose of waste without understanding where it goes and how it affects the planet. We continue to pollute the natural resources essential to our survival, ignoring the fact that when we destroy nature, we destroy ourselves.

Insaan believed climate change was caused by an endless need to develop, advance, progress. But most of the world didn't seem to care about resolving this issue. The world's struggle to accept the reality of climate change scared him and he realised that violence against nature was as important an issue as the violence of war. He approached this global challenge the same way he had approached his previous experiments, attempting to solve it within the community. Insaan was confident that the youth could create a green space in town that would be open to the local people.

The volunteers had decided from the beginning of the project that they would only ask for funds from Afghan organisations and businesses. They didn't want to rely on any international funds, partly because once anything was built in Afghanistan using foreign money, signage went up stating where the money came from. The group thought it was an insulting reminder about the nation's reliance on foreign development funds.

Insaan and the volunteers approached the owner of the biggest hotel in town for assistance.

'I will give a small amount for some soil because nothing will grow on that hard, rocky ground. But you'll have to remove the stones first,' the hotel owner said.

Boosted by their first pledge, the volunteers engaged in the laborious process of removing all the smaller stones with shovels. After that, a provincial reconstruction team from ISAF agreed to move the larger boulders and level the site with tractors and bulldozers. Once the area was cleared, the owner of the hotel brought a few trucks of agricultural soil to the park.

The volunteers then approached the provincial agricultural department and the local municipality to provide tree saplings. But the two bodies seemed unable to agree with one another and kept shifting responsibility between them as to who should assist the group. This bureaucratic bickering went on for some months, which frustrated the volunteers. They couldn't understand why it was so difficult to build something that was in the interest of the community and the government. During this project they learned that government agencies were slow machines, encumbered by inefficient bureaucracy. Insaan supported and encouraged the volunteers from behind the scenes.

'Don't give up. Never give up.'

Insaan could see that success would be a necessary motivator to empower the movement and its members, and failure had the potential to undermine their self-belief and derail their momentum.

Insaan was proud to see his volunteers respond to the challenges with determination and optimism. It was the volunteers who did the legwork of going between the bureaucrats, demanding funding; and it was the volunteers who returned again and again to the plot of land to prepare the ground. Finally their persistence paid off.

'Fine. Go and collect your saplings,' a public servant at the department of agriculture said, and practically threw the approval letter at the ecstatic youth.

The group then designed the garden, marking out various plots and pathways, and reached an agreement with a local civil society group to make bricks for the signage of the park. And then the hardy saplings took root. The peace park was taking shape.

One day, after all their hard work, Insaan received a call from a major US NGO with an offer of financial support. Tied to a US$10,000 offer to help with the garden was signage to acknowledge funding.

Insaan relayed the offer to the volunteers, wondering if they could look past the money and remember the agreement they had made at the beginning of the project. It was such a large sum of money – could they stand by their convictions and turn it down?

They discussed the offer and came back to Insaan with their answer: 'We don't want their funds.'

By the time the group eventually launched the peace park in October 2009, the once-arid plot of boulders was looking like a fertile oasis. The local people could now walk along tree-lined paths or sit on park benches and enjoy the lush green grass. The youth, with their own hands, had turned a place of stone into a park of beauty. The governor said in front of the local media: 'I must confess, I didn't believe that the youth could do this. Unfortunately, through the years of war and conflict we've lost some values. We've lost self-sufficiency and self-belief. Everyone waits for a foreign NGO to place a stone or brick before doing anything. Building this peace park is an example that we can build our own country and not be dependent on others. We thank the Afghan youth that this can be done.'

On a sign erected naming the park, the youth had a volunteer write their own message on one side of the signboard in beautiful calligraphic Dari: 'Why not love? Why not bring peace?'

Insaan and the volunteers had talked about the indomitable strength of love and the group had agreed it was a belief they wanted to nurture. When Insaan shared their message for the signage with a staff member at one of the international NGOs, the foreigner said: 'Are you sure you want to use this phrase, *Why not love*? Are you sure people will understand this?'

'What do you mean?' Insaan asked.

'It sounds naive. There is a war going on in the country,' the foreigner said, as if they weren't aware.

'They believe in it. I believe in it,' Insaan said indignantly.

When the youth heard about this interaction, they were outraged. Did this foreigner think so lowly of the Afghan people?

'Let her see the park,' they said, and Insaan felt vindicated for his hopeful message.

But maybe this woman's concern was prophetic, because on three occasions unknown people came to the park to vandalise their message of love. The culprits threw red paint on the sign like splashes of blood; they destroyed it by scratching the paint away and chipping off the bricks. It was hard for the volunteers to not feel personally attacked by these acts of vandalism. Nevertheless, each time their sign was defaced, the youth diligently rewrote their message.

To raise funds for the garden, Insaan and the youth published a book of photographs. The book sold out its small print run and they raised enough money to buy a marble dove from Kabul. Insaan and Asghar collected the dove, and Asghar swaddled the symbol of peace like his own child, carefully carrying it all the way back to the mountains. With the help of a volunteer bricklayer, the dove was mounted on the signboard. Just as the vandals destroyed their signboard, over time they slowly chipped away at the dove.

After every act of vandalism, Insaan took the opportunity to discuss with the group what it meant to work for peace, what it meant to do something worthwhile, of value. The anonymous acts of vandalism and violence showed the youth how easy it was to attack their fragile message. It took more courage and strength to build a mission of peace and love than it did to support the status quo, to remain in the cycle of violence. The greater and stronger their movement became, the more ferocious these attacks would become. Insaan was sure that projects they built with great love would be destroyed, but he urged the youth to never give up.

Eventually the dove was torn off the signage completely and was not replaced. But the youth took the opportunity to change the sign to a permanent and more durable marble stone, which vandals were not able to destroy. It read: 'Even a little of our love is stronger than the wars of the world.'

Chapter 6

What Does Equality Mean?

One morning, as the sun crept over the Hindu Kush, a group of young women and men rode bicycles through the streets of Kabul, celebrating their commitment to equality with a display of defiance. People on the street stopped and stared at their unusual procession. Some people shouted encouragement; others did a double-take at the sight of women on bikes. But there were detractors too. One man shouted: 'You're a disgrace to Islam'.

This was the community's bicycle club. Every Friday, a group of around twenty young men and women would set out just after dawn and ride for a couple of hours through the nearly empty streets of Kabul. For security reasons they chose different routes every week, sometimes in parks, sometimes on the road.

Because of the numerous cultural and religious restrictions on women's movements in Afghanistan, many women did not have the opportunity to exercise and maintain their physical health. A woman going into the streets in Afghanistan was usually covered in numerous layers to protect her modesty, encumbering her ability to move freely. If there was a man with the woman, she walked behind him.

To encourage women to join the bicycle club, the community arranged classes. Every Tuesday morning for one hour, the centre was closed to male volunteers, and bicycles were provided so the female volunteers could practise in private. When the women felt confident enough, they could then join the group's regular morning rides through the city using borrowed bikes.

One of the riders was a particularly small boy, about the size of a nine-year-old, dressed in trackpants, a grey jumper with its hood pulled low over his forehead and a black scarf that covered the bottom half of his face. Out of the small hole in the hood peered a little round face with almond-shaped eyes. I realised this wasn't a boy.

'On the street I am called Ali, but when I am at the centre, I am Chehrah,' the young woman said. 'I ride my bike disguised as a boy because I am scared of having acid thrown on me.'

Chehrah was born a refugee, in Pakistan. Her family moved back to Kabul when she was five years old, but it had not been a happy return, with the death of her father in a car accident. She first heard about the community on Facebook, made contact and asked to join. She started working with the food cooperative and then taught with the street kids school. When she joined the bicycle club, she enjoyed a new-found self-confidence and freedom. She acquired a bike of her own and began riding to and from the community and her university classes. Her bike was her favourite way to travel. It was a quiet, cheap mode of transport that didn't pollute the city. The public transport system was unreliable and at times unsafe, and she couldn't afford to taxi everywhere. Where previously she had been restricted by chaperone customs, now she could move about the city as she pleased.

She was happier in Kabul now that she had friends. The community helped her to believe in the future of Afghanistan and encouraged her to work for women's rights; she just hoped her disapproving mother would come to understand that.

The community was not the only group who organised for women to ride bicycles in Afghanistan. There was a national women's cycling team, but even they faced harassment, discrimination and violence from citizens in Kabul.[1] There was also a skateboarding school and NGO called Skateistan – established by Australian Oliver Percovich in 2008 – which started in the streets of Kabul and later moved to a skate park and indoor facility.[2]

'Women don't ride bikes in Afghanistan and Afghans never see men and women riding bikes together,' Chehrah said. 'But the community are committed to encouraging progressive views of women.'

The bicycle was an enormously liberating option for the female volunteers. Indeed, throughout history it had been a major step forward in emancipating women. Perhaps those bicycle rides would be the first revolutions in Afghanistan's liberation from war and its movement towards equality. But this also showed me just how difficult it was for female volunteers to join the community.

TARA PLANTED HER feet firmly on the floor of the public bus, and she tried to sway with the movement of the vehicle to avoid falling into any of the other passengers. She had to be alert and smart to find safe spaces like the one she was in now, where she could avoid contact with men. When the public buses in Kabul were full like this there were frequent complaints about the behaviour of male passengers.

Tara was on edge. She was eighteen years old and it was the first time she had left her house without being accompanied by a member of her family. Well, that wasn't entirely true. Her parents allowed her to travel to school on her own. But this trip was different. This time she didn't have permission to travel alone. This time she had lied to her parents. Today she was visiting a community of young people who were dedicated to building peace in Afghanistan. She was told this was a community where men and women from different ethnic groups worked together to run community development projects. She was told the community was not affiliated with any particular political party or religious sect. The stories about this community were so remarkable that when Tara first heard them she thought her friend Mina was lying or joking. What's more, Tara was surprised to learn that Mina had been teaching street kids with this community group for six months without receiving any salary. The stories were fantastical enough to lure Tara out of her parents' home on this risky and unauthorised excursion.

Tara had finished school and wanted to go to university to study international relations, with the hope of being a diplomat. But her future study depended upon her family: if they were happy with her going to university she would go; if her family decided not to let her, she would not go. This adventure risked her entire future. Just thinking about the consequences of being caught caused her hands to flutter in panic. She had to breathe slowly and deeply to calm herself. At first she had thought Mina mad for telling such strange stories, but perhaps she was the mad one.

'Is the group safe? Are there safe spaces?' Tara asked in the days prior to her visit.

Tara's father was a general in the Afghan army and because of this she had been raised in an environment with additional restrictions for security. Her father and the family were at increased risk and had been threatened before by the Taliban; her teenaged brother had been killed in a suspected targeted attack. Tara's father's life in the military made her visit to the community even more complicated. How could she explain to her father, a man who dedicated his life to fighting wars, her desire to meet with a group of nonviolent activists? She decided to keep her visit to the community secret.

'There are rules,' Mina said. 'We don't take photos of people without permission. We don't post content on social media without permission. Volunteers only come to the centre if they have work to do. A man and a woman cannot be in a room together alone. The community does its best to ensure the safety and privacy of every member.'

Hearing these rules had comforted Tara somewhat, but she still felt fearful of the unknown. Rules alone didn't protect people in Afghanistan.

It was an hour's bus ride from her home to the community centre. By the time she arrived she was sweating profusely under her headscarf and desperate to be free of the crowded bus. She was greeted by Mina, who accompanied her to the centre. Mina had told her that strangers to the community had to be introduced when they first entered the building. It was a safety measure that Tara appreciated. According to Mina, the community used to have an open-door policy that allowed anyone to enter off the street. But this put people at risk. Twice the community had suspected the authorities of trying to plant people in the group; both those volunteers were asked to leave. Mina told her that many of the women used fake names when coming to the community to protect themselves. Tara wondered if she should too.

Mina stopped at the gate of a falling-apart building.

'Ready?' Mina asked.

Tara took a deep breath and nodded.

Tara stepped over the threshold of the centre and entered a new world. A group of young men and women stood in the yard, immersed in a conversation about their work. Among them were Pashtuns, Hazaras, Tajiks and Uzbeks. Public interactions like this, between young men and women who were not family, were not common. Tara went to school with classmates of different ethnicities, but they tended to be separated by their ethnicity and gender. Despite her parents' awful experiences during the war, they had raised her to respect other people regardless of their background. Perhaps this was because her family members were Tajik and Pashtun. But she knew that others felt differently. She had seen the ugly face of discrimination in the area where she lived in Kabul. She saw the way the different ethnic groups would make negative comments about each other to such an extent that the Hazaras were forced out of the area.

Mina smiled and said hello to the volunteers as she walked in. Tara followed close behind her, keeping her eyes averted, her cheeks aflame with shyness. Custom dictated that women should be accompanied by a male escort, usually family, in their travel and interactions. Even if she wanted to speak to one of these strangers she had been raised to avoid such contact. She didn't look at any of the strangers' faces and she didn't want them to look at her face.

Mina led Tara up a flight of stairs and into a small office with cushions placed around the edges. There were two people inside the room: a hawk-nosed young Pashtun man wearing blue robes and a leather jacket, and a young Hazara woman dressed in black pants, blouse and a lavender hijab. The young woman wore little ornamentation, just one silver bracelet that Tara could see, and she wasn't wearing make-up. Her simple, dignified appearance made Tara feel like a painted doll. Mina introduced the duo as Abdul and Hojar.

'These are the two managers of the community,' Mina said.

Abdul had blue eyes and his skin colour was a deep red. His prominent Adam's apple looked like a rock in his throat. He placed his hand on his heart in greeting. Tara looked to the floor and said nothing. Hojar's serious face transformed into a warm smile when greeting Tara.

'Welcome to our community,' Hojar said, before talking generally about the group's activities and aims. She finished with: 'People join this community for many different reasons. There are some who join because they are angry; others because they are grieving. Some join due to a sense of responsibility; because they see no-one else doing the work that needs to be done. We would be very happy if you would volunteer with the group and embrace this core philosophy.'

Tara didn't say a word in response. She kept completely quiet throughout the exchange and tried to remain composed, but her head was spinning. The whole meeting was surreal, but here were these two young people, Abdul and Hojar, confirming all that Mina had said about this group.

Tara was most impressed by Hojar and her ability to express herself. In many areas of Afghanistan, women weren't allowed to go to school; they didn't have the opportunity to go outside of their homes, much less to say anything once outside. But Hojar was able to express her opinions in the meeting without fear and for Tara that was a new experience. While Hojar spoke, she also had the confidence to look her listeners in the face. Tara had never acquired those kinds of communication skills – she had never even thought of it as a possibility.

Any woman who could gain those skills and be able to find her voice in a context outside of her home showed bravery. Tara instantly idolised Hojar. Tara wanted to be as strong as Hojar, she wanted to learn those skills. But there were still many challenges she had to overcome before she could return to the community.

It took Tara some time to gather the courage to ask her family for permission to visit the community regularly; even then she proceeded cautiously. She approached her mother first. Her mother came from an open-minded family. Her brothers and sisters were doctors and engineers and most of them lived abroad. Tara's mother had also travelled overseas. She was very supportive of Tara's education and had never prevented her from studying. When her mother heard about the community, she immediately supported Tara and did her utmost to give her daughter the opportunity to leave the house.

'Your aunties' and uncles' successes arrived because they educated themselves. If you are to serve society so should you.'

At first Tara could only visit the community one day a week. While her mother took full responsibility over the household chores, Tara would rush to the community to work with the street kids, and then she would rush back so she could reach home before her father and brothers.

Tara had wanted to tell her father about the community, but she was worried about how he would react. As a soldier he had risked his life for Afghanistan, and she didn't want him to think she was ashamed of him or that she was ungrateful for his service.

It was Tara's mother who assured her father that the community was safe and persuaded him to let her attend the group. This was a long process and it took almost a year to properly allay his fears. Here was his daughter, who was not freely able to go to the bazaar for safety reasons, regularly travelling alone to a community centre where she worked with young men. Her father came to understand how much this community group meant to her and over time he felt comfortable with the arrangement.

When Tara first visited the group, she had been wary of the social nature of the community. It was dangerous for a woman's reputation to associate with such groups in Afghanistan. Hojar spoke to her about how the group managed such interactions.

'There have been some behavioural issues with some of the volunteers in the past. We do not judge these young people for their behaviour. We have many young men and women who aren't accustomed to socialising together. They are trying to figure out who they are, learning to interact with other people and the other gender. Most of the volunteers are traumatised by the ongoing effects of war on them and their families. Sometimes they can be inadvertently inappropriate. Flirtatiousness makes many of the youth uncomfortable and makes the centre an unsafe place, especially for women. As such, the volunteers have agreed to be strict with this type of behaviour for our own protection.'

Tara understood that female members had to observe social expectations to avoid drawing attention to the group. It was expected that they should dress and behave appropriately. Having the community as a safe space also gave her the opportunity to learn how to speak with men. Slowly she overcame her shyness and became a more confident woman like Hojar.

Tara did not need convincing of the worth of nonviolence – she knew how violence had directly and indirectly affected her family. Once she'd started volunteering she could see how each member of the community embraced the philosophy of nonviolence and then put it into practice to achieve small, local changes. She saw firsthand the effectiveness of local actions and became more and more convinced that social change was possible.

ONE AFTERNOON AT the centre, I was sitting with Insaan, Hojar and the Stalwarts eating pumpkin seeds when I broached a sensitive topic.

'Do you think gender equality is possible in Afghanistan?'

A hush settled over the room. Hafizullah stared at his feet; Horse laughed nervously but didn't answer my question; Hojar stared at the young men, with flashing eyes.

'I can't speak to this idea,' Muslimyor said with a scowl, and then stood up and left the room. Insaan's face didn't change expression but I noticed him observing everything.

I found their reactions to my question strange – they were usually willing to discuss their views. The question didn't seem so radical considering one of the three pillars of the community was to strive for equality.

The cracking of pumpkin seeds filled the silence.

'In 2012 the religious council of Afghanistan announced that women are inferior to men,' Insaan explained. 'President Karzai's office approved the message.'[3]

I asked the group what they thought of a president approving a decree that told people what to believe.

'We live in the Islamic Republic of Afghanistan, so the constitution of the Afghan government is based on Islamic principles,' Hafizullah said. 'Religion is our politics and our politics are our religion.'

'The Afghan mind does not separate religion from politics or life or social issues,' Insaan said. 'From birth, in the home and in public spaces, that is how they have ordered their lives.'

None of the men felt comfortable making a statement that could be perceived to challenge their religion or their religious government. Hafizullah looked uncomfortable with the entire discussion but he felt as if he should contribute.

'It is difficult to discuss these concepts in Afghanistan because each community has a different definition or practice of equality, and people have to behave according to those ideas in that area,' Hafizullah said.

'For example, in Kabul, a woman may not think it fair to wear the burqa. But in the villages, the woman herself may feel more comfortable wearing the burqa.'

While the men found it difficult to speak about equality, Hojar did not.

'That religious decree was established by men,' Hojar said. 'In Afghanistan women must submit to whatever men say. That is the custom. In all the years Karzai was president his wife didn't have a public persona – the highest-ranking political personality in Afghanistan didn't feel free enough to have his wife as a public figure.'

'I can't comment on gender equality,' Horse said. 'But the independent human rights commission has done a lot of work over the years in raising awareness of the rights of women. During and after the Taliban period there were, and there still are, people who adopted the view that women shouldn't go to school and if they did they could only study up to a certain age. Nowadays more and more people are becoming aware that girls have the right to go to school. This is one example of change.'

Horse was finding the middle ground. He didn't address the idea of gender equality in our discussion, but he supported the advancement of women's rights. Perhaps his approach would be the formula for progress in Afghanistan.

'There are more and more reports of violence against women who want to speak out,' Hojar said, with feeling. 'These women face violence in their own homes and their own communities. Women are fighting for their voice and facing the consequences for it. Just look at what happened to Farkhunda.'

Farkhunda was an Afghan woman in her twenties who had an argument with a mullah outside a mosque in Kabul. The mullah falsely, and publicly, accused her of burning the Quran. A mob of angry men dragged her out into the street and then stomped on her, beat her with sticks, stoned her and drove a car over her. The mob dumped her body in the Kabul River and set it on fire. Those who weren't participating in the violence either watched or filmed the attack on their phones. This was in 2015.[4]

'That's why we are so concerned about the behaviour of our volunteers at the centre,' Insaan said. 'Because women are still being stoned in 21st-century Afghanistan. International experts on women's issues have ranked Afghanistan as one of the most dangerous countries in the world for women, particularly regarding non-sexual violence, access to healthcare and access to economic resources.[5] We rely on the wisdom of the female volunteers to navigate society's expectations. For everybody's wellbeing, the volunteers need to understand the limitations of our work and the struggle of women in our society.'

'So, when the community says one of its goals is equality what does that mean?' I asked.

'For now, we are focusing our efforts on ethnic equality and cooperation,' Insaan said.

Insaan's reply acknowledged that religious equality was seldom talked about anywhere in Afghanistan. Even equality between Sunnis and Shias was difficult to discuss. That was why the volunteers thought it would take two generations to achieve change: that wasn't being negative, that was being realistic.

'Teaching in Afghanistan is a process. Imagine students from this political and social environment coming to the door of nonviolence, or equality, or sustainability for the first time. The average person will take three years of consistent hard work to start considering the ideas, because they have never encountered these philosophies before. Over the years I have seen how the volunteers have changed within their personal lives, even if it means distancing themselves from the traditions of their own family. They will be the ones who, in their social context, among their communities and their families, will bring out this personal change at the appropriate time. That's why I have hope. But on a public level it's much slower.'

The conversation that evening made an impact on me – the weight of resistance, the taboos and the self-censorship. I had underestimated the dangers the community faced and the degree of caution they had to show, even in discussing theoretical concepts of equality, and it made me realise how hard it would be to safely effect change in this conservative society.

Later that night, when I was alone with Insaan, I confessed to him my concerns.

'You are one criticism away from serious harm. One slanderous remark away from mob rule,' I said.

Insaan smiled sadly.

'I imagine it sometimes. I may become the object of the mob's anger. The community will not be able to help me. If they do, they will have the same fate as I. I won't be surprised at their helplessness, but I will be disappointed.'

Insaan sighed. 'I would rather be on the hopeful side because that is what it means to strive for change. It is a hopeful endeavour. Those people in the past who opposed unacceptable laws like that of slavery did not know they would be successful and they faced dangerous opposition. That's why threats to the community traumatise us so much. We need to be prepared to be harmed.'

When I went to bed that evening, I couldn't stop thinking of the horrific murder of Farkhunda and the very real possibility that something similar could happen to any of the female volunteers I met, like Hojar.

THE RAIN DROPPED, heavy and miserable, turning the dusty city to mud. The older streets of Kabul that hadn't been rebuilt flooded – in previous years heavy rainfall could shut down the entire city. Rivers of trash were pushed downstream, clogging drains. I sat with Hojar in the office of the Community Centre. She stared out the window in a pensive mood: from her vantage point on the second floor of the centre, she could see the dry community garden, now benefiting from the downpour.

Hojar had spent all morning at the centre meticulously organising the community finances with the other community manager, Abdul. Hojar was proud when the community offered her the position. Even if she could have found another job after graduating from university she would have preferred working with the community. She believed in their mission, but she was not so naive to think they would achieve such grand ideals in their lifetime.

When she took on the role, Hojar had been worried that the other volunteers would be upset that she, a Hazara and a woman, was now manager. There was no official hierarchy of authority in the community. The role was purely administrative, but she was mindful it could cause rivalry among the other volunteers; indeed, money had been the cause of rifts and infighting between ex-volunteers and the community in the past. She was also concerned about how the community would continue to finance its projects. Their benefactors and donors would not be able to support them forever and for this reason she didn't think such funding was sustainable. But she had accepted the offer nonetheless because she was committed to doing the practical work, the concrete action of the community.

'When I was young I accepted my role in society because I didn't know there was any other way,' she said, still looking thoughtfully out the window. 'However, my experiences of war and my family circumstances caused me to lose patience with society's expectations of me. Now, I think of myself as rebellious.'

She looked at me with a determined smile, as if to emphasise her last remark. Hojar didn't think she was a special case in wanting more freedom as a woman. She thought lots of Afghan women felt the same as her and she took heart from the brave activists – the human rights advocates, politicians, feminist writers and artists and many others all over the country – who pushed back against the patriarchal structure. However, she believed there was still a lot of work to do.

'Since 2001, when the US and NATO forces invaded Afghanistan, the term "women's rights" has been repeated almost like a slogan. But in reality, they haven't taken solid shape.'

One of the justifications given by the United States for invading was to liberate Afghan women from the persecution and oppression of the Taliban. Yet the United States was aware of the oppression of women in Afghanistan before 9/11 and was silent on the matter. Meanwhile it financed the perpetrators.

In truth, advancing women's rights in Afghanistan was much more complex than dismantling the Taliban regime. Attitudes and policies towards women in Afghanistan had been built upon historical, political, cultural and religious patriarchies. Gender dynamics were not solely based on Islamic interpretation. The pre-Islamic Pashtunwali code of ethics, which functioned in modern Pashtun tribal communities and ran parallel to Islam, also informed Afghan culture. Policies about women's issues, which included access to education and employment, marriage rights and inheritance rights, differed depending upon the ruling party of the time – meaning it had been shaped by Afghan royalty, military commanders, warlords, communists, the Soviets, the Taliban, the United States and NATO.

And so, even in 2017, more than a decade since the Taliban regime had been overthrown, Hojar didn't think there was a strong, national women's rights movement. But she was willing to start building the foundations for future generations. She felt that people's lack of responsibility for the country contributed to the fact that life had not improved in the past decades. She thought people were missing the only things that were truly important: creating a better future, sharing love, building peaceful societies.

When I looked at Hojar, I saw the spirit of the community. She was fierce yet compassionate. She would stand up for what she believed, but she would also listen to the opinions of others. Not only was she an integral part of the community's past, she held the keys to the community's future.

There was a knock on the door of the office and Insaan entered. Over the years, Hojar had come to think of Insaan as family, like an older brother. Now that she had taken on the responsibility of work at the centre she felt as if they were working side by side towards a common vision.

Soon after, other volunteers joined us, arriving for the weekly meeting for project coordinators.

Tea and boiled lollies were served on a metal platter and everyone was forced to squash in together in the small space, on cushions, on the floor, perched on the bookshelf. Abdul started the meeting by reiterating their mission statement and then the coordinators chanted their usual mantra.

'We want to change from me to we.'

THE MOUNTAINS, 2009

Like most mornings Hojar woke at three o'clock to make the bread. The synchronised sound of her four brothers' snoring acted as an aggravating metronome for her work. The amount of housework she was expected to do every day was frustrating because she had much more to do than her brothers and it prevented her from doing her schoolwork.

After kneading the dough, Hojar and her sister had to milk the goats and sheep. By the time they came back their mother had started the fire in the *tandoor* to bake the bread. Her mother prepared breakfast while she and her sister fetched the water from the spring. It wasn't uncommon for her older brother Mahdi to still be asleep when breakfast was being served. Today was no different.

'Why are you still sleeping? Why didn't you help us?' Hojar complained, but Mahdi just rolled over and snored louder.

She was not the only one who had trouble with lazy Mahdi. Her brother Ali had risen early to start work on the land while Mahdi slept. When Ali returned and found Mahdi sleeping he aimed a kick at the lump, which earned him a satisfying yelp, but then Mahdi rolled over and resumed his snoring.

'I'm hungry,' Musharat announced, implying breakfast should be ready.

Their mother dropped a loaf of unleavened bread in front of Musharat and then returned to her cushion where she lay down and turned her back to the family. Hojar placed tea in front of Musharat and Ali and tried to coax the younger children to eat, pretending her mother's bout of depression was nothing to worry about. But all of the children were painfully aware of the woman suffering silently in the corner of the room.

Once everyone had finished breakfast, Hojar cleaned up and the children got ready for school. Only now did Mahdi wake up, make his tea, eat the leftover bread and leave Hojar to clean up his mess.

'You are a woman, this is your job,' he told Hojar.

'I am not your slave,' Hojar shouted back at him. But he left for school, and there was nothing she could do but clean up after him, because that was her role as a woman in the house. *I am not a woman,* she thought, *I am a slave.* And now she would be late for school.

As much as she hated the way her brothers treated her, she didn't blame them. They didn't invent the system. It was society that had established and now accepted these gender roles. It was the villagers who told her brothers that studying was not useful for a girl. It was the villagers who told her mother, 'Your daughter is all grown up,' when Hojar was thirteen years old, which meant they thought she was ready for marriage. It was the villagers who expected her to get married, stay in the house and assume her role as a wife and a mother for the rest of her life.

Most women in her village and in the rural areas were expected to marry at a young age. But Hojar didn't want to marry. She wanted to study, she wanted to work, and she wanted to escape from these mountains. Her father taught her to value her education and had always encouraged her to study. When she was seven, he enrolled her in school. The Taliban had only just left the province and very few fathers in the village would allow their daughters to study. Nobody was sure if the Taliban would return or not.

Hojar wanted to complete her schooling, even though she only ever heard negative comments about her wishes from the other villagers. Sometimes she felt the restrictions and accusations came from all directions and it was not a pressure that led to progress. Hojar believed that the marriage of women so young was setting the entire society back: not only would society lose the girl, but the girl would lose herself. Now that she was fifteen – and still unmarried – she was determined to finish school.

That evening after dinner Hojar's mother approached her.

'We need to speak about marriage,' she said. 'I married a kind and handsome man when I was thirteen. Was it so bad for me?'

Hojar looked at the ground and picked at the floor. Usually Hojar tried to change the subject but today she felt her frustration building up inside her and she knew she could not suppress it.

'If I marry young according to the expectations of the people and my life is ruined, it doesn't affect them at all. Their lives will not get worse, but I will have to suffer because they talked me into getting married against my will. This is not what I want. I don't want to live according to the expectations of the village. Let them talk. This is my life.'

Even at that young age, she found the strength within herself to tell her mother the truth. Hojar's mother looked up at her daughter with love in her eyes.

'You've already had a hard life. I don't want you to suffer the way I did. So work hard, study hard and follow your dreams,' her mother said.

BEFORE NEVER-ENDING WAR there existed a different Afghanistan to the country I knew. My former travel partner, Martin, first visited Afghanistan in 1976, before the Soviet invasion. He drove a Volkswagen from Pakistan to Iran, taking the Khyber Pass to Kabul. Then he drove along what was at that time Afghanistan's only highway to Ghazni, Kandahar, Herat, and across the western border. He joined the throngs of hippies who passed through Afghanistan on their way from Europe to India, searching for the next cheap, exotic frontier. This was the country of Rumi the poet, Eastern mysticism, the giant Buddhas in Bamiyan and many other famous archaeological sites; bazaars of colourful fabrics, rugs and blankets; turbaned nomad families on camels; mountain treks, glaciers, blue-tiled mosques and cheap hashish. Women, both Afghans and foreigners, could freely walk the streets.

The majority of Afghans were farmers who had never been to school. Dirt roads between provinces were populated by horses, donkeys, camels and bullock carts. Half the children born did not live past their fifth birthday and the Afghan life expectancy was only fifty years. Outside the wealthy urban centres, it was a country suspended between modernity and the Middle Ages.[6] There wasn't much industry, there weren't many jobs, but there was peace. The next time Martin entered Afghanistan was in 2004. The streets were full of beggars, soldiers and the ruined shells of collapsed infrastructure. It felt like the country had gone back in time.

Maya and her extended family were Tajiks from Herat, who had migrated to Australia over the past four decades in dribs and drabs. I had known the family for most of my life. The Tajiks are a Persian-speaking people and approximately seven million ethnic Tajiks live in Tajikistan, one of Afghanistan's northern neighbours.[7] Tajikistan became an independent sovereign nation when the Soviet Union disintegrated in 1991; however, Tajik communities can be found in numerous countries in Central Asia.[8]

Maya was born in the mid 1960s. She lived in an eight-bedroom house with twelve members of her extended family in an affluent area of the new city of Herat. Maya's upbringing in Afghanistan was 'the best of childhoods' but she acknowledged that she was from a wealthy Tajik family and was more privileged than most Afghans.

As a child Maya used to play in her house and visit her friends, neighbours and family who lived in the area. Children played a game called bat ball, which was similar to baseball or cricket, on the smaller, quieter streets near their homes. They used to make their own balls by shredding a bicycle tube into strips about half a centimetre wide and wrapping the rubber pieces around a small rock. Once they had a reasonable-sized ball, they would wrap it in cotton thread and then use a needle to finely crochet it. Everyone had a homemade ball, but if a child owned a soccer ball they were the king of the street, with a hundred followers.

Maya used to go to school in the morning until midday when she would come home and have lunch with her family. In the afternoon she would study or have a siesta or go to school with her girlfriends for a few hours. At her school there was a canteen where she and her friends socialised, while the boys played sports. She enjoyed the simple pleasure of being able to walk to and from school. She never expected that one day it would be a radical act.

Socialising with the other gender wasn't socially acceptable, even in the more liberal city of Herat. For the most part marriages were arranged, although Maya had friends who got engaged to people they met at university. Maya was the eldest of seven sisters and by custom she should have married first.

'I don't want you to find me a husband,' Maya told her mother. 'I will introduce a man to you.'

But her mother refused this proposal as she believed it would embarrass the family.

'If you don't want to marry a man I choose for you, then don't marry at all.'

Maya never married.

The happiest days for Maya were celebrating the numerous festivals of Afghanistan. Her two favourites were the Eid festival, which marked the end of Ramadan, and Nowruz, the Persian New Year. Nowruz celebrations lasted for two or three weeks and were preceded by weeks of excitement and preparation, which included making sweets.

Maya didn't grow up with a television. Instead she listened to BBC Persian radio, which was broadcast in Iran and Afghanistan. BBC was a window through which she could see the rest of the world. In 1975 she listened to the Muhammad Ali and Joe Frazier fight, the 'Thrilla in Manila'. It was from the BBC that she learned about the Israel–Palestine conflict and why there were impoverished Palestinian refugees in Herat who came knocking on people's doors asking for donations. She always wanted to go to Palestine to help the refugees. She never thought that one day she would become a refugee herself.

Maya grew up reading Simone de Beauvoir and Jean-Paul Sartre. She and her friends spent their university days sitting and reading books, discussing topics like feminism. Her friends wore jeans or pants or leggings. Some of her friends even used to wear miniskirts or sleeveless tops, but usually not outside the house. Maya recognised that in rural areas women often preferred to wear burqas and follow purdah, and in those days 80 per cent of people lived outside of the urban centres.[9] It wasn't until the Taliban took control that strict dress codes for women were enforced nationwide.

There weren't many NGOs, missionaries or foreign companies in Afghanistan in those days. There were embassies, but the general public rarely interacted with the diplomats. People were accustomed to seeing travellers; they could distinguish between the tour bus tourists and the dirty-feet, torn-clothed hippies. The local Heratis didn't know about the hippie philosophies and they joked that these tourists were international beggars. For the most part, though, Maya's family and their neighbours respected the tourists because they were well-behaved and polite.

As a young woman Maya didn't feel she was worse off than any woman in a Western country. When she saw the tourists travelling around Afghanistan, she thought she could do the same. This wasn't to say Afghanistan was a completely liberal society. The country, its cultures and its traditions, especially in the rural areas, were still ruled by a patriarchal system and women were expected to conform to social and religious restrictions. The older generation of women who worked in Herat were usually teachers, nurses or midwives. Those were the only careers they were allowed to pursue. When she finished high school, she wanted to enrol in university. She planned to travel around Afghanistan during her university holidays, and then maybe get a scholarship to go overseas to study.

The Afghanistan Maya knew changed forever on Christmas Eve 1979 when the Soviet Union invaded. The Afghan people divided into groups of fighters called Mujahedin, or soldiers of God, and war began.

During the Soviet invasion, Herat was infiltrated by outsiders from Mujahedin militia as well as by Soviets and Afghans connected with the communist regime. In a city where everyone used to know each other, the general public learned to be frightened of strange men wielding guns, regardless of who they claimed they were fighting for. It was a lawless society where thugs and ruffians suddenly had armies and money. They targeted wealthy, influential families, demanding money or property or even kidnapping family members. In some instances, they took people's wives and daughters. Many people fled from Herat to become refugees in Iran and Pakistan to avoid such a fate. Even though Maya's family lived in a safe area, close to the governor's house and next door to a police station, they were still fearful of Mujahedin approaches.

When Maya graduated from high school she enrolled in engineering at the Kabul Polytechnic University. It was the mid 1980s, when war was raging all across the country. Maya was twenty years old and she was publicly forthright with her views against the communist regime. One day a group of men hustled her into a stairwell in one of the university buildings and searched her and her handbag. She was lucky they stopped her in the stairwell; she had heard of a basement in the university where those opposed to the state were taken and never returned. The men didn't find anything on her and let her go. She walked away from the experience wondering how close she had come to being disappeared. When she returned to her room in the university boarding house she discovered it had been ransacked. That night she stayed with her sister-in-law and the next day she returned to Herat. After that day the feeling of crosshairs between her shoulderblades never left her.

There wasn't a university for engineering in Herat and so she found a job with a bank. The local Mujahedin, who knew her family, knew that she was wealthy and didn't need to work for money. They were suspicious that she was helping the regime. Maya became worried that they were following her, so she only left the house to go to work and then she would come straight home.

Once, Maya's bus was stopped by Mujahedin. They kept the women on the bus and took the men outside, where they searched them and checked their identity cards. If they believed a man was part of the communist regime they would kidnap the man or kill him on the spot. One of the Mujahedin came inside the bus and asked, 'Do any of you have a pen?'

Maya instinctively reached inside her handbag to offer a pen but was stopped by a pinch on the leg, a warning from the woman next to her.

Why would he come on the bus and ask the women for a pen when there were so many men outside? It was likely a trap: the Mujahedin were trying to catch any educated women and label them as communists. She could have been killed for that pen.

After two years working for the bank, Maya could no longer bear the fear of Mujahedin scrutiny. Several times she sensed that she was being followed and initially she convinced herself she was being silly. After she was followed from home to her office, she stopped working and placed herself under virtual house arrest.

Maya's family eventually left Afghanistan in 1988, unable to tolerate the hardships of the war. Maya's brother, Mahdi, was fourteen years old and they were worried he would be conscripted into the army or be taken by the Mujahedin. They closed the doors to their house, not taking anything with them, with the intention of returning to Afghanistan once the Soviets had left the country. Maya's family crossed the Iranian border and settled in the city of Mashhad. An uncle subsequently sponsored the family's resettlement in Australia with the UNHCR. The day Maya found out her family wasn't going back to Afghanistan she cried day and night until she had no more tears left to shed. To her, leaving her home was like poking out her own eyes. She felt lost. She attached her personality, her identity, to her home, her country, her history, her land. Thirty years later, she still dreamed of Herat, but the beautiful Afghanistan she once knew no longer existed.

Chapter 7

Lessons and Actions in Nonviolence

THE MOUNTAINS, 2009

Muslimyor woke up with frost-caked eyelashes and eyebrows. When he opened his eyes, a thin seal of ice that had formed between his lids cracked. While his bare face was numb from overnight exposure, the rest of his body was insulated from the bitter cold by the body warmth of the ten other volunteers in the tent. He was lying on his back, on cushions and blankets, covered in a sleeping bag. They were so tight in the tent he could hardly move. A bird cuckooed the rising sun, which was beginning to shine through the blue, white and red makeshift tent made of woven PVC plastic. Thick snow had piled up against the sides of the tent overnight and condensation clung to the walls.

The volunteers had been sleeping out for four nights now as part of a peace vigil to deliver a message to US President Barack Obama. It was October 2009 and President Obama had just been awarded the Nobel Peace Prize, which upset and confused the group. Only a few months earlier the US senate overwhelmingly approved a US$106 billion emergency spending bill to expand the war in Afghanistan and to continue the war in Iraq.[1] Here were these young Afghan men, trying to broadcast their message of peace and nonviolence to the world, and, while their efforts were being ignored, the man who had just ordered thousands more soldiers be deployed to their country was awarded the most prestigious peace prize in the world.

'Really we should feel sorry for America,' Insaan said. 'Martin Luther King once said, a nation that continues year after year to spend more money on military defence than on programs of social uplift is approaching spiritual death.'

When Insaan broke the news to the group, he showed them a picture of President Obama sitting at a desk in his office; behind him were photographs of Martin Luther King and Mahatma Gandhi. Muslimyor couldn't believe the contradiction.

'This decision re-defines war as peace,' Insaan said.

The volunteers discussed what protest action they would like to take and decided they wanted to deliver a message to President Obama. They planned to remain in a tent vigil in the peace park until the president received their message, one they hoped to spread through national and international media networks.

'Why do you want to do this?' Insaan asked.

'We don't think the US or NATO military forces are effective in the process of reconciliation in Afghanistan,' Arif said.

'For how long will you keep vigil?' Insaan asked them.

'We won't leave the tent until President Obama has accepted our message,' Muslimyor said.

'I don't think you know how long it will take for him to receive your message,' Insaan said. 'It may never happen. Do you really want to do this?'

'Yes, of course,' the volunteers replied, wondering why Insaan would question such positive action.

'You told us if you have a voice then you should speak, regardless of the result,' Muslimyor said. 'If we don't say anything, what will the result be?'

'Okay then. Let's do it,' Insaan said. 'As long as you remember that the value of the vigil is not dependent on whether the politicians answer you or whether it has any effective results. You may be ridiculed for your protest, but the process will be important to help you think through peace and find that motivation and determination for peace within you.'

A few days later their vigil commenced with a cultural program in the peace park that included the playing of a flute, the singing of songs and Insaan's delivery of a message of peace, before a small crowd of local people and politicians.

'Salam alaikum,' Insaan addressed the crowd. 'We welcome you and the possibility of peace to this forgotten but gorgeous place. We are the youth of the mountains who do not represent any political or religious views except for those views which make us truly human, capable of acting in love and truth. We are tired of war and we share with brothers and sisters everywhere a common aspiration to live in peace. We wish to converse as equal, fellow human beings, without the need for guns and bombs.

'We desire to patiently build our nation, to trek on our own paths, build our own parks and choose which of our own mountains to climb. We desire the dignity of working with our own hands and walking with our own legs ...'

Although Muslimyor portrayed outward confidence to the rest of the youth that Obama would answer them, the longer the vigil went on the more he doubted their success. Why would the president of the most powerful country in the world notice a group of young people sleeping in a tent in a war-torn country? The inevitable disappointment of not being noticed was made more painful by the ridicule from passers-by, who laughed at them for staying in the crude tent.

At the outset Muslimyor could tell that Insaan thought they were naive to attempt a vigil and that he didn't expect them to go through with the idea. But the volunteers stuck with it, only leaving the vigil to go to school; by day, Insaan manned the tent. The volunteers spent every night in the tent, their evening conversations dimly lit by a kerosene lamp and their meals cooked on a gas stove. The freezing nights were endured, and the youth were united during the vigil by solidarity and a sense of purpose.

Already the vigil had been a pivotal experience for Muslimyor. Until then he wasn't aware of any other group of young people who held a vigil for a particular purpose, let alone to deliver a message to a world leader. He had been proud of Insaan's opening address at the start of the vigil. He hoped President Obama would receive their message with an open and honest heart, as their idols Gandhi and Martin Luther King would have done. He hoped they would receive a reply from President Obama soon.

Muslimyor crawled from the small tent in time to watch the sun rise over the mountains, bathing the park in orange light. Looking at the peace park afresh, he noticed the trees they had planted were growing well in the dry clay. Perhaps there was hope for life in this rocky garden.

The Tajik youth began to stir and prepare themselves for their morning prayer. On the first morning of the vigil, Muslimyor had learned about the different style of prayer of the Tajiks, who were Sunni. Arif prayed at a different time to what Muslimyor thought was appropriate and Muslimyor had laughed at him. The next morning, Arif saw him praying with a small piece of soil in front of him and the Tajik took the opportunity to laugh at him in return and say something unpleasant about the soil. After a brief argument, they sat down together and discussed their differences. Then, critically, they came to an understanding, accepted their differences and moved on. When Muslimyor had first met Insaan and the Tajik members of the group it had felt very strange but gradually his discomfort had receded, so by now he was starting to see Arif and the others as friends.

That morning the volunteers learnt the US ambassador would visit their camp. The group had alerted the US embassy staff about the vigil and by chance the ambassador had been in the region for an election issue. Muslimyor was excited and felt sure the message would get to President Obama now. Before the ambassador arrived, Americans dressed in plain clothes and flak jackets, wearing headphones, inspected the site and asked many questions. They cordoned off the area and checked all the possible routes to the park. Muslimyor felt the atmosphere become strange and he was insulted by the security personnel's paranoia and suspicion. In his eyes, this meant that the ambassador didn't trust the volunteers.

A small ceremony was held to welcome the dignitaries. The volunteers sat on park benches while Insaan addressed the ambassador, a retired general and US Security Coordinator for Afghanistan. Soldiers stood at the ready to protect him.

'We, the people of Afghanistan, have a proverb that says, "Mountains cannot reach mountains, only man can reach man". Today you have reached out to us and we are touched. We thank you and hope that you will be able to take our simple message of peace from Afghanistan to reach out to the Nobel Peace Prize Winner President Obama and to the world, in the same wonderful way you have encouraged us with your visit this morning.'

When Insaan finished, he offered the ambassador a framed photo of the tent vigil to give to President Obama.

In response the ambassador said he would deliver their message to President Obama and send them his reply; in return he requested the volunteers pack up their tent and stop the vigil.

After the ambassador had left, Insaan sat the volunteers down and spoke to them.

'I know the ambassador said he would deliver the message but in all likelihood he will not. You will not get an answer. This is politics.'

The vigil in the peace park ended after seven days. Insaan maintained contact with the ambassador by email long after, reminding him of the promise he made to this hopeful group of youth. As far as they knew, the ambassador never delivered their message to President Obama.

THE MOUNTAINS, 2010

After the tent vigil Hafizullah became more involved in the group's activities and started to make friends. The group consisted of about fifteen regular participants; however, the larger events such as the peace treks attracted more than one hundred people. They would often meet at the peace park or Insaan's house or office.

Hafizullah was one of the lucky ones in the group. He didn't have direct experience of conflict, yet whatever peace Hafizullah and his family enjoyed, it felt fragile to him. Like it needed to be cared for. His parents knew about the group, but he was sure they didn't fully understand the group's philosophies and viewed their activities with a degree of mistrust.

'What does the word "nonviolence" mean to you?' Insaan once asked the group.

The young men looked at each other, unsure how to respond.

'To not fight each other?' Muslimyor guessed.

'Do you think it's just about physical fighting? Do you think people can be violent in other ways? Can we be violent to animals or even our planet?' Insaan asked.

'Nonviolence is a way of life,' Insaan had told them. 'We *practise* nonviolence. When peace is our goal, nonviolence is our method. We hope to use dialogue and discussion to solve a problem rather than force.'

After a number of successful community-building projects, Insaan suggested it was time to push themselves outside of their comfort zones.

'We should reach out to other youth in other provinces of Afghanistan,' Insaan said. 'We should make peace with the Pashtun people.'

Their first foray was to reach out to young Pashtuns in Kandahar province, the heartland of the Taliban. They made contact with the youth directorate in Kandahar and started to foster a relationship with a group of young people there. They bought second-hand leather from the bazaar and cut and sewed the leather into cell phone pouches. On one side of the pouch they sewed the word *peace*. There was no way they could get the pouches to Kandahar themselves but Insaan had contacts in an international NGO who helped them deliver the pouches, which included a note with the group's contact details. When the youth in Kandahar received their cell phone pouches, they called Insaan and the group.

'We can't believe this. We can't believe that Hazaras, without even knowing us, would demonstrate such love for us. You have done an impossible thing. It has done a lot for our spirits to know that we are not alone.'

The group were thrilled to hear from the young Pashtuns from Kandahar. Many of the volunteers had never had any interactions with Pashtun people before and a simple offer of friendship had encouraged them all. For Hafizullah, the reaction from the Kandahar youth made him think that there really was a desire for peace and friendship around the country and that perhaps this work could spread.

After their success with the young people of Kandahar, Insaan arranged for the group to visit the youth directorate in Daykundi, a predominantly Hazara-populated province in central Afghanistan that had been hit hard by the drought.

THE ENGINE OF the helicopter gurgled and coughed, and the blades slowly began to rotate. Hafizullah tried looking up at the blades by lowering his head against the glass and twisting his neck upwards. Muslimyor was practically climbing over him from the next seat to get a look. Nadir and Arif were plastered to the window on the other side of the machine. Insaan watched on from the middle with a small smile. It was the first time any of the young men had been in a helicopter – usually choppers were something to fear.

The blades began to spin faster and faster, whipping up dust on the tarmac; and then, with a wobble, the helicopter lifted off the ground. The young men inhaled sharply, slightly fearful, but also full of adrenaline. The helicopter seemed to hang in the air, hardly moving, until suddenly they were high off the ground, looking down on the mountains they had lived amongst their whole lives but never seen from above. The noise of the blades was deafening, and their vibrations made Hafizullah's brain rattle around his skull. Muslimyor tried shouting to Hafizullah, who was next to him, but he was drowned out; they could only point at the villages as they rose higher. It was hard for them to take it all in; they'd never been on a flight before, and now they were on their way to Daykundi.

From the helicopter they could see the impact of drought on the landscape, with the province's famous almond trees shrivelled and lifeless. But Daykundi's poppy fields were thriving and at the bazaar Insaan noticed people hanging around selling heroin.

After a poor night's sleep sharing flea-infested mattresses, the group met thirty Daykundi youth. They had not planned to meet a particular ethnic group and they didn't ask the Daykundi youth about their ethnic backgrounds. Hafizullah and Muslimyor were many years younger than any of the other people present at the meeting, which gave them cause to feel nervous. Using slides on an overhead projector, Muslimyor explained to the Daykundi youth their objective.

'We want to reach out to as many young people as possible, across ethnic groups and provinces, and join together in peace.'

One of the Daykundi youth stood up and responded: 'I can't believe I am hearing this from a fellow Afghan. I can't believe that you are so young and yet you seem so sincere and serious. You have inspired us to do more in the Daykundi province.'

The group were encouraged by these comments and by their experience in Daykundi. The volunteers remained in close contact with the youth in Daykundi province long after the visit. Although Insaan found it difficult to pinpoint an exact time when the movement was birthed, reaching out to other young people in other provinces was a key moment in the evolution of the group. Little by little the volunteers were growing in confidence and belief that they could encourage other Afghans to unite under the goal of peace.

Insaan's ambition did not end there. It was time to look beyond Afghanistan.

'You know, there is a whole world of peace activists who may be interested in connecting with you,' Insaan said. 'Would you be interested in reaching out to them?'

THE MOUNTAINS, 2010

Horse walked home bubbling with excitement. He had just spent his morning with Insaan, Muslimyor, Hafizullah and the other young members of their group and his mind felt alive with fresh thoughts and ideas. Since Muslimyor had introduced him to Nadir, Horse had begun working morning shifts at the chip shop before he went to school. Through that work he became friends with Nadir and Hafizullah and he heard their stories about the group 'working for peace' as Muslimyor had called it. He met Insaan, who would visit the shop on his motorbike, and he became interested in their unusual activities and conversations.

Horse arrived home to find his uncles helping his mother fix a broken door. Their ramshackle house was always in need of some repair; this door was just the latest issue in a long list. His brothers and sisters were all too young to help with this kind of work, so they relied on the generosity of their extended family to pitch in. While he was grateful to his uncles for their help, he also felt ashamed. This was a father's job, but they were a family abandoned, which placed an unfair strain on his mother.

As she washed and pummelled the clothes of her seven children, Horse told her about his day.

'Insaan told us about an Indian man named Gandhi whose country was colonised by the British Empire, but he defeated their great army without using violence. Then we spoke about how we could help promote peace in Afghanistan.'

His mother gave him a puzzled look, more focused on her work than anything Horse said to her. While she was too busy to listen, his uncles had overheard his comments.

'You're just a group of children. If the politicians can't bring peace what can you do?' one of his uncles said.

'Insaan says that we can't rely on the politicians to do this type of work. That if Afghans want peace, we have to work for it ourselves.'

His uncles laughed at him, and Horse wasn't sure how to respond to their cynicism. He thought of real, solid examples of their work that he could explain to his uncles, so he told them about the peace pouches they made for a group of young Pashtuns in Kandahar.

'You sent gifts to these wild people? These Pashtuns from Kandahar who killed your family members?' his uncles said, becoming upset. 'Better to give the presents to your family members.'

Before this project Horse had never sought out Pashtun people. All his life Horse had been told by his family and by the local people that Pashtun people were dangerous and so he had become frightened of them, even though his one living example of a Pashtun person contradicted that reputation. His father had a Pashtun friend who used to visit their house. He would carry rolls of cloth to sell in the villages. The man had a long beard and when he spoke in Dari he had a thick accent that made him hard to understand. Horse didn't think of that man as wild, but that didn't stop him thinking the rest might be.

He understood that for many of his relatives the traumas of war were still too recent. When the Taliban came to the region during the civil war, his family fled to Kabul. Local men, including Horse's father, were enlisted and armed to fight against the Taliban. Horse's father was fined for losing his weapon, but his family could not afford to pay, so his father ran away. The local government said that Horse's family needed to send a family member in place of his father. Horse's uncle was sent to Mazar-i-Sharif to fight against the Taliban. He disappeared while in battle. It was a shameful story for Horse, but it was not the worst when it came to his father.

Despite knowing how much his community hated and distrusted Pashtuns, it hadn't really occurred to Horse how radical the act of making those peace pouches might be until he tried to explain the idea to his family members. But when he thought about it now, with his uncles' angry faces confronting him, he realised they were offering friendship to a group of people hated by his community, a group of people who lived in the heartland of the Taliban.

'You're too young to understand that these kinds of activities are mad,' his uncles said.

But Horse disagreed. When he was still a new member of the group, he became friends with Arif, a Tajik. At the time, Arif's family were fighting with Horse's family. Horse's uncles believed that Arif's family helped the Taliban during the war, a common accusation levelled at Tajik families by Hazara families in the region. There were indeed some Tajik families who had sided with the Taliban during the civil war; whether they did so out of fear or because they were Sunni Muslims like the Taliban was hard to determine. As it was, when the Taliban left the valley, many Tajiks left too; those who remained faced great animosity from Hazaras that had not cooled in the years since the fall of the Taliban. Horse had questioned if he should continue to be a part of this group when a Taliban-sympathiser was sitting across from him.

Within their peace circle Insaan asked them to speak about how the war affected them.

'When I was young, one of my sisters disappeared during the war,' Arif said, holding back tears. 'And then my parents were killed by a Hazara soldier.'

Horse was rocked by these revelations. It was impossible not to feel compassion for this young man who opened his heart to their group, to Hazaras, and seemed to bear them no ill will. Talk of philosophy and peace were entirely new discussions for Horse and he admitted to himself it was the first time he had ever been challenged to think deeply. Now he had a Tajik friend too.

THE COMMUNITY'S COMMITMENT to nonviolence and ethnic harmony in Afghanistan was remarkable considering the history of conflict in the country. Although the modern state of Afghanistan was founded in 1747, internal tribal rivalries, divisions and wars were commonplace throughout the 18th and 19th centuries.[2] Shared ethnicity did not necessarily ensure cooperation in Afghanistan; tribal politics was much more complicated than that.[3]

Apart from its own internal politics, Afghanistan's geopolitical position in the middle of the Eurasian steppe made it vulnerable to invasion and occupation from foreign empires. During the 19th and 20th centuries,

Afghanistan fought three wars with the British Empire. In the post–World War II power vacuum, the battle for supremacy in the new world order between the Soviet Union and the United States engulfed Afghanistan.

Between 1956 and 1978 King Zahir Shah managed the competing interests of the two superpowers, accepting over $500 million in economic aid from the United States and $2.5 billion in economic and military aid from the Soviet Union. These resources helped build roads and infrastructure across the country.[4]

During the 1960s King Zahir Shah began to implement democratic reforms: a new constitution introduced a constitutional monarchy with a parliament, elections, freedoms for the press, civil rights, women's rights and universal suffrage. In this semi-democracy, underground political parties emerged but the king retained paramount power. The socialists and the communists who wanted to revolutionise Afghan society and politics clashed with the political groups and Islamic groups who supported the king and Islamic traditions.[5]

King Zahir Shah's reign and the Durrani dynasty was overthrown by the king's cousin and former prime minister, General Mohammed Daoud Khan, in a military coup in 1973. Daoud established a republic with support from the burgeoning communist party, the People's Democratic Party of Afghanistan (PDPA), and appointed himself president.

After just five years in charge, Daoud's regime was ousted by Afghan army officers aligned with the PDPA. Daoud and eighteen members of his family were executed. The Saur Revolution, as this coup would later be known, marked the end of even pseudo-democracy in Afghanistan.[6]

Following the assassination of Daoud, the Khalq (People) faction of the PDPA took power with the support of the Soviet Union and installed Nur Muhammad Taraki as president. They began implementing reforms as part of their mission to create a secular, socialist state, which was deeply unpopular with the religious elite and the traditional, rural areas of Afghanistan, where people feared communists were trying to eradicate Afghan customs and beliefs. Efforts to distribute land equally were opposed by the powerful landlords who would eventually join the Mujahedin militia groups in fighting the Soviet occupation.

The country became governed by brute force. Taraki's government captured, imprisoned and assassinated key figures in communities: heads of family, heads of tribes, religious leaders.[7] It was reported that more than 27,000 political prisoners were executed or disappeared between April 1978 and December 1979.[8] Rebellions broke out across the country.

The communist revolution was faltering when in September 1979, Taraki's deputy, Hafizullah Amin, had Taraki assassinated – smothered with a pillow – and assumed the presidency. Amin's rule was short-lived but just as ferocious as Taraki's, characterised by brutal assaults on villages.[9] Meanwhile an Islamic revolution in Afghanistan's neighbourhood resulted in Ayatollah Ruhollah Khomeini declaring Iran an Islamic republic. The Soviet Union was concerned that a weakening Afghan state on its southern border was vulnerable to either Islamic extremism or US influence. A rise in Islamist groups could empower similar movements in the Soviet Union's Muslim-majority Central Asian republics, and the Soviets feared that an Islamist Afghanistan could ally itself with Iran and Pakistan.[10]

On Christmas Eve 1979 the Soviet Union stationed troops in Afghanistan, ostensibly in an attempt to stabilise the regime in Kabul. Three days later, on 27 December, Soviet troops laid siege to the Tajbeg Palace (the Queen's Palace), and murdered President Amin. The Soviet Union then installed Babrak Karmal, from the Parcham (Flag) faction of the PDPA, as ruler. It didn't take long for nearly 100,000 Soviet troops, 750 tanks and 2100 combat vehicles and aircraft, including MiG fighter jets and helicopter gunships, to take control of major cities, roads and airfields across the country.[11]

A resistance movement formed: a nationwide, tribal jihad of 19th-century muskets, WWI-era rifles and AK-47s, led by clan chiefs, religious scholars and warlords. Ethnic groups and religious factions at first were largely united against the foreign, infidel enemy. The United States, China, Iran, Saudi Arabia and Pakistan supplied money and arms to the different Mujahedin groups to fight the Russians, attempting to influence the outcome of the war and position themselves favourably in the region.

Soon every part of the country, every valley and every district, was ruled by a Mujahedin commander – a warlord – and his militia. The Islamists, holding strict religious views, were one such group. They were a minor political player in Afghanistan prior to the war; however, financial backing from Pakistan, Saudi Arabia and the CIA brought them greater power and influence. This would later pave the way for the rise of the Taliban, Osama bin Laden, al-Qaeda and other such groups.[12]

The country steadily descended into suspicion, division and chaos. Opposition against the Russians formed along tribal, regional and religious lines. The different Shia and Sunni factions became divided by the foreign nations that supported them. Saudi Arabia supported Sunnis and Iran supported Shias. Civilians who didn't join a militia group were labelled communists or infidels. These were the first steps towards turning Afghanistan into a state of warlords.[13]

By the time the Red Army withdrew from the country in February 1989, 1.5 million Afghans were dead. Civil war erupted in Afghanistan as the tribes sought to overthrow Najibullah's communist Afghan regime, which had remained in power with the support of Soviet weaponry and financial aid. Afghanistan quickly became divided into a confusing array of bickering warlord fiefdoms divided by ethnic groups, religious sects, tribal loyalties and shifting allegiances, all vying for power, all terrorising the Afghan people.

Burhanuddin Rabbani, his military commander Ahmad Shah Massoud, and their Tajik forces known as the Jamiat-e Islami controlled Panjshir and the north-east of the country. Another Tajik, Ismail Khan, held three provinces centred around Herat. Gulbuddin Hekmatyar and his Islamist Pashtun fighters, the Hezb-i-Islami, who were supported by the CIA and Pakistan's Inter-Service Intelligence (ISI), occupied a small region near Kabul. General Rashid Dostum's Uzbek forces controlled provinces in the north. Shia Hazara forces, supported by the Shia Iranian government, controlled central Afghanistan. Pashtun tribes in the south were at war without any unifying leadership.[14]

Once the Soviets had been defeated, the United States backed away from Afghanistan, and the millions of dollars of military aid they provided to the Mujahedin was not replaced by humanitarian aid. Support of the government ceased after the Soviet Union collapsed in 1991. The warring factions of the civil war looted the major cities and demolished the nation's infrastructure – roads, hospitals, schools, shops, houses, power and telephone lines, water and sewer pipes, everything was destroyed. Thousands of young men flocked to the various factions. Homes were seized, civilians were kidnapped, women were raped, markets were raided, agricultural fields became war zones and minefields, and the country fell into anarchy. In this environment, Mujahedin rule became tyrannical, and severe restrictions were placed upon women and their movements.[15]

As Najibullah's government began to topple, the Mujahedin armies crept towards Kabul. Hekmatyar and his Pashtun fighters approached Kabul from the south, while from the north, Rabbani, Massoud, and their Tajik forces allied with General Dostum and his Uzbek army. Najibullah was overthrown and an ensuing battle for Kabul was won by the Tajik and Uzbek forces.[16] It was only the second time in 300 years that Pashtuns had lost control of the capital.[17]

Rabbani, Massoud and the Tajiks formed a government in Kabul, with Rabbani as president of an internationally recognised regime. Meanwhile Hekmatyar rallied his Pashtun forces and commenced a long-term siege of the city, using shelling and urban warfare to fight for control, in the process killing thousands of civilians and earning him the title the Butcher of Kabul.

Out of this turmoil emerged a group of Pashtun fighters from the south of Afghanistan. They were headed by their spiritual leader, Mullah Mohammed Omar, and were determined to bring peace and Islamic justice to a country that had suffered through years of lawlessness and chaotic warfare. A large majority of their supporters were religious students from Afghanistan and Pakistan, educated at Islamic religious schools called 'madrasas'.[18] They called themselves the Taliban, which means 'students' in Pashto.[19] They were children of the jihad, born into conflict, displaced by violence, raised in refugee camps, educated in all-male schools by barely literate mullahs, with hardly any contact with women, disconnected from Afghan society, history and tradition.[20]

With Hekmatyar failing to unite the Pashtun warlords and take control of the nation, the Pakistani ISI and the CIA saw the Taliban as the new potential rulers of Afghanistan, who could be favourable to Pakistan and the United States and could help secure trade routes to the newly independent Central Asian states. In November 1994 the Taliban captured Kandahar, Afghanistan's second biggest city, with relative ease. By September 1996 the Taliban had seized Kabul from President Rabbani and established the Islamic Emirate of Afghanistan, with Mullah Omar as the head of state. When the Taliban found former president Najibullah, they beat him, tortured him, castrated him, tied him to the back of a car and dragged him around the streets of Kabul, before shooting him and hanging him from a post outside the presidential palace.[21]

It could be said that initially many Afghan civilians welcomed the Taliban, who were seen as Robin Hood–style characters, saving the country from the corrupt warlords and making the roads and the areas under their control safe. This illusion of justice was dispelled the moment the Taliban came to power in the southern provinces and enforced a controversial interpretation of sharia that was lacking in historical perspective or tradition.

The Taliban refused to accept modernism and Western culture, and imposed sharia punishments for violations of their laws such as stoning, amputation and public execution. Most of their edicts (such as bans on music, television, kite flying, keeping birds, beard shaving, British and American hairstyles, sorcery and more) had no basis in the Quran. They targeted Shia Muslims, particularly Hazaras, and they severely restricted women and their rights, closing down girls' schools, banning women from work, and forcing them to wear the burqa at all times in public. The reality of what the Taliban were offering Afghanistan no doubt scared Afghan civilians, especially women and non-Pashtuns, but it did not deter Pakistan, Saudi Arabia and the United States from supporting the group's early push for power. Meanwhile Russia, Iran and India backed the Rabbani regime in Kabul.[22]

The Taliban swept through Afghanistan capturing territories and instilling their version of sharia law, but they were met with stiff opposition from the other ethnic tribes. Time after time villages of innocent civilians were massacred by marauding forces of one ethnicity or the other. In 1993 Pashtun and Tajik forces commanded by Ahmad Shah Massoud, the Lion of Panjshir, rampaged through Afshar district in west Kabul, torturing and killing the local population. They destroyed 5000 homes and abducted and enslaved survivors.[23] In 1997 Uzbek soldiers massacred 3000 Taliban prisoners-of-war in Mazar-i-Sharif.[24] One year later the Taliban took revenge by murdering 8000 civilians in the same city, particularly targeting Hazaras. In 2001 the Dasht-i-Leili massacre saw Uzbek forces once again kill several thousand Taliban prisoners, shooting them and killing them by suffocation in shipping containers.[25]

With the country in turmoil and atrocities being committed on all sides, the world's major oil companies had a different focus. The untapped gas and oil resources in Central Asia were there to exploit and Afghanistan was a useful thoroughfare. When Bill Clinton's US government supported US oil company Unocal and Saudi Arabian oil company Delta, in negotiating pipeline deals with the Taliban, global politics once again shifted around the strategic and economic benefit of control over Afghanistan. If the Taliban could bring peace to Afghanistan, the United States could route pipelines through the country. The pipeline projects ultimately failed due to the fraught politics of the region, but it proved that the United States was ready to talk to anyone as long as there was a potential financial benefit.[26]

By 2001 the Taliban ruled about 90 per cent of Afghanistan, but they never took complete control of the country and they failed to gain the support of much of the Afghan population.[27] The Taliban became increasingly isolated and reviled by the international community, particularly because of their treatment of women. They never received widespread international recognition as a legitimate government of Afghanistan, but this didn't stop Pakistan, Saudi Arabia and the United Arab Emirates all supporting the Taliban's 'Islamic Emirate'.

And then September 11 changed everything.

Chapter 8

Countering a Legacy of Mistrust

Muslimyor's eyelids drooped perilously close to a deep slumber.

'Muslimyor,' Insaan said in his ear, placing his hand gently on Muslimyor's shoulder.

As soft as Insaan's touch was, it startled Muslimyor. He shot up out of his chair with a yelp.

Muslimyor looked around and noticed that all the other group members were asleep. Hafizullah was snoring loudly like a bull, Horse whistled through his nose every time he breathed out, and Nadir was drooling.

'I'm awake,' he mumbled. 'Let me wash my face.'

It was two in the morning and they had been speaking on the phone with international guests for twelve hours already. There was another twelve hours to go. They had laid down mattresses and cushions on the floor of the chip shop to make it more comfortable, but all this had done was allow Hafizullah to fall asleep mid conversation. Insaan called this new program the World Peace Exchange. Their intention was to deliver their message of peace to the world, one conversation at a time.

The program was a product of Insaan's attempts to connect with people outside Afghanistan. During the tent vigil Insaan had been contacted by an American activist called Daniel Johnson. Daniel had seen a post on the internet asking the international community to join their vigil and he wanted to be involved.

'I will be standing with you, listening to you,' Daniel said.

'A phone call from America? Wow. The world is listening to us,' the boys had said.

Daniel threw his support behind their vigil and organised for a group of twenty people to hold a solidarity vigil in Washington at the same time. This empowered the boys to continue their demonstration. After that first phone call Insaan asked Daniel to keep in touch.

'We need this,' Insaan said.

Daniel continued to call the community and share stories and experiences with the young men. Both Daniel and Insaan thought these conversations were encouraging and they decided to get other friends and organisations involved. Insaan and Daniel had talked about their concerns that people didn't listen to each other anymore; they had stopped exchanging ideas. In honour of these discussions, in late 2009 they started the World Peace Exchange. They hosted these conversations on a monthly basis, and they made the sessions twenty-four hours long so they could cover all the different time zones of the world. Insaan stayed awake to translate the sessions, while the boys took it in turns to sleep.

'We must get our message out there,' Insaan said to them.

The World Peace Exchange was the group's first contact with the international community. Before this program, Muslimyor didn't know any other people from any other country. When he began to participate in the calls, he was fascinated to hear the different languages and accents of the foreigners, and their different world views. It was the first time he had heard the English language. He could hear that people cared for him, people who didn't know him and who didn't have a reason to care for him. He'd become friends with people who otherwise he would never have met. He never realised that the human family was so big.

'We don't have to fight. We can talk. We can have conversations and negotiations,' one of the callers from the United States had once said to him.

Simply put, that thinking was a revelation to Muslimyor. The common view of his village was that Afghans needed to fight the war to ensure peace and security.

Through the World Peace Exchange program Muslimyor began to see that there were other human beings who were interested in talking about peace and exchanging ideas about how to work together. There were people elsewhere who were working for the same cause. Through the program he learned that his story was important and that people wanted to hear it – he had become a peace activist.

THE MOUNTAINS, 2010

Insaan had been making attempts to connect with the international community and international peace groups for years before Daniel Johnson responded. One of his targets was Mary Smith, part of a small but very committed peace group in the United Kingdom whose mission was to speak against the economic and military wars of the UK government.

During the slow evolution of the World Peace Exchange program, Insaan read on Mary's online blog that she would be in Kabul. So Insaan and Nadir called her from the chip shop and invited her to see them.

That was all it took. After that one phone call she came to visit the group in October 2010.

Insaan and the young men met Mary at the small airport in the mountains. Asghar introduced himself and hoisted one of her heavy suitcases on his back to carry it across the gravel car park.

'Please don't,' Mary said. 'It will be too heavy for you.'

'No problem,' said Asghar. 'I am a mountain boy.'

Mary was then taxied to the group's potato chip store where they shared a simple but delicious meal of potatoes and rice.

'Our potatoes are the best in Afghanistan,' Insaan said enthusiastically and told her the story of how the chip shop came to be.

Insaan interpreted the introductions and conversations between Mary and the young Afghan men. They told Mary about their families and their villages, about the work they were doing with Insaan and their aspirations to be good people. Mary, in turn, told them about her life.

'I was a high school teacher and I moved into the poorest neighbourhood in London for work. At that time, there were refugees moving into our area. I couldn't understand why anyone would want to move into our area, but then they told me they were fleeing terrible persecution and death squads. Because of that I became involved in efforts to advocate against war. That work and civil disobedience campaigns prepared me to take a stronger step and go into a war zone and resist the United Kingdom's involvement in Iraq and Afghanistan. I worry that in my country the dominant religion has become militarism.'

'You are a very good person,' Horse said. 'Thank you for helping us.'

The young men were excited to show off their home to Mary and had arranged a day trip to a local lake.

'They say most of the area's wildlife has been lost,' Insaan said to Mary. 'But I have been told that it still contains wild goat, wild sheep, wolves, foxes, and fish in the lake.'

'We want the people of the world to come to our lake for friendship and peace,' Horse said. 'Maybe if they see our nature they will believe that Afghanistan can be a beautiful country.'

The young men then offered a gift to Mary: a set of plastic letters forming the Dari alphabet. En route to the lake, they helped Mary learn to read the characters.

Mary was completely unprepared for the beauty of the lapis-coloured lake. Young children frolicked in the shallows; families picnicked on the lawns; newlyweds operated pedal-powered boats, shaded by sun umbrellas. *How did the world not know of this serenity? How could such a place exist in a country like Afghanistan?*

Mary left Afghanistan feeling moved by her meeting with these bright and kindly young men, and deeply impressed by the multilingual Insaan, who struck her as a talented and versatile person. Most impressive of all was that he genuinely enjoyed building new and purposeful relationships. She had enjoyed his warmth, and his wit and laughter enlivened her experiences there.

'We needed this, Mary,' Insaan said. 'We needed to show the young men that they are not alone in this battle, that there is a global community of peaceful-minded people standing with them. Thank you for visiting us.'

This was by no means the end of their friendship; this was just the beginning.

I SAT ON a cushion in the Community Centre, wrapped in a blanket, shivering uncontrollably, staring at a computer screen. Next to me, Tara was furiously scribbling notes as she listened to various exchanges from around the world. Tara too was wrapped in blankets, trying to stay warm.

The tips of her fingers, which emerged from fingerless gloves, were pink from the cold and from the effort of gripping her pen. Insaan, Horse, Hojar and five other volunteers were also huddled around the computer, cocooned in layers of clothing and quilts, little marshmallows of linen. We were gathered together for that month's World Peace Exchange.

'My daughter was killed by a bulldozer in Palestine, trying to stop homes being destroyed by the Israeli government,' an American woman said. 'Her graphic and awful killing was witnessed by civilians, but there has been no accountability. The Israeli government say they have done nothing wrong.'

The crackly Skype connection cut out every so often, but I imagined it was much better than when the program first started in 2009 and the youth used their cell phones to make the calls.

'Our youth can relate to the Palestinians and their grievances; they are both peoples trapped within artificial borders created by the international community,' Insaan said.

'This planet does not have borders,' a young man named Abdul said. 'Borders were created by human beings. These artificial divides separate us and together we can overcome these obstacles to stand together to support all humanity.'

'It is encouraging to know that people all over the world are fighting in defence of displaced and dispossessed people,' Tara said, her voice wavering slightly. 'Your daughter's sacrifice for a community that was not her own is an example of how the world can be seen as a global village.'

Conversation turned to the situation in Afghanistan.

'Spring brings fresh worries of attacks from insurgent groups and retaliation by the government military. Afghans have experienced this over so many years that each spring and new year makes us think, who will die this year? Who else will we lose?' Abdul said.

'Life has become so unpredictable that we can't look ahead for more than one month,' Horse said. 'When we leave our homes in the morning, we wonder if we will return home that evening.'

'Leaving the house is an act of courage, going to school is an act of courage. You are all courageous,' the American woman said.

A tribal elder from the Standing Rock indigenous community in the United States joined the conversation.

'Why can't we treat Mother Earth with kindness and respect? Plundering her for profit is a crime against your mother, against all our mothers.' He cried as he spoke and, before Insaan had a chance to translate his words, the youth began to cry, touched by the emotion in his voice.

'We can still save our mother. We just need to wake up.'

'When we stood in solidarity with the people of Standing Rock, we were not just standing up for their water. We were standing for our water, for the world's water,' said Abdul, referring to a previous action by the community.

The group had supported the Standing Rock tribe while they protested against government and business negotiating indigenous land and jeopardising clean water sources for the sake of oil extraction and pipelines.[1] At the same time, the well of the community's rented house in Kabul dried up. For ten days the community fetched water in containers on a wheelbarrow while the well was deepened. There was great relief when the pump successfully delivered water to their well again. Muslimyor felt that the street kids shouldn't be kept ignorant of the water crisis and incorporated water-saving messages into lessons, games and activities that were shared with neighbours. These two synchronous actions in different parts of the world were the embodiment of the peace exchange.

At the end of the three-hour conversation, everyone was starving. The calls were emotionally draining, and they needed a break. Kebabs were served and people warmed their hands with toasted bread.

I sat with Tara who told me she enjoyed the diversity of people she met through the conversations. These intense exchanges were better than any class she had ever attended at school, and she had been exposed to ideas that she'd never imagined before.

As valuable as the conversations were, reaching out to the international community had its risks. After decades of the international community intervening and meddling in Afghan affairs, people had little faith in Western ideas and philosophies. In modern-day Afghanistan, associating with foreigners risked misunderstandings and dangerous accusations.

I WALKED WITH Insaan amongst a field of mudbrick homes, tarpaulin roofs stretched across thick sticks, weighted down by rocks. We were walking through one of the fifty or more internally displaced people (IDP) camps in Kabul.[2] The camp was established in 2008 on government-owned land and accommodated roughly 1000 IDPs (predominantly Pashtun and Tajik people).

We pushed aside a piece of green material that covered a gap in the mudbrick street wall and entered a muddy courtyard littered with trash. A man stood in the centre of the yard, a clutch of grubby children gathered around him. He was well dressed, with a *paqool* perched on his head: dignified amid abject poverty. He was a farmer from Helmand province and his family had been displaced by the violence.

'Our house was destroyed during fighting between American and Taliban forces,' he said.

The farmer and his family of twelve, including his parents, fled by car to Kabul. That was seven years ago. All of his children were born in the camp. He had not found work since arriving in Kabul. I wondered how they survived.

It had been sixteen years since the United States invaded Afghanistan and there were still more than one million conflict-induced IDPs and the number was rising. Between January and November 2016, 486,000 more Afghans were internally displaced as a result of intensification of the conflict.[3]

When the United States invaded they promised a new age of democracy and liberty. So, where did it all go wrong?

During the Soviet invasion, thousands of foreign fighters joined the jihad. Among them was the son of a billionaire Yemeni construction magnate, a Saudi student called Osama bin Laden. In 1989, while fighting in Afghanistan, bin Laden established al-Qaeda, a militant Sunni Islamist organisation, some of whose combatants were originally trained by US forces and whose weapons were supplied by the US government.

In 1996 bin Laden returned to Afghanistan, allied with the Taliban, and began to build al-Qaeda's influence in the country. Al-Qaeda very quickly became a power in Afghanistan, from which it launched what it called a global jihad against the United States and its allies, and organised the 9/11 terrorist attacks.[4] On 11 September 2001, two aeroplanes were deliberately flown into the Twin Towers of the World Trade Center in New York, with another plane hitting the Pentagon in Virginia, and a fourth crashing in Pennsylvania, causing nearly 3000 deaths.[5]

In October 2001 bin Laden broadcast a statement, filmed from the cave of an Afghan mountainside, addressing the attacks.

'What America is tasting now is something insignificant compared to what we have tasted for scores of years. Our nation [the Islamic world] has been tasting this humiliation and this degradation for more than eighty years. Its sons are killed, its blood is shed, its sanctuaries are attacked, and no-one hears, and no-one heeds.'[6]

In the aftermath of the 9/11 attacks, President George W Bush declared a 'War on Terror' and the United States began the military invasion of Afghanistan, demanding the Taliban extradite bin Laden and expel al-Qaeda from Afghanistan. In October 2001 the United States and Britain, with allies including Australia, initiated the inauspiciously named 'Operation Enduring Freedom' and joined the already existing United Islamic Front for the Salvation of Afghanistan (more commonly known as the Northern Alliance), a coalition of Tajik, Uzbek and Hazara forces opposed to the Taliban.[7] By December 2001 the allied forces had captured the Taliban stronghold, Kandahar, and dismantled the Taliban regime.

Under the influence of the United States, its allies and the UN, an agreement was signed on 5 December 2001 in Germany by a diverse collective of competing Afghan groups, excluding the defeated Taliban. Supported financially and politically by the United States, the UN and the international community, the Bonn Agreement outlined the post-2001 peace-building process in Afghanistan, which aimed to promote liberal democracy, a multi-ethnic representative government, facilitate socioeconomic development and rebuild permanent state institutions.[8] The process was to be protected and supported by the NATO-led security mission ISAF.

By the time the Bonn Agreement was finalised, Afghanistan was in crisis. The country had been left to rot by the Taliban, who did little to rebuild the nation and had resisted international NGO support for the people. A five-year drought had ruined the nation's agriculture, destroying 70 per cent of the country's livestock and leaving the nation reliant on international food aid. One quarter of children born in Afghanistan were dying of preventable diseases before the age of five: typhoid and cholera epidemics were rampant, and pneumonia and malaria had re-emerged as public health threats.[9] Despite the nation's dire condition, Afghans began returning to the country, filled with optimism. More than two million refugees returned to the country in 2002 alone.[10]

Shah Marai was working in Kabul as a photographer for Agence France-Presse (AFP) when the United States defeated the Taliban. 'Then one morning, the Taliban were gone, vanishing into thin air. You should have seen it. The streets were filled with people. It was like people were coming out from the shadows into the light of life again,' he wrote for the AFP.[11]

Justifying the invasion was an exercise in spin and opacity. Despite their claims, the United States was not motivated to help build a democratic, peaceful Afghanistan and restore rights for women. The invasion was largely driven by retribution for the 9/11 attacks. Moreover, the so-called War on Terror was a pretext for maintaining US military presence in the Middle East. US presence in Afghanistan kept alive the opportunity to develop oil and gas pipelines in the region and offered potential future access to Afghanistan's wealthy natural resources such as copper, iron ore and rare earth elements. Most importantly, Afghanistan was strategically placed between China, Russia, India, Pakistan and Iran.[12] All of this had the Afghan people concerned that their country would once again become a proxy battleground between world powers.

The Afghan invasion provided the United States and its allies with an opportunity to stabilise Afghanistan and the failing states of South and Central Asia – a region in turmoil, a region regarded as the homeland of terrorism. However, instead of consolidating and securing the region to protect it against a tide of insurgents, in 2003 the Bush administration used the false pretext of 'Weapons of Mass Destruction' to shift its crosshairs to Iraq and its oil supplies, to invade Iraq in March 2003.

While the United States and its forty-six member 'coalition of the willing', which included Australia and the United Kingdom, prepared to invade Iraq, roads weren't being built in Afghanistan; 95 per cent of the people were without electricity; the country's infrastructure remained in ruins; the army, police, civil service and judiciary was in disarray; and the new Afghan government was financially bankrupt. While the agricultural industry struggled, opium production flourished. A narcotics trade that had been abolished by the Taliban in 2000 was exploited by US-funded warlords.[13]

The US government's initial unwillingness to partake in rebuilding the Afghan nation resulted in a delayed and confused multinational aid effort, comprising more than forty countries, including all the NATO members. Each of the international donors disbursing aid in Afghanistan had their own agenda and separate agreement with the government. Donors were inclined to fund areas that were appealing to their constituents back home, rather than coordinating aid with the Afghan government's priorities, which led to gaps in many development areas.[14] The Special Inspector General for Afghanistan Reconstruction, the US government's leading oversight authority on Afghanistan reconstruction (formed as late as 2008), repeatedly criticised the international community's nation-building efforts. Even though the United States spent over US$100 billion on relief and reconstruction from 2002 to 2014, most of the projects were undermined by poor planning, shoddy construction, mechanical failures and inadequate oversight.[15] The failures of the international reconstruction mission led to a loss of faith amongst the Afghan people that the international community could rebuild their country.

Martin was working in Kabul in 2004 and 2005, before the re-emergence of the Taliban in 2006. At that time, there were several thousand foreigners living and working in the city and there was a roaring social scene. Businesses like those on the now-lifeless Chicken Street thrived. It was not hard to find accounts of foreign restaurants, underground bars, pool parties and tennis clubs.

'For a decade, Afghanistan attracted adventurers, do-gooders, racketeers and reporters like flypaper,' wrote *Guardian* journalist Sune Engel Rasmussen. 'Many got stuck in an intoxicating "Kabubble" of adrenaline and booze. Stories abound of drinking in brothels, drag racing through empty streets at night and making out at Taliban-themed costume parties.'[16]

Martin recalled his experiences of parties in Kabul, parties hosted by NGOs, and remembered it as a time of excess.

'It was disgusting. In the middle of poverty and war, there were parties with four hundred people, five hundred people, supplied with as much alcohol as you could want. There were drugs, prostitutes; it was such a contrast to the life outside. It was an insult to the neighbours.'

Just as the US strategy for nation-building in Afghanistan failed, their military strategy undermined the later peace-building process. During the

2001 invasion, the United States avoided major deployments of American ground troops by relying on air strikes and drones, and funding and arming local militia from the Northern Alliance in the north and Pashtun warlords in the south to fight the Taliban.[17] Civil war–era warlords were empowered to return from exile to participate in the war against the Taliban and al-Qaeda.[18] After the collapse of the Taliban, rather than support the Afghan government and national security forces, the United States paid those same warlords to keep the peace. Many of these warlords revived poppy cultivation and engaged in other criminal behaviour in order to finance their armies; soon the trade, which had been wiped out by the Taliban in 2000 and 2001 in their attempts to achieve international recognition as a legitimate state, provided more than 90 per cent of the world's opium and heroin supply.[19] Once again, the Afghan people suffered the consequences as millions became addicted.[20] The revival of these warlords, the war criminals of the last decade, led to the widespread corruption and disintegration of state institutions, already weakened as a result of three decades of conflict.[21]

The US and NATO's failure to consolidate peace in Afghanistan allowed for a revival of the Taliban and other insurgent groups. Although the Taliban regime was defeated in 2001, the politics and the ideologies of the group were not. During the first years of foreign occupation, the Taliban remained operational in Afghanistan thanks to narcotics production and trafficking, and support from countries like Pakistan that harboured retreating Taliban and al-Qaeda operatives during the 2001 invasion. The armed Islamic groups fighting and supporting the Taliban's war in Afghanistan were often based in the tribal regions of Pakistan and were a powerful influence on Pakistan's domestic politics. Steve Coll's book *Directorate S* referenced US intelligence agencies' reports that Pakistan's Inter-Services Intelligence (ISI) was training and supporting as many as 100,000 armed militants in 128 different camps in Pakistan.[22]

It may seem strange that a US ally would protect enemies of the United States, but Pakistan had been playing this double act for years. American investigative journalist and political writer Seymour M Hersh wrote that the ISI believed that maintaining a relationship with the Taliban leadership inside Afghanistan was essential to national security.

'The ISI's strategic aim is to balance Indian influence in Kabul; the Taliban is also seen in Pakistan as a source of jihadist shock troops who would back Pakistan against India in a confrontation over Kashmir. The Pakistanis also know that their trump card against aggression from India is a strong relationship with the United States.'[23]

In 2003, after the United States and Britain turned their attention to Iraq, the Taliban launched an insurgency against the Afghan government and ISAF. Al-Qaeda, an Afghan group called the Haqqani Network, Gulbuddin Hekmatyar's Hezb-i-Islami forces and other smaller outfits also opposed the government. But it was in 2006 that the violence began to escalate dramatically, and the tide began to turn against the international forces.

The United States and ISAF's military strategy, which relied upon aerial bombardments, drone attacks and night raids, caused indiscriminate killings of civilians and destruction of property, agriculture and livelihoods. There were also numerous instances of rogue brutality, such as when American soldier Robert Bales snuck away from his military outpost in Kandahar province one night in 2012 and raided two villages, slaughtering sixteen unarmed Afghan civilians, including old men, mothers and children, inside their homes, and then set their bodies on fire.[24] In Urozgan province, in 2012, an 'elite' Australian soldier kicked a handcuffed, innocent civilian shepherd named Ali Jan off a cliff and then executed him.[25] In 2009 another elite Australian soldier on his first deployment to Afghanistan executed an elderly, unarmed detainee as part of a 'blooding' ritual encouraged by higher-ranking soldiers. On the same mission, the prosthetic leg of a murdered Afghan was souvenired and taken back to Australia to be used as a novelty beer-drinking vessel.[26] Afghanistan had once again become a land where foreign soldiers could commit unsanctioned and illegal violence towards innocent civilians with impunity.

In its War on Terror, the United States had decided they were going to rewrite the rules of war and trash international human rights agreements and expectations. The United States introduced at least six different prison systems where they could interrogate and torture prisoners outside the US jurisdiction of law. This included Guantanamo Bay in Cuba, prisons at Bagram and Kandahar, a dozen secret jails at temporary military encampments, jails run by Afghan warlords and the Afghan government, jails run by the ISI in Pakistan, and 'places of rendition' by which the CIA transported prisoners to allied countries where they could be interrogated and tortured by local intelligence agencies. The United States deemed al-Qaeda and Taliban forces as 'illegal enemy combatants', and denied them Prisoner of War status and the associated protections under the Geneva Conventions and the US Constitution.[27]

Over time, details emerged of CIA and MI6 programs to detain and interrogate terrorism suspects in the years after 9/11. Afghan males, some of whom were teenagers as young as thirteen years old, were disappeared in the night and subjected to torture breathtaking in its malicious creativity: waterboarding, sensory deprivation, sleep deprivation, rectal feeding, rectal hydration, beatings with pipes, electric shocks, near asphyxiation, attack dogs, preying upon phobias, humiliation, nudity, rape, sexual assault, and so on.[28] Suspects were held in these so-called 'black sites', under such conditions, indefinitely. Some died in custody, some were sent to Guantanamo. If they were lucky enough to be set free, they returned to their families as shells of their former selves, no doubt radicalised against Western democracy. Often these terrorism suspects were innocent, accused as part of a local dispute or political manoeuvre. Those who disappeared in custody were known as 'ghosts'. This was a war in which the 'champions of liberty' debased their own legal principles.[29] By 2018 there were still forty men held in Guantanamo, of whom only nine were facing or had faced trials. The others were known as 'forever prisoners'.[30]

When the United States invaded Afghanistan they promised a new age of democracy and liberty, but instead they doomed the Afghan people to another decade and more of war, torture, bombings, grief and death. Since the commencement of Operation Enduring Freedom, tens of thousands of civilians had been killed in direct violence in Afghanistan.[31]

The decade-long manhunt for Osama bin Laden ended on 2 May 2011 when a US Navy SEAL team raided his Abbottabad compound in Pakistan and shot him in the head. According to Seymour M Hersh's account, Pakistan's ISI had been holding bin Laden hostage at the Abbottabad compound since 2006. The ISI was using bin Laden as leverage against Taliban and al-Qaeda activities inside Afghanistan and Pakistan, but they eventually arranged his murder 'to ensure the continued release of American military aid'.[32]

The assassination of Osama bin Laden was 'job complete' for the United States, according to then US Secretary of State Hillary Clinton. In December 2014 the United States and its allies withdrew the majority of their combat troops from Afghanistan and transferred full responsibility for security of the country to the Afghan National Security Forces.[33] By 2018 there were still 15,000 US troops in Afghanistan. The US-led military intervention had cost close to US$1 trillion but it had failed to stabilise Afghanistan.[34] The Taliban and other armed opposition groups were the strongest they had been since 2001, and the withdrawal of international troops and the reduction of economic support by the international community left the country on the brink of collapse.

After the transition of international forces from combat roles to advisory and training roles, the Taliban mounted and sustained its strongest military campaign in years, and the war became bloodier than ever. The United States and its allies had lost the war. Afghanistan had been torn asunder once more, a divided society left to piece together the fragments of a once beautiful country. Peace negotiations were the last hope for a political resolution to the conflict, but they were unreliable at best.

In 2017, as I stood with Insaan and this family from Helmand province amongst the makeshift mud homes, it was clear the biggest losers in this disaster were the same ones who had suffered through the Soviet war, the warlord era and the Taliban regime: the Afghan people.

Chapter 9

Violence Comes to the Mountains

When violence eventually came to the village, Insaan didn't see it coming. He had considered the fact that the people who issued the first threat were probably still intent on doing him harm. His friends were still protecting him and were obviously still wary of trouble. But so much time had passed since the first threat that he had become accustomed to living in a perpetual state of hypervigilance, almost to the point where his protection became normalised. He conceded that when his antagonists refused to meet him to address the root grievances, their original sentiments were allowed to simmer. In hindsight, he could see they were simply waiting for the right opportunity to drive him out.

The day his peaceful life in the mountains was brought to an end, Insaan had been in the city all day working at his office. He rode his bicycle from the city to his village's valley, alongside the river, at the feet of the giants of Afghanistan. He passed farmers tending fields of potatoes, shepherds leading their goats along maroon-coloured dirt roads shaded by healthy poplar trees. Insaan left his bicycle at the bottom of the rise that led up to his house, and then he climbed the slope on foot. As he walked, he noticed a strange black stain on the skyline, but it didn't occur to him that the source of that stain was his own home. When he reached the top of the rise, he saw a crowd had gathered at the front of his house; he saw his charred possessions laid out on the ground like evidence at a crime scene. He felt his heart pounding, but he managed to detach himself from his emotions, observing and capturing all the details, trying to analyse and understand what was happening.

Insaan noticed the soot on his scattered possessions and the acrid smell synonymous with a recently extinguished fire. The crowd was chattering, excited and horrified, discussing who might be responsible for this attack. This was a scandalous event for the peaceful village. When Insaan arrived, the villagers turned to look at him, faces downcast and ashamed. It was clear to Insaan that everything he owned had been destroyed or was missing. Asghar approached Insaan and without a word handed him his bag. Within it were his most valuable items, his identity documents. All of his money had been stolen.

Asghar had been in the field, digging up potatoes, when he saw a thick black cloud of smoke hovering over the village. It took him a second to realise it was coming from his and Insaan's house. He ran through the fields, head lowered, knees pumping, breathing heavily from panic and exertion. As he drew closer, Asghar could see smoke streaming out of the building. He tried to open the door but released the red-hot handle immediately with a yelp. He broke the glass of one of the windows with a rock, flicked the latch, and climbed through the opening into a confusion of smoke and flame. Asghar was blinded by the smoke and terrified, but he wanted to make sure Insaan was not inside. He grabbed Insaan's document bag and climbed back out the window. By this time some other villagers had arrived to throw soil and water on the flames, but it was too late. The room was destroyed.

Insaan stayed in his landlord's room that night, accompanied by his bodyguards, Nadir and Zee. None of them could sleep, too shocked by the events of the evening. Insaan wondered who may have been responsible for the fire and theft. He reasoned that they hadn't wanted to hurt him, as he was in town at work. If he could resolve this conflict at a local level, if he could find out who did it, he could stop it becoming a life-threatening matter. Nobody in the village had seen the culprit or culprits. Asghar had been the first person on the scene, by which time the fire was well and truly underway. Whoever it was, the message was clear: they wanted Insaan to leave.

In the days after the fire, a rumour spread in the village that Insaan had set his own room on fire. Then the accusations became more dangerous for him: it was put about that Insaan had kidnapped a villager.

Insaan sought advice from his colleagues.

'Leave tomorrow. They are going to kill you,' they told Insaan.

'But I am innocent,' Insaan said.

'That doesn't matter. This is Afghanistan.'

Insaan realised his time in the mountains was over. He was being forced to abandon this life he had carved out for himself, drummed out of the village by unknown and implacable enemies. He would have to leave those villagers and families who had trusted him, protected him and become his friends and family, and he grieved this loss like a death. He didn't bear a grudge against the perpetrators. His only regret was that he didn't get the opportunity to sit down with them and make peace. He said his goodbyes, none of which were easy, and removed himself from the village.

Although Insaan felt cheated by circumstance, he wasn't ready to give up the struggle. He always knew that if he stayed in the mountains, the work would have remained parochial. He decided he would relocate to Kabul where he could spread the influence and reach of the work. It was going to be personally difficult for him to settle in a new city and to establish and educate a new group of young people. But the work and the philosophies were a transferable process of ideas; even if this movement couldn't be restarted in Kabul, the struggle would continue in a different setting and a different era. When those philosophies become common practice, that's when war would be abolished.

After Insaan left, Zee refused to clear away the incinerated remains of Insaan's room, keeping it as a charred memorial to Insaan and his attempt to bring peace to a community.

Part 2

ARE HUMANS CAPABLE OF ABOLISHING WAR?

You are not a drop in the ocean.
You are the entire ocean, in a drop.

– Rumi

Chapter 10

Restarting in Kabul

Insaan arrived in Kabul wrung-out, angry and defiant. After living in the mountains of central Afghanistan working for peace, he had fled his little village and he was lucky to still be alive. He was determined to restart the peace work he had begun, so he made the decision to relocate to Kabul. He did not ask and he did not expect anyone to join him; however, Arif, Nadir and Asghar decided they would come with him to the capital. They said they wanted to explore their own opportunities for studying in Kabul, but Insaan realised this was just one of their reasons. He had found himself in the unlikely situation where Afghans were protecting him and one another, regardless of ethnicity and religion – this was what he had hoped for when he first started the community.

The organisation Insaan worked for in the mountains offered him housing in Kabul temporarily, until he found his feet. He accepted and the four of them agreed to live together. Arif was eighteen years old and had finished his final exams at school. Nadir was sixteen and still at school. Asghar was thirteen and Insaan had agreed with Asghar's family that he would look out for him in Kabul.

Insaan knew from his recent experience in the mountains that moving in with three teenagers was going to be difficult. He had already become accustomed to the uncertain nature of life in a war zone. He had changed from the man he once was, a man who needed structure, who lived to a strict five-year plan. After spending more than six years in the mountains, contemplating his purpose, that man had been scrubbed out. The way he lived, the way he interacted with people, and his understanding of community had changed dramatically from his early years. Where he was raised, 'community' was his family living together in an apartment block where he didn't know his neighbours. He was cordial with them, he didn't fight with them, but he didn't relate to them either. However, in the village in the mountains everybody knew one another. People had to interact with each other daily, whether they liked their neighbours or not, and they relied upon each other. He had lost his sense of privacy in the mountains. The social barriers he erected to protect himself and his individuality had been torn away and he now embraced the idea of strength through community. Insaan thought of the Afghan proverb: 'If you have one stick you can break it very easily, but if you have a bundle of sticks you can't break them.'

Insaan was in conversation with Mary Smith and Daniel Johnson. In the past they had mentioned the possibility of providing financial support if Insaan wanted to develop the work. He made a gloomy assessment of his life: he was transitioning between jobs and cities, he was still in shock after his unplanned departure, and he had to pay rent. He needed help. But he was worried about receiving financial assistance – he feared that involving money could negatively affect his relationships with the teenagers, and the nature of the work. That's what money did, especially in a war zone, where survival was an issue. He discussed his fears with Mary and Daniel, but they left it up to him to decide whether he could go through this personal transition from an independent actor and independent group to receiving financial support. After much soul-searching, Insaan eventually reasoned that without a home to rent he could not stay in Kabul. He agreed to accept the money to help him pay rent with the knowledge that this decision would change the dynamics between him, the youth and any young people who would later join the group.

The group relocated to a small, three-room apartment. It was fairly cold, without much sunlight and with no garden. After living in the mountains, none of them liked the apartment, but they made do for the time being. They laid mattresses in the rooms and they had a sofa donated to them by a friend; apart from that there was no other furniture in the place.

Arif enrolled at an electrical trade school and Nadir and Asghar would enrol at high school after the winter holidays.

Insaan first saw Kabul in 2004 after he crossed the Afghanistan–Pakistan border. At the time, the city infrastructure was sparse and dominated by low-rise, single-storey buildings, pockmarked and cracked with bullet holes. The tallest building in Kabul was the brutalist, eighteen-storey Ministry of Communications structure, which rose above the city like a brown thumb. There weren't many cars on the unsealed dirt and gravel roads. Herds of sheep and goats walked the streets, stopping to eat the accumulated rubbish on the pavement. Beggars and war veterans sat in gutters. Street kids burned incense to chase away bad spirits. Women with and without burqas could be seen in public. Insaan saw military convoys, but there weren't many international or Afghan soldiers patrolling the streets. That job was left to private security and policemen. His overall impression was of a city flattened by war.

The city had changed a lot in seven years. It had become more crowded, as refugees returned to Afghanistan and the rural communities fled the fighting. The city wasn't able to cope with the huge influx of people and the number of beggars in the street had increased. Heroin addicts congregated under bridges, their desperate, devastated condition visible to anyone who passed. Shantytowns and displaced people's camps had sprung up all over the city. In some parts of Kabul the sewerage was overflowing, and the streets were putrid. The air pollution was worse. There had been drought; water levels around Kabul were dropping every year. Insaan noticed the river and its tributaries were clogged with plastic and trash and all sorts of rubbish; the water was black and foul. By 2012 only 27 per cent of Afghans had access to safe drinking water and 5 per cent to adequate sanitation.[1]

The city was growing outwards and upwards. New shopping centre complexes were built, including the first to be serviced with an elevator. Lavish new wedding halls were used as examples of progress. The garish 'poppy palaces' of the military elite, built on the skimmed profits of opium production and corruption, bedazzled the eye with pink hues and glass facades and showed that there was prosperity and wealth for those in power. The city was becoming marked by fortified compounds of government and NGO buildings. The outskirts of Kabul were consuming local townships, amalgamating them into the greater cityscape. With growth came land grabbing and conflict, usually perpetrated by high-ranking officials from the police, military or government.

Within Kabul there hadn't been a surge in military presence, but 60 kilometres outside of the city there was the enormous American military base Bagram: a well-lit, electrified foreign city surrounded by the darkness of Afghan villages. It had been a decade since the United States had defeated the Taliban, yet, aside from Kabul and a few other major cities, almost no-one in Afghanistan had access to electricity.

In 2004 there was still a lot of optimism among Afghans for a better future. But by 2011 much of that had evaporated. Insaan saw little progress being made in rebuilding the capital, despite the millions of dollars of international development and aid money, and there was hardly any concrete, long-term, sustainable development in rural areas of the country.

Insaan was disappointed to learn that the work of civil society groups in Kabul had been significantly complicated by the militarisation of aid by United States and NATO. Military forces were performing aid work, and most of the development funding was channelled through the US military – America's attempt to win 'Hearts and Minds'. Many civil society organisations and NGOs relied on foreign military for funding and security; they became colonised without knowing it. Kabul represented to Insaan how not to build a city.

That winter, Insaan first thought about inviting a Pashtun youth to join their house. This was an intentional move, based on their experiments in peace in the mountains, to pursue the concept of community. In the mountains he had seen young men of different ethnic groups overcome their prejudices and perceived differences by building relationships with people from other ethnic groups. He felt ready to restart his experiments in peace in Kabul. The goal was for these young people to commit to living together, to build alternative ways of connecting that would counter the socioeconomic, environmental and military violence in Afghanistan. He wanted to set an example to the rest of Afghanistan to convince people that peace was possible.

Insaan discussed the idea with Mary.

'You're going to have a tough time,' Mary said. 'You're going to have teenage rebellion, teenage romance. It's going to be quite a way from peace and abolition of war.'

'Give me three years,' Insaan replied.

Insaan then brought the young men together in a meeting and floated the possibility, asking: 'Would you like to make this a multi-ethnic live-in community?'

The young men deliberated on this radical idea to live with strangers of different ethnic groups. Could they trust each other? Would they be safe? Yet in a way they had already begun the process: Arif was Tajik, and Nadir and Asghar were Hazara. With the boldness of youth and the desire for change, they responded in the affirmative.

'Yes, let's do it.'

So began their search for a fifth member of the community.

INSAAN, THE STALWARTS and I walked down narrow mudbrick walkways in the bitter cold. The occasional covered-up pedestrian hurried past into the night without offering any greeting. The streets were otherwise empty and mist was starting to descend upon the city, creating a sense of eeriness that was both beautiful and unnerving. For me, Afghanistan had never been so quiet, and I felt a thrill at being outside at night. I had been living under the assumption that there was an unofficial evening curfew. Not even with the adventurous Martin did I walk the streets after dark.

We stopped at a rusty door embedded in a hard mud wall and knocked. A young woman opened the door slightly and peeked out at us. When she saw who it was, she squealed with delight and ushered us inside. We passed through a courtyard and a garden of trees and flowering shrubs, invisible from the street, and entered the main house. A young man greeted us, grinning fiercely, shaking hands and kissing cheeks. In the context of widespread societal distrust, it was uncommon for Afghans to invite strangers and foreigners into their homes. What's more, male guests usually wouldn't see the female members of the family except for the children. But I was beginning to expect this type of radical behaviour from the members of the community.

In the next room was the reason we had come: a sleeping newborn and a toddler in an orange onesie. The young man and his wife were proud to show off their young family. It was toasty warm inside and we sat on comfortable cushions on the floor, alongside the couple's bed and the baby's cot. On the floor in front of us the couple had prepared a generous feast of spinach, chicken, rice, bread, pickled vegetables and tea.

'Paiman was the first Pashtun man in the community,' Insaan said. 'Paiman and Zarrina met in the community.'

Paiman and Zarrina shared a loving look.

'In Afghan families, when the older sons reach a certain age, usually around eighteen, the family begin to talk of marriage,' Paiman said in English. He had a strong accent and he spoke quickly and stuttered a little, as if he was too excited to form his words properly so they piled into each other.

'The custom is that the parents will look for a suitable spouse by talking to their relatives and friends about who can arrange something. In the provinces outside of Kabul, neither the man nor the woman is part of the process. They aren't asked their opinion. But we did not follow this tradition.'

Paiman looked slyly at his wife.

'I got to know Zarrina when she was working with the seamstresses in the tailoring and duvet projects. The first time we met, marriage was not on my mind at all. She was a fellow volunteer, nothing more.'

Zarrina rolled her eyes and Muslimyor laughed like a hyena, which earned him a disapproving glare from Hojar.

'But gradually those thoughts came to my mind,' Paiman said, chuckling as he spoke.

Everyone joined in the laughter now.

'I invited my aunt to attend one of the community events so she could meet Zarrina. That's when our friendship began.'

After three months of conversations, Paiman and Zarrina became close friends and they started talking about marriage. The problem was Paiman was Pashtun, Zarrina was Tajik, and it was going to be difficult to negotiate the families' different expectations and traditions. But they were willing to take the risk and Paiman sent his aunt to Zarrina's family to ask for her hand in marriage.

Within Paiman's family there were relatives who said he should marry a Pashtun girl, while some of Zarrina's family members wanted her to marry one of her relatives. The custom of marrying cousins was founded in a strange crossover between tradition, trust and geography. People in Afghanistan, especially people in rural areas, could be suspicious of strangers. This was partly due to the history of ethnic and religious conflict in Afghanistan, but also because of isolation. On the rare occasion there was a marriage with someone other than a relative, it was usually someone the family knew well, and it was usually within the same ethnic group and faith. Once people started moving to cities, broadening their social circles, breaking down barriers of suspicion and distrust, new marriage traditions emerged.

'My family was worried that if I married Paiman he would make me live in the provinces with donkeys,' Zarrina said.

Paiman and Zarrina agreed to be firm in their decision, recognising there would be relatives on both sides of the family who would never be happy with their marriage – and with change and progress in general. In the face of their determination, the families relented, and the young couple wed.

'It's our lives, our marriage, not theirs,' Zarrina said.

I could see how important their happiness was to the community members. Afghanistan needed positive stories – especially interethnic ones – and what could be more heartwarming than seeing the love in a household such as this: Zarrina doting over their baby girl, Paiman bouncing their son on his knee.

'And now they are raising the next generation of peace activists,' Insaan said.

We all laughed but we also recognised the truth and hope in the statement. Perhaps this next generation would be the ones to bring peace to Afghanistan.

KABUL, 2012

Paiman sat down next to Arif in the cafeteria of their college. The two friends lived in the same dormitory together and they were both studying to be electricians.

'How is your little friendship circle going?' Paiman asked Arif.

Arif swivelled in his seat, checking to see who was in the room and Paiman laughed at his reaction. Paiman had an almost wolfish look about him when he smiled or laughed. His lips stayed close together at the front and peeled away at the molars as if he was baring his teeth in a snarl.

'It's okay, I checked the room before saying anything,' Paiman said to a visibly upset Arif and laughed again, smiling at the empty room, as if for support.

'You shouldn't joke about that,' Arif said.

Arif liked to confide in Paiman about the group's philosophies and activities, but he was careful to only mention the group when he was in trusted company. There were people of varying origins, backgrounds and beliefs at the institute and he didn't know who he could trust.

'I have a proposition for you,' Arif said to Paiman. He looked particularly nervous today. 'We want to start a multi-ethnic live-in community. We would like you to join us. What do you think?'

Paiman leaned back in his chair and whistled through his teeth. That was a hell of a question for a Monday morning.

Paiman grew up in an eastern province of Afghanistan, in a district predominantly populated by Pashtun people. The local people viewed any outsider with entrenched suspicion; to some, all foreigners were military. And here was Arif, a Tajik man, asking Paiman to live with Tajiks and Hazaras. No wonder Arif had been so worried about the other classmates eavesdropping on their conversations. Paiman was suspicious but curious. He had known Arif for a year and in that time a level of trust had developed between them. But now he wondered if Arif had befriended him as some kind of plot. Anything was possible in Afghanistan.

'I'll think about it,' Paiman said.

Paiman was eighteen years old when he came to Kabul to further his studies. He had barely socialised with a Tajik person or a Hazara person before moving to the capital. His Dari was limited. His childhood was one of farming and growing up in nature and he was thankful for that. But the less idyllic backdrop for his early years was living with fear of attacks and witnessing fighting between local groups. By the time he was in the tenth grade, in about 2007, the intensity of the fighting had escalated, the night raids had increased and international troops were swarming the area.

Paiman asked his father for advice about Arif's offer.

'In the days before the Soviets came, the different ethnic groups of Afghanistan lived together without problems. After the Soviet invasion I had the experience of being a Sunni refugee in Iran, a Shia country, and I was never discriminated against for my religion. But eventually the wars divided Afghanistan and the region,' his father said. 'You know how to discern character. If you are happy with the group, then I trust you.'

After speaking to his father, Paiman realised that Afghans could be and should be striving for harmony. For Paiman and his family, war only meant loss – of family, of wealth, of land. He was already convinced that there needed to be a different way: but what was the solution? Paiman came back to Arif and agreed to meet Insaan.

When Paiman came to the apartment he couldn't settle his nerves. Arif's caution in speaking about the group in public had spooked Paiman a little. He felt as if he was doing something wrong by coming to this group. He was almost surprised to find the apartment was quite normal; he didn't know what he imagined, a secret underground lair? Arif introduced him to Insaan and a teenager called Asghar. Paiman had heard so much about Insaan over the last few months that he expected to recognise him, but this man was a stranger. Insaan was instantly welcoming. He smiled broadly and encouraged him to sit. Their short introduction ended with a question.

'Can you teach me Pashto?' Insaan asked Paiman.

After all of Paiman's anxiety about visiting the group, here was a simple request from a man to learn the Pashto language. Why should he refuse that?

Paiman started giving language lessons and visiting the live-in community, stepping stones to his involvement with the group. While members of the group spoke different languages and their accents were different, over time Paiman could see there was friendship there. He reasoned that if people from different ethnic groups could become friends, the distance between them could be narrowed; by extension he thought it might be possible for them to sit down with one another and live together. And so, aged twenty, he agreed to live with the group as their first Pashtun member.

Chapter 11

Establishing a School of the Street

The first floor of the Community Centre was full of young children dressed in ragged jumpers and muddy pants. Their shaved heads, grubby necks and weathered faces were turned towards one end of the large room where musicians performed. Behind them a giant love heart made out of red balloons had been pinned to the wall. The crowd represented many of Afghanistan's diverse ethnic groups: there were Hazara children of Mongol descent; green-eyed, dark-skinned Pashtun children; white-faced Tajiks; and Turkic Uzbeks. Little boys gazed in awe at the pretty young female volunteers on the edge of the crowds; phones rang; young girls at the front whispered and giggled; children were roughly pushed in and out of the room by volunteers acting as ushers. Every time the door was opened the performances were interrupted by a cacophony of whistles, shouts and laughing from the hallway outside. Heads in the crowd swivelled this way and that, not sure where to look.

This was the community's street kids school, weekly classes run by the volunteers for one hundred vulnerable children. These young children were all street workers before they joined the community's school. Every Friday for the past year the students had been attending classes in Dari, English, mathematics, nonviolence and tailoring. To encourage families to enrol their children in government schools for the other six days of the week, the community supplemented the lost income of the studying child by providing monthly food gifts of rice and oil.

'They say there are more than two million Afghan children who work to supplement their families' incomes,'[1] Insaan said. 'There are 60,000 children who work the streets of Kabul. This is supposed to be the future of the country and they don't even know how to read or write.[2] Do you know how much it costs to keep one US soldier in Afghanistan for one year? 2.1 million dollars.'[3]

A talented *dambura* player began to perform and the crowd went silent. The young audience members watched with wonder at his skills. One enthusiastic member started a clap that triggered convulsions of disapproval from the onlooking volunteers: 'shhhhhs', wagging fingers and stern looks.

'Over fifty per cent of the population is under twenty and that percentage is growing,' Insaan said. 'One of the measures of society is how we treat our children. Not just our own children, but all children. What kind of world are we offering them?'

Insaan's face seemed to sag with sadness, as he contemplated the children's and the nation's hardships. He caught me observing him and forced his face into a positive smile.

'The students arranged this party for themselves to celebrate the completion of their first year of school at the centre,' Insaan said with a laugh.

Insaan motioned for one of the students to approach us.

'This is Arash,' Insaan said. 'He is an Uzbek from the north of Afghanistan.'

The Uzbeks were the fourth largest ethnic group in Afghanistan, descended from Turkic tribes that migrated to Central Asia following the Mongol invasions of the 13th century. In 1991, following the breakup of the Soviet Union, the Uzbeks formed their own nation state of Uzbekistan, which borders Afghanistan. However, Uzbek communities can be found in various countries throughout the region.[4]

Arash said he was fifteen years old and he had a convoluted system to calculate it. 'My mother told me I was born when Hamid Karzai was president. Karzai was president for about twelve or thirteen years and now Ashraf Ghani has been president for two years, so I am fifteen.'

Births were rarely registered in Afghanistan, especially in rural areas, and people without a connection to international visitors weren't accustomed to counting their age.

Arash had lived a life of poverty. When he was nine years old he lost his father, a street cart vendor, when he became 'collateral damage' in the bombing of a mosque.

'My father was a good man who always told me to go to school, so I could have a brighter future. He didn't want me to work as a child. But once my father died, I knew that I had to work to support my family.'

Arash was now responsible for his three younger brothers and sister. He had been working on the streets ever since. He used scales to take the weight of passers-by – for each person he weighed, he would earn 5 Afghanis (10 cents) – but then he changed to boot polishing. There were frequent bombings where he worked in the city and he was also scared of being chased by police with batons. Arash shrugged – that was life.

Arash had never liked school. When he was eleven, a local religious leader was forcing all the children in his neighbourhood to go to a religious school. If they didn't attend, he would hit them across the shoulders and legs with twisted metal wire. If the students couldn't memorise texts, the teacher would hit them. Arash developed a great hatred for that mullah and for school.

'My father would have approved of this community,' Arash said. 'They are helping me be a better person. In Afghan society there is a lot of discrimination. Ethnic groups behave in a bad way towards each other. In the home, when people get angry, the tendency is to try and solve the problem with violence. I learned from the community that change starts with ourselves. I try not to discriminate against other people and to control myself when I am angry. I don't want to fight anymore.'

Arash didn't believe there was any difference between a Sunni and a Shia, or even a Muslim or a non-Muslim.

'We are all human beings,' he said with a smile.

Arash wanted to finish high school and go to university.

When I looked at the students, I was reminded of the begging street children who tugged at my pockets asking for a dollar. Now here was this young man named Arash amazing me with his eloquence and self-awareness. These were the children who sacrificed their schooling, polishing shoes and selling cigarettes to help support their impoverished families. Now this community was doing their best to support them and their families.

When Arash returned to the other students, Insaan resumed speaking.

'Civil society in Afghanistan has broken down and been replaced by international NGOs who operate to their own agendas. We need independent civil institutions to provide a platform for civilians to influence the direction of their society. However, the individual alone can't rebuild civil society. Only with collective community power can we force change. Individuals see themselves as victims, but together we are leaders and actors for change. All of our projects are devoted to community building. It is a long, difficult, fragile process which we have been working towards for many years and if we want to change Afghan society for the better, we will be working on this for many years to come. If we want to build a peaceful future for Afghanistan, we need to educate the future generations.'

KABUL, 2012

Horse woke up to bomb blasts; his eyes went instinctively left and right, and his first thought was, *is everyone okay*? He had become so accustomed to waking up to the boom and clatter of violence that explosions were now his alarm clocks. He tried to ascertain whether the blasts were close by, and when he judged them to not be an immediate threat, he rose from his mattress on the floor and set about his morning routine. He and Muslimyor were scheduled to prepare breakfast for the community.

Kabul had been a difficult adjustment for Horse after being raised in the relatively peaceful mountains. On top of the violence in the capital, the city life of busy streets, crowds of people, air and noise pollution could be overwhelming. When he walked the streets of Kabul, amongst people from all over Afghanistan, he felt lost and alone.

But there were positives to take out of the move as well. Life in the rural areas was more labour intensive than in the city. In Kabul he had more time to focus on his studies and the schools and teachers were better than in the mountains. The transition to Kabul was made easier by his friends in the community. Insaan and Asghar had phoned Muslimyor and Horse, telling them about their live-in community and inviting them to join, but for Horse the economic reality first made the move seem impossible. He simply could not afford to live in Kabul. His family were having significant financial difficulties and there was talk of him returning to work as a shepherd to earn some money to counter their debt. Insaan suggested Horse could join a small project the community was funding, the production of a short film, but this seemed like a short-term solution to what was a lifelong struggle for Horse and his family. What would he do for money after the filming was completed? Muslimyor was much more cavalier about the idea and it was his enthusiasm and determination that convinced Horse to join the community. Their families were only happy if both of them went, so they could watch out for each other. So, the two fourteen-year-olds moved to Kabul together to work and further their schooling, but also to join the community and reunite with their old friends.

Arriving 'in community', as they called it, had been exciting and strange. 'Parliament house', so named because of its proximity to the national assembly in Kabul, was bigger than the previous apartment the group were renting, with one large room at the front of the house and two smaller rooms at the back. This extra space was appreciated considering there were now ten young men living in the house. This included four new members: Zilal, Baddar, Hamza and Soban.

Because this was a multi-ethnic community in which members took turns to cook, different kinds of food would appear at the table every day. Each ethnicity would cook in their own ethnic style, particular to their region. Some of the residents had grown up in Iran, so they prepared Iranian dishes, which Horse ate for the first time. Pashtuns added all sorts of spices and peppers in their food, but Horse preferred the Hazara cooking, which used tomato purees.

There was a constant hubbub of activity and discussion around the house; a manic energy filled the community. Everything was different and new and possible. The group was in its infancy, planning and preparing for the future, exploring different ideas for projects to devote their time to. Meanwhile the new community members had to transfer schools and settle into their new living arrangements.

Also emerging from the rubble of war at that time were a host of civil society groups. The community reached out to several of these groups in Kabul, inviting them to visit their community and see their practice. However, Insaan had reservations about the independence and makeup of some of these networks, as it was not hard for political organisations or government informers to infiltrate groups and manipulate their ideologies. This became an ongoing concern of the community.

The community registered themselves as an official group, a legal necessity to operate in Afghanistan. For the purposes of registration, they were required to submit a constitution, prompting lengthy discussions about their core values and the drawing up of a written charter. The community agreed that the gross inequalities of Afghanistan caused injustice and crippled human potential and they identified the concerns they wanted to address: children, especially girls, who were denied the right to formal education; women, particularly widows, who were denied the right to engage in the economy and earn a fair wage; and vulnerable families unable to afford basic items to ensure their survival. During this period, they came to an agreement as to who could live in the community, how they could be admitted and what the purpose of the community was.

Horse and Muslimyor laid out bread and tea for breakfast and, as community members joined the meal, they continued the discussion about the group's priorities.

'I think we should sponsor a program for seamstresses. If we can create jobs for women this will help all families,' Arif said. The group agreed wholeheartedly.

'Surely we must devote time and effort to helping refugees and displaced people,' said Paiman.

'This problem is too great,' said Baddar. 'What could we do to help?'

'We should not refrain from assisting just because problems appear overwhelming,' said Insaan.

'We could help fund small business loans using the model Insaan ran in the mountains,' suggested Muslimyor.

'There is a street kid who works for an old man selling soup. Perhaps we could provide him a loan so he could run his own soup business rather than working for someone else?' said Hamza.

And so it went, an endless spitball of ideas on how to improve their communities, until they finally committed to a project.

'I knew a street kid in Quetta, Pakistan,' Insaan told the community. 'His name was Amaan and he was a friend of mine. I will forever regret that I didn't do enough to help him. I would like to start a school to support street kids like Amaan.'

QUETTA, PAKISTAN, 2002

Amaan's skullcap sat on the back of his head; a thick bushy fringe covered his forehead. After a long day of sifting through dumpsters and piles of trash, his feet were bone-white with dust and dried mud. Amaan was a twelve-year-old, green-eyed Afghan Pashtun refugee who collected and sold rubbish to earn a few rupees so he and his grandmother could survive. Insaan had invited Amaan and his grandmother to his house to share some delicious Pakistani mangoes.

Amaan and Insaan did not share a common language; neither of them spoke Urdu very well and Insaan did not speak Pashto. Despite the vast difference in age and the limitations on their communication, Amaan was Insaan's friend and one of the first refugees he had come to know in Pakistan. They had met on the grim streets of Quetta, when Insaan noticed Amaan collecting rubbish. Insaan offered him a smile and in return Amaan came and sat next to Insaan and shared an apple with him. It was an offer of friendship, but for Insaan it was so much more.

While working in Quetta, Insaan was confronted with the misery and hardship of more than one million Afghan refugees. Every day he walked amongst thousands of tents that sprawled in each direction for miles, creating a makeshift city of refugees. Each tent housed a family and their trauma. There was a child who had picked up what he thought was a toy, and it had blown his arm off. There was the woman covered in burns after pulling her dead children out of the fiery wreckage of a destroyed home. Surrounded by so much suffering, there were times when Insaan felt overwhelmed by the hopelessness. As a young man he had come to Pakistan with the naive desire to change the world, but when he was confronted by the magnitude of the crisis in Pakistan he had no idea what help he could be.

For Insaan, Amaan became the human face of the Afghan refugee crisis in Pakistan. When the scale of the disaster almost became too much for Insaan, he had befriended one refugee: one insignificant child from Kandahar, an orphan amongst a million fleeing the violence in Afghanistan. That sharing of food after a hard day's work became a ritual for Insaan and Amaan and over the months a friendship of sorts emerged.

That day, Amaan sat opposite Insaan, chewing thoughtfully on a mango pip. Smeared juice had wiped clean a patch of grime on his cheek. Amaan looked up and caught Insaan contemplating him.

'What?' he asked.

'Nothing. Take a photo with me. Smile,' Insaan said.

That simple request angered Amaan's grandmother.

'What reason does he have to smile?' she asked.

She was right, Insaan thought. Her simple question made Insaan doubt his worth to these people once again. All of his education and knowledge and he couldn't even give this boy one convincing reason to smile.

'We are leaving, Insaan,' Amaan said, with tears in his eyes. 'My grandmother and I are going to Iran. Life here in Quetta is difficult.'

Insaan couldn't understand why they thought life in Iran would be easier. There could be life-threatening challenges for a Sunni Pashtun to take refuge in Iran, a Farsi-speaking, Shia Muslim country. Insaan wanted to offer him viable alternatives but he had nothing to say. There was no solution to Amaan's problem; there was no simple solution for any of the refugees displaced in Pakistan. Insaan had come to Quetta wanting to help refugees like Amaan. Insaan had been so happy to be able to provide medical help there to many, but now, faced with Amaan's answerless dilemma, he realised how proud and vain he had been.

And now young Amaan was leaving, and it was highly likely they would never meet again. Perhaps Amaan would die on the journey, or he would end up in one of the madrassas that trained boys in jihad. Perhaps he would become one of the hunted and demonised Afghan insurgents. Insaan was thrown by their decision and was scarcely able to offer any warmth or support for the distraught child and his frail grandmother. Instead Insaan remained silent and looked out the window to a dreary late afternoon sky.

When Amaan and his grandmother left, Insaan cried like he had never cried before: deep sobs that dredged up guilt and inadequacy. It was in this low moment that Insaan felt a firm determination take root inside of him. He would find a way to help these people.

KABUL, 2012

Ever since Quetta, Insaan held a place in his heart for street kids. He felt that he needed to do something in compensation for what he didn't do for Amaan and all the street kids on the border of Pakistan and Afghanistan. Amaan deserved more than what he got from humanity; all the street kids did. Humanity could employ so many methods to help them, but instead they spent money on dropping bombs on their heads. When Insaan suggested starting a school for street kids, the community was immediately on board with the idea. They initially enrolled five Hazara and Pashtun children from a refugee camp as part of a three-month pilot program teaching literacy. Muslimyor became one of the three teachers involved in the school.

When Muslimyor came to Kabul, he had enrolled in a government school and assumed responsibilities in the community, starting with managing the community accounts. When he first joined the multi-ethnic community, he was fearful the volunteers from the other ethnic groups would be informers or spies. Paiman was sporting a healthy beard that reinforced Muslimyor's fears and stereotypes of Pashtuns. He had no idea if Paiman or any of the other Pashtuns and Tajiks were decent human beings. There were opportunities to harm the community, even if it was just passing on information to friends or family. It took an entire year for Muslimyor's suspicion to subside.

Muslimyor built trust in the other community members through conversations and actions, by simply being together, working on shared projects and talking. The community arranged regular peace circles where each member of the community expressed their feelings. For Muslimyor it was an eye-opener to share opinions about the different traditions of each ethnic group – even to reveal a dislike of some of their own traditions – and learn how other ethnic groups suffered through the war at the hands of the Taliban. This made him see that his new housemates were not supportive of extremist views and practices. Honest communication within the community helped to strengthen their friendships, and deliberately opening their lives to one another allowed them space to consider each other as equals.

Chapter 12

A Pashtun Perspective

Abdul was Hojar's fellow community manager. He was almost regal in his appearance and manner, with immaculate clothes, perfectly combed hair and precise language. There was a rhythm to his movements, even when he walked. I had seen him lead the community's dance group, beating the drum, nodding his head, controlling the rhythm, directing the dancers when to spin and how to step.

Insaan introduced Abdul to me as the community's Badshah Khan, a Pashtun leader who was called the 'Frontier Gandhi'. After meeting Gandhi in 1919, Badshah Khan educated and organised members of Pashtun tribes into a nonviolent resistance against British occupation. The *Khudai Khidmatgar*, the Servants of God, as they called themselves, refused to cooperate with the British and instead practised self-reliance, even when British repression became increasingly brutal.[1] A likeness of Khan decorated the entrance to the Community Centre; stencilled underneath it was his fundamental belief: 'My religion is truth, love and service to God and humankind.'

Abdul arrived at the Peace House one morning, visibly agitated. When he greeted me, I could tell that something was wrong; his eyes looked bloodshot and he couldn't stop pacing back and forth. Eventually he stuttered out some words to the group.

'Last night, at one in the morning, I received a threatening phone call. The caller spoke in Pashto and purported to be a Talib. He told me

I should feel ashamed to work with international visitors and threatened to harm me.'

Abdul's wife was frightened because she overheard the phone call. She wanted him to quit the community.

'Last year my cousin was threatened by the Taliban and he fled the country to Saudi Arabia,' Abdul said. As he spoke, he swallowed nervously.

'You will all remember the previous threat made against the seamstresses,' Insaan said. 'A letter with the letterhead of the Taliban which we ascertained was fake. Perhaps it is the same person.'

'The caller spoke in Pashto, but he had a Dari accent,' Abdul said.

I looked around at the worried expressions on the community members' faces as they discussed the best course of action. How easy it was to threaten someone's life in Afghanistan. That unknown caller could have been anyone and yet the community had to take every threat seriously.

'I will call the number,' Horse decided.

Horse placed the call on loudspeaker and Insaan and the rest of the community members crowded around the phone. A man answered and Horse spoke to him in Dari. Abdul rocked back and forth on his haunches, biting his knuckles. As Horse spoke, Abdul wanted to interject, but Insaan waved him down and mouthed to be quiet. A helicopter flew overhead, rattling the windows. When the conversation finally ended, everyone fell back onto their respective cushions, breathing a collective sigh.

'He was Hazara,' Hafizullah said and the rest of the group agreed. The man had used particular language and mannerisms that identified his ethnicity.

'He denied responsibility for the call and said his friend did it as a joke,' Insaan said. 'He said his "friend" knows Abdul but he wouldn't say who it was.'

'The threat might be another chapter in the ongoing feud with …' Abdul trailed off, not finishing the thought. The rest of the community became quiet, but eventually Insaan explained the substance of the feud.

'This volunteer previously lived with the community and he felt he wasn't supported by the community or by our international friends. He left the group and has been upset with me and the community ever since,' Insaan said.

Insaan looked pained speaking about it and the community members were clearly uncomfortable.

'This wasn't the first time a former volunteer had turned against the community, but this time was particularly painful. The community had thought of him as a friend. We still do. But Afghanistan is a conflict-ridden country, full of people who are often traumatised and psychologically unwell,' Insaan said. 'These arguments are a product of war. People are in survival mode. I don't blame these ex-volunteers, in fact I sympathise with them. But these threats make life in community very stressful.'

After the excitement of the threat had died and everyone had calmed down, I asked Abdul how he was feeling.

'When I am threatened like this, I do not regret my involvement with the group. In fact, it makes me proud. They will not deter me from my mission.'

AFGHANISTAN HAS A complicated history of migration throughout the different phases of its modern conflict. Afghanistan was the world's biggest source of refugees for more than thirty years, before Syria surpassed it in 2014, but it was also the site of the largest repatriation operation in the world when more than six million refugees returned to the country after the fall of the Taliban.[2] Much of the Afghan population has either been a refugee at some point or has a family background of displacement. Many Afghans have spent their lives crossing borders.

During the decades of conflict, millions of Afghan refugees fled to the neighbouring countries of Iran or Pakistan where they waited for the fighting in Afghanistan to subside. Afghan refugees settled and raised families there, although they were never offered citizenship or permanent residency and were susceptible to discrimination, violence and even deportation.[3] While conditions were often difficult for Afghan refugees in the region, it is hard to imagine the social, political and economic impact this era of mass movement had on Afghanistan's neighbours. Nowadays, Pakistan and Iran host approximately three million Afghans each and for many Afghans born and raised there, they first set foot in Afghanistan after deportation.[4] Abdul was one such person.

Abdul was born a 'temporary person' in a refugee camp in Pakistan in 1992, first entering Afghanistan twelve years later. His parents were originally from Paktia, a Pashtun province in the east of the country. After the Soviet invasion, aerial bombing drove people to live a half-life between caves in the mountains by day and tense periods in their darkened villages by night. The men of Paktia armed themselves in the name of jihad. Almost all livestock and wildlife were slaughtered, and some days families resorted to eating wild grass and plants. After the planes had bombed their mud homes, the tanks came. The Soviets made the women watch as they tied their husbands, sons and brothers to the tanks and dragged them on the ground until they were beyond dead. The surviving villagers fled across the mountains on foot, walking for days, many of them without shoes, until they crossed the border into Pakistan, blistered and broken.

Abdul's family fled Afghanistan in the 1980s, arriving in Pakistan, like most others, without money and to a system largely unprepared for the influx. The Pakistan government hastily established a tent camp for Afghan refugees, aid from different countries of the world slowly arrived and gradually a settlement formed. The people in the camp were from different provinces and different tribes of Afghanistan, but they were all Pashtun. Pashtuns would usually use a council of elders in the area, a *jirga*, to resolve disputes. But in Pakistan, their traditional judicial system had been uprooted. Strict Pashtun culture dictated that women should be veiled from the public eye, remaining inside the house or covered when they were in public.[5] But in the refugee camps, without privacy, the traditions of purdah couldn't be maintained. They built mud walls and houses, partially to improve their shelters, but also to provide privacy so they could better practise their traditions. Men tried to work odd jobs or pick up small businesses to earn a living. Over time, life settled down.

Abdul's mother had married just before she fled to Pakistan as a refugee, but her husband was killed during the war. Afghan culture dictated that it was possible for the brother of the deceased husband to marry the sister-in-law as a way to support the widow.[6] It was under these circumstances that Abdul's parents were married.

By the time Abdul was born, there were nine people in Abdul's family – his parents, four brothers, two sisters and himself – all living in the one small mud hut in a squalid refugee camp. When Abdul was young and started going to school, he thought they were living in another province of Pakistan. When he learnt he was from Afghanistan and not from Pakistan, and he began to hear news of the war between the US forces and the Taliban, he began to wish he was not from such a miserable country.

Abdul worked every day after school. He collected old slippers and sandals and iron to sell to second-hand stores. Using the earnings from that small venture he bought ice-cream from a factory, storing it in an icebox and carrying it on his shoulders to an area where women and children collected water. He used those profits to buy other items to sell – henna, hair dye, chewing gum, hair clips – and kept them in a metal box. One morning he found his box broken open on the street and the items stolen. It was a demoralising blow for the young entrepreneur, but there was nothing else for him to do: he started again.

A few years after the US invasion of Afghanistan and the fall of the Taliban, word came to the refugee camp that the Pakistan government was forcing Afghan refugees to return home. Abdul's family heard the government were going to demolish the camp and remove the tents. Many of the refugees in the camp, including Abdul's family, no longer had homes in Afghanistan to which they could return. Their home and the agricultural land around it had most likely been destroyed, and if it wasn't, their land was sure to be occupied by others.

Abdul's family knew it would be a difficult return to Afghanistan, but they didn't feel like they had any other choice; the Pakistan government appeared determined to force the refugees back. It was 2004 and the family decided to restart their life, not in Paktia, but in Kabul, where they had relatives. They didn't know what to expect on the other side of the border; Afghanistan was still a war zone after all. The family drove their truck to Kurram Agency, in the Federally Administered Tribal Areas of Pakistan, where there was a processing centre for returnees to Afghanistan. The authorities took biometric eye data before issuing the family cash for their transport back to Afghanistan.

When they arrived in Kabul the city was heaving with an influx of returning refugees, but with the help of their relatives Abdul's family settled near the Babur Gardens, renting a room on a hill of houses.

Abdul enrolled in the sixth grade at school, but they spoke Dari there and he could only speak Pashto. The other students ridiculed him for being stupid and he came last in his class that year. It took him many years to stop missing his friends in Pakistan and settle in Kabul. It was only once he joined the community that he made friends and felt like he had found his people and his place.

While Abdul was studying at high school, his twenty-one-year-old brother was killed in a car accident, leaving his father the only breadwinner. After the funeral costs the family became financially destitute, so in the school holidays Abdul worked as a labourer, reconstructing the centuries-old Babur Gardens, the resting place of the first Mughal emperor in Afghanistan. In the mornings Abdul worked alongside terraced green lawns, shade trees and marble-tombed splendour. After that he went to Mandayee market, the biggest bazaar in the city, where he carried goods in a wheelbarrow for customers for a fee.

Abdul's family lived behind the Babur Gardens for two years until they could no longer afford the 1000 Afghanis (US$25) monthly rent. One of Abdul's uncles had built a house for himself on a vacant plot of land on a hill in Kabul and he advised the family to mark out an area on the empty hill for themselves; this was government land, but people were taking whatever land they could find.

'Land grabbing' caused a huge amount of conflict in Afghanistan. Land laws in Afghanistan were inconsistent, overlapping and incomplete. Everyone had a claim to land, whether it was a historical claim linked to ancestors or from documents bought during different regimes, drawn up under different legal systems or purchased with different currencies. Most land was transferred informally, without legally recognised deeds, titles or means to prove ownership. If a dispute over land went to the courts, the decision could be bought for the right sum. There was no clear policy to settle refugees, displaced people and returnees and there was no land allocation program at that time. Everyone was claiming land for themselves, so Abdul's family did likewise. It was lucky for them that they did. An audit in 2015 of the distribution of land to returnees under the Land Allocation Scheme revealed a decade of institutional corruption and nepotism within Afghanistan's Ministry of Refugees and Repatriations. The best land was distributed to friends and families of the influential.

The empty land that was far from the cities, which did not have access to water and electricity, which was in the middle of conflict zones, was allocated to the returning refugees.[7]

Abdul and his family went to the hill to dig ditches to reserve some land, but they were worried by the gangs of Tajik people from Panjshir province who controlled the land. These gangs were selling land as if they were the rightful owners and they were pocketing the money. Abdul's mother was the one who negotiated the deal without paying any bribes, but it was by no means easy. The Panjshiris tried to intimidate the family off the land and there were a few times when Abdul's mother picked up a shovel to threaten them. Once they had secured land from the clutches of the Panjshiris, they began building their home.

It was dry land and there was no water on the hill, so Abdul and his mother had to lug water containers up the slope to their plot and wet the ground to make bricks of mud. Because it was government land and technically stolen land, the police would regularly pass by and try to chase them off the plot or destroy their bricks. It took them many months to construct one room and they had to pay bribes to stop the police from harassing them.

It had been a trying few years, but Abdul's family considered themselves lucky they were no longer landless. Those two rooms would end up being the foundations for their family home, which would grow over the years and would end up accommodating Abdul and his future wife.

KABUL, 2012

Abdul slung his bag over one shoulder and trudged out of school, thinking about his daunting college entrance exams. He was in his final year at school and nothing mattered more to Abdul than success in those exams. He was so preoccupied that he walked straight into two strangers at the school gate: one young Pashtun man and one young Hazara man. The shorter man, the Hazara, said, 'Salam,' and tried to place his cheek to Abdul's cheek. It was the first time a Hazara had tried to greet him like this in his life. Abdul was taken aback and not at all comfortable greeting a Hazara stranger like this, but he was too surprised to protest. Instead he mimicked the gesture with great trepidation.

'My name is Paiman and this is Nadir,' the Pashtun man said. 'We are members of a community dedicated to nonviolence and building peace in Afghanistan.'

Paiman delivered a prepared speech about the group and then invited Abdul to come to the house to learn more about the group and their activities.

'Can I have your phone number?' he asked Abdul.

Abdul had already decided that this was probably some trick to endanger or embarrass Pashtun people and yet Paiman's direct request put him on the spot and he found himself providing Paiman with his number, mainly out of politeness.

For two weeks Abdul avoided Paiman's calls or made up an excuse and hung up. Then Paiman told him about an event the community was organising that was so unique and peculiar, Abdul couldn't deny his curiosity. The community was arranging a lunch at a restaurant for young people from the different provinces and ethnic groups of Afghanistan.

The day of the lunch, Abdul met Paiman near the restaurant. It was raining and it was the first time Abdul had visited this part of Kabul, which heightened his anxiety. They walked into the packed restaurant together, Abdul preparing himself in case he needed to flee. He stood at the back of the room and watched the attendees take turns to stand up, say where they were from and explain a bit about themselves.

Abdul counted representatives from twenty-seven out of Afghanistan's thirty-four provinces. Then the entire room engaged in a group discussion about the challenges that Afghanistan faced and how they could help solve those problems. Abdul was enthralled by what was happening and when Paiman next asked him to his house, he accepted.

After overcoming his initial suspicions, Abdul became a regular visitor to the house. The community introduced Abdul to their activities and philosophies, and he started to warm to the group; he even had meals together with the Hazaras. One day Paiman asked him, 'Would you consider living with us?'

The thought was exhilarating: to join a community working for a better future, to become fully involved in their activities, to live outside of his home with a group of other young people. Abdul asked his family's advice, but their response was a curt, 'No.' The concept seemed dangerous to them. They couldn't understand why he was even considering such an absurd idea.

'What if I stay just one night per week and if at any time I feel uncomfortable then I will leave?' he asked.

His parents weren't happy with the arrangement, but they trusted him.

'You are old enough and smart enough to judge the situation for yourself,' they said. 'Be careful.'

And so, his transition into community life began. He would stay for one or two days, and then return to his family home for a few days. Eventually he was put on the roster for cooking and cleaning and he was left with no other choice but to move in.

Chapter 13

Everyone has Considered Escaping

KABUL, 2012

Violence was not like the Hollywood movies that Muslimyor occasionally watched on Insaan's laptop. There was no suspenseful music to warn you of imminent disaster. Somehow those movies managed to create excitement out of explosions and gunfights. In reality, violence was sudden and terrifying, tearing apart an otherwise peaceful day.

One day Muslimyor and Horse were in school when the nearby parliament was attacked by the Taliban. The sound of gunfire clattered into their classrooms, familiar staccato bursts and yet a sound to which Muslimyor would never grow accustomed.

Muslimyor watched the colour drain from his female teacher's face.

'Sit still, please. Don't move,' she said nervously, then left the room.

White-knuckled, with jaws clenched, students traded nervous looks. Nobody knew what to do. Muslimyor resisted the urge to run. The noise of gunfire played out in the background like elevator music. After some minutes, the teacher returned looking a little more composed, smiling, trying to project calmness.

'It's just gunfire, it will settle down. Just don't move,' she tried to say confidently, but her trembling hands and voice gave her away.

She resumed the lesson, but each volley of bullets made her jump and she eventually left the class again, wringing her hands. Muslimyor and his classmates endured this agonising pantomime for twenty minutes, throughout which the firing never ceased. Muslimyor was growing more and more frightened; if the fighting reached his school they would be trapped and massacred. This time when the teacher returned she told them to go directly home.

The students rushed to the door of the classroom, creating a bottleneck at the exit. Muslimyor jumped out the window, ran across the schoolyard, found Horse in his classroom, and they dashed out of the school into even more chaotic scenes. Next to Muslimyor's school there was a primary school, and he could hear the crying of the schoolchildren as he passed the gates; the teachers had closed the main gate to the school because some of the students were too small to go home alone. Muslimyor saw mothers running towards the school, some barefoot. Parents who were waiting at the gate were shouting over the wall for their children; older students climbed the wall to get home.

As Muslimyor and Horse ran through the streets, the gunfire seemed to follow them. They feared that each time they turned a corner they would run into fighting. When they arrived at the community they were panting with terror and relief, grateful to be home alive.

After quickly embracing the other volunteers and members of the community, they joined in and began calling those members who were not home or missing. They needed to warn those who may not have been aware of the danger. Insaan later rebuked them for not being reachable during the blasts, but really he was terrified.

During a moment of relative calm, a bomb exploded nearby. *Doof.*

A young street kid who was visiting the community that day said, 'Oh, that's nothing, that's just another bomb.'

But this didn't stop him or the others rushing to the back room of the house. They huddled together, nervously trying to make jokes to take their minds off imminent danger.

'If you go outside, wear your turbans,' Muslimyor laughed, and wrapped his head in a scarf. Above the door, a sign read 'Peace on Earth'.

'Why do you think we are in this room?' Insaan asked the street kid.

'The Taliban has come. In the other room, if a rocket strikes, we may all die. Here at least one of us may survive,' the little boy said.

Muslimyor and the other community members couldn't sleep that night. They sheltered in the room curled up against each other, an intimate sharing of pain and fear. The windows vibrated with the *boom, boom, boom* of every type of blast. The cumulative effect of each explosion pushed Muslimyor closer and closer to the edge of sanity. The uncertainty, the anxiety, the unprocessed anger, a desperation for something better; all contributed to a growing desire to escape. To run away and never come back. Suddenly he was shouting and banging his head on the wall and Insaan and Horse were holding him back; he was crying and close to breaking down.

'It's okay, it's okay,' Insaan said, over and over again. 'It's not your fault. This is not something that is within our control. The bombs are not dropped by us. We are not the ones who are persistently killing. It's not our fault.'

In the hearts of Afghans who lived in chronic war, that was not 'just another bomb'. It was trauma – persistent, relentless trauma. At times, it felt as if they could not escape from this anguish, as if this violence was the natural order of things in Afghanistan. But as Insaan soothed him, Muslimyor felt his anger slowly subside. He looked around at his friends and felt the bonds between them all. This community was all that was keeping Muslimyor going. On his own, he would not have stopped banging his head against the wall. On his own, he would have given up.

MOST AFGHANS, AT some point in their life, contemplated the idea of leaving the country to seek safety and prosperity in another country. Each bombing, each escalation of conflict caused Afghans to revisit this dilemma. For many, the images of safe, wealthy Western countries plastered all over the media were too tempting to resist. Many brazen young men, full of daring and curiosity, were willing to risk treacherous journeys for a chance at a new life. Many talented and ambitious Afghans were fleeing the country, which was causing a national brain drain. Some people faced an immediate need to flee and for others there was a final tipping point that pushed people into the decision to leave. Faced with unemployment and financial insecurity in a country at war, many believed they had nothing to lose by leaving for Europe. The reality was that finances were what prevented many people from leaving. Even those who owned assets and properties would not be able to offload their wealth. It was rare for people to buy into a war-torn country like Afghanistan.[1]

For the ordinary Afghan, acquiring a legal visa to a foreign country was nearly impossible. Safe and legal resettlement options for Afghan refugees in the region were more or less non-existent. Iran and Pakistan were overwhelmed by generations of Afghan displacement and life in the Central Asian states for refugees offered few opportunities. This caused many Afghans to look further abroad, to the prospect of work and safety in Europe or Australia.

An asylum seeker's journey from Afghanistan, to seek protection in a Western country, followed at-times illegal and dangerous routes across multiple countries at the risk of death or kidnapping. Over the years, thousands had drowned or were lost in the Mediterranean Sea en route to Europe or in the waters between Indonesia and Australia. One of the volunteers, Tara, told me how her sister's family fled the insecurity of Ghazni to seek refuge in Europe. Their boat capsized at sea and the entire family disappeared.

Despite these barriers and risks, the Afghan diaspora had spread to the farthest reaches of the world. One of the community members, Taqi, had two cousins who flew to Indonesia and then risked their lives on a boat journey to Australia in early 2012. That was before Australia reintroduced its policy of detaining refugees who arrived by boat in island prisons. Taqi's cousins settled in Perth and had since assisted family members to migrate; Taqi himself was unwilling to attempt it because it had become too dangerous.[2]

Every community member I spoke to had considered leaving Afghanistan, but Abdul summed up his concerns best of all. He wouldn't leave as a refugee because he thought he would forfeit the value and respect he had earned in Afghanistan. He believed that in Western countries refugees were not judged on the content of their character, that they were stigmatised just by being a person who fled danger. For him, it was also simple: his home was his home and he wouldn't be happy without his family.

What was rarely considered in this decision-making process was deportation back to Afghanistan.

THE SAFE HOUSE was a cold, basic concrete apartment not far from the Peace House. The decor was spartan, just the bare essentials: a few cushions, some kitchen items and little else. The location was kept secret to protect its tenants: the deportees.

When deportees first arrived in the country, they were offered two weeks' accommodation in a reception centre provided by the International Organisation for Migration; after that time they had to find their own accommodation. Without family and friendship networks, many returnees found it difficult to find housing. Rent in Kabul was expensive, accommodation was limited, and there wasn't a rental market like in Western countries. Deportees often ended up in slums or on the street. Abdul Ghafoor, founder of the Afghanistan Migrant Advice and Support Organisation, set up a safe house for those deportees who had nowhere else to go. The deportees were allowed to stay in the house for one month, but they could always ask for more time if they were desperate.

Abdul Ghafoor was born and raised in Quetta, Pakistan, after his family fled Afghanistan during the Soviet conflict. He was working for an international organisation called Right to Play when threats to the organisation by armed groups jeopardised his work and his life. He fled to Norway to seek asylum in October 2010. When his application for asylum failed in March 2013, he was deported to Afghanistan, a country in which he had never set foot. He used his negative experiences to benefit others, establishing an organisation in Kabul that assisted other returnees and deportees.

The community regularly donated duvets to Abdul Ghafoor and his organisation, delivered to the safe house in a taxi overflowing with colourful bedding. I climbed a flight of stairs, arms loaded with duvets. At the top of the stairs, I passed my burden to a surly-looking Tajik and a Hazara.

'I lived and worked in Germany for six years before being deported,' the Hazara said, gripping his new pink duvet.

'I lived there for two years,' the Tajik man said. 'My family are citizens in Germany but still they deported me.'

'President Ashraf Ghani signed a deportation agreement with the German government. After that we were forcibly deported,' the Hazara man said.

They were referring to a deal agreed upon by the European Union and Afghanistan, which allowed the EU to deport tens of thousands of Afghans in exchange for providing billions of dollars of development aid to Afghanistan.[3]

One of the deportees residing in the safe house was absent. He had been badly injured in a bombing of the Supreme Court two weeks after being deported by Germany to 'safe' Kabul. His face had been severely burned from the blast.

Deportees were returned to 'safe zones' of Afghanistan, so determined by the deporting nation. Many of the so-called safe zones were isolated because travel around Afghanistan was considered extremely dangerous due to the resurgent influence of the Taliban and other armed groups over rural parts of the country. The Taliban controlled several highways surrounding Kabul, including the 'Death Road' to central Afghanistan and Ghazni province. The country's battered Ring Road, a highway network more than 2000 kilometres long, built by international donors at a cost of US$3 billion, was still not complete after more than a decade of work.[4] Parts of it remained unfinished while other sections had repeatedly fallen under insurgent control. On much of its length, only heavily armed military convoys could travel safely because of the risk of insurgent roadblocks and bombings. The Hazara man was too scared to return to his home province of Ghazni to see his family.

Deportees were especially at risk from armed groups such as the Taliban because they had been to Western countries. They could be accused of being a spy, of working with foreign troops or governments, of being a Christian missionary, or they could be viewed as wealthy after spending time in the West. This meant that many people could not leave the areas to which they were being returned. For those who were not returned to their areas of origin they could easily become isolated.

The previous year, Martin and I had spoken to a man who was deported to Afghanistan after being denied asylum in Norway. He returned to his family in Jaghori district in Ghazni province but would regularly travel to Kabul to find work. It was during one of these trips from Jaghori to Kabul that he was captured by the Taliban. He was one of the lucky few who were released alive.[5]

'So what are you going to do?' I asked the two men. 'Find work?'

'There is no work in Kabul,' the Tajik man said.

'What about your family?' I asked. 'Can they help you?'

'My family don't understand what deportation is,' he said. 'They think I'm a criminal.'

I thought his answer was crushing. The man looked humiliated, almost as if he saw himself as a failure. For deportees, there was a risk this isolation and desperation could exacerbate already existing mental health issues, which could result in drug addiction, alcoholism and homelessness.

'I will go to Iran in a few days' time to see some family and then from there decide what to do next,' the Hazara man said.

'I will go back to Germany as soon as I can, and I will continue to go back, ten times if I have to, until they accept me,' the Tajik man said.

I said my goodbyes to the men and left them in the dank apartment, holding their donated duvets. These two desperate figures were in geopolitical and humanitarian limbo. Raised in a country destroyed by foreign invading powers, they engaged people smugglers to help them seek protection. Upon reaching safety they were refused asylum by countries that had sent troops to fight in Afghanistan and then they were deported back to danger by these champions of liberty and human rights. Now they were going to re-enter this broken system; they were going to risk their lives again, because they didn't see any other way out.

I SAT WITH Insaan, Muslimyor, Horse and Hojar around a floral mat sharing bowls of potato and onion soup. We pulled apart unleavened bread with our hands and then dipped it in the broth. Hojar poured steaming tea out of a pot into glass cups. The tea was bitter, something the Afghans remedied by adding numerous teaspoons of sugar into the cup.

'I saw on the news this morning that President Ashraf Ghani praised Afghan mothers for raising the future fighters of Afghanistan,' Muslimyor said. 'I wonder if Afghans actually believe this war propaganda?' He barked a series of short sharp laughs that sounded like gunfire. I'd noticed he was often the one to start a debate.

Muslimyor and Horse had just returned from their morning classes of mathematics, chemistry and physics. Horse considered Muslimyor's question, fingering the scar on his cheek.

'For most, the ethics of war is trumped by the need to survive,' Horse responded. 'Everyone knows someone working for an armed group, whether it be for the Taliban or a local militia. It is a good source of income. When there are no jobs people will do whatever they need to do to survive. To not provide for your family is shameful.'

'I don't think Afghans understand how to escape from war,' Hojar said. 'They can't see whether the war will end peacefully or violently. We have been at war for too long.'

There was a loud bang and the windows of the Community Centre rattled, as if the front door had been slammed very hard. But the windows kept shaking and the bang increased into a roaring crescendo that was far too loud for a door. A pane of glass shattered and a door was forced open.

Everyone stood up, panic stricken, except me. I realised something bad had happened, but my mind couldn't work out what.

Insaan picked up his camera and hid behind his lens. Hojar's face paled and she quickly moved against the wall, sliding down into a sitting position. Although Muslimyor had experienced blasts like this many times before, he still felt confused and giddy. He pointed to a plume of smoke that appeared over the back wall of the yard outside and I at last understood what was happening. It was a bomb. It could have been a few streets away, or it could have been a kilometre away, it was hard to tell. The *rat-tat-tat* of gunfire started. Hafizullah was thought to be in the area near the bombing, with a couple of street kids, buying supplies from the market. They tried calling him but they couldn't get through; phone lines were usually busy after a bombing, making it difficult to connect with loved ones.

I felt oddly distant from the drama, as if I was an audience member in a theatre. I wasn't frightened because I couldn't comprehend the danger. I couldn't imagine the fighting would breach the walls of the Community Centre. How little I understood gun battles and violence in Afghanistan. Each time a bomb went off I cocked my head and tried to work out how close it was to our location, like tracking thunder. The neighbours' children began crying and I shook a little inside because although I thought I was safe, I knew somewhere in Kabul someone was dying.

Horse tried to contact his family members. One of his brothers who had been selling potato pancakes near the area of the bomb blast was safe but his little brother, Ali, was missing. Horse worried that the blast had triggered one of Ali's epileptic fits. Horse finally got hold of his mother and she assured him all his brothers and sisters were safe.

We learned that there were two coordinated attacks in the city that day. A car bomb was detonated near a police headquarters in the west of the city, not far from the Community Centre, and then gunfire broke out between security forces and the gunmen who were barricaded inside the building. A second attack occurred minutes later at an office of Afghanistan's main intelligence agency, the National Directorate for Security, in east Kabul.[6]

Sirens erupted into the afternoon air and the gunfire in the street became more intense. The group continued to make calls to check on their loved ones. Everyone was worried about Hafizullah. It had been hours since the explosions and we still hadn't been able to reach him.

Insaan tried to perform some simple, normal tasks, but he couldn't concentrate. The tea he put on the stove boiled over. He wanted to check on the Peace House, but it still wasn't safe for the three-minute walk.

And then finally Muslimyor and Hafizullah spoke on the phone. Hafizullah guessed he was about a few hundred metres away from the bomb when it blew concrete, smoke and flaming timber onto the street. Dust filled his mouth and nostrils when he breathed in, and his ears felt like they were full of water. He was shocked by the explosion, but he had responsibility for the two street kids. Wind blew the smoke plume in their direction and a combination of dust and plastic and ash fell from the sky like spice into a cooking pot. Hafizullah took each child by the hand and carefully escorted them home.

Hours later we were still hearing gunfire and bombs, and the youth were still questioning their movements around the city. I wasn't allowed to leave the Community Centre. Horse needed to go to the bank to withdraw some money, but he felt dizzy and his stomach felt like lead. He asked Muslimyor to accompany him. Hojar went outside but stayed low in case of bullets. She was on high alert, and every time an ambulance screamed past her she jumped in fright. Everyone on the street was talking about the attack, even the young children. Hojar had a meeting that afternoon but she couldn't remember what she was supposed to talk about.

By the time the fighting had stopped, it was reported that fifteen people, including eleven civilians, were dead and another fifty were wounded.[7] Afghan Taliban militants claimed responsibility for the attacks. There had already been two attacks in Kabul that year and it was only March.[8] On 10 January a car bomb had exploded in the centre of the city, killing at least thirty people and wounding seventy others.[9] The Taliban claimed responsibility for that attack. On 7 February, twenty-two people were killed and forty-one wounded in a suicide blast at Afghanistan's Supreme Court in Kabul.[10] That time the Islamic State claimed responsibility.

That evening we gathered together at the Community Centre to debrief on our experiences and how we were feeling.

'When I heard the blast, I was transported to my home in the mountains,' Hojar said. 'I was six years old and bombs were dropping around me, shaking the earth and shattering the glass windows in my house. I was paralysed by fear and I fell. I thought assailants were going to come into the yard and through the roof at any moment.'

I admitted to the group that this was my first bombing and that perhaps I was in shock.

'The response from the government today will be to kill the terrorists,' Insaan said. 'That is the response the world has to all forms of terrorism. Kill. Go and kill all of them. This is how we, as a world, respond to fear. We fear the Taliban and all the terrorists, but we ignore the terrorism which is inside us and then we inflict more terror. We are fighting a war and it's not working because war doesn't solve war. It's not very logical: socially, psychologically, emotionally. We just make everybody afraid.'

I looked at these teenagers and marvelled at their grit and their resolve. This was their everyday. This was normal in Kabul. These people were footnotes to the global war on terror.

Chapter 14

Giving and Receiving Education

During my stay in Afghanistan, some of the volunteers at the centre were overcome with a strange fever. Throughout the building, students were huddled in corners secretively scribbling on paper. Conversations were held in whispers. Every so often a paper-swap would be made and the students involved would retire to a quiet space to examine the other's work.

'They are writing their applications for the elite university tests,' Insaan explained. 'Look at how stressed they are. It's madness.'

Perhaps it was madness, but I could understand it. This was a stressful enough experience in a safe, prosperous nation like Australia, where there were many different educational paths and opportunities. In Afghanistan there were fewer quality universities, fewer places for students, and many more people to compete with. The consequences of success or failure in their university applications were much more extreme. For them, a good education was not only the stepping stone to a successful career; it was a potential escape route out of the country to the United States and Europe. For these young people, a good education was a survival technique. Even so, Insaan found their desperation unsettling. Later that day he started a discussion, perhaps to take the pressure off.

'Does having a university education mean you are an intelligent and successful person?' Insaan asked the community members. 'I think there are many different forms of intelligence. For example, Horse, you are intelligent because you can survive in the mountains of Afghanistan.

You know how to farm the land. I am a doctor, but when I came to the mountains I didn't know these things. So perhaps, you are more intelligent than me?'

Insaan believed one of the challenges the world faced was the presumption of superiority. This was a judgement, of human beings and of human societies. Presumed superiority existed all over the world, of one tribe, or nation, or religion, saying to another that they are better, they are more intelligent. One form of intelligence could be the ability to understand that all human societies could contribute to the advancement of humanity as a whole. Intelligent humans would select the best parts of other societies and incorporate those ideas into their own society. Intelligent humans would learn to cooperate rather than wage wars.

'It's very easy for society to define intelligence or success or tell you how to fulfil your potential as a human being. Tell me, if money and success weren't an issue, what would you really want to do with your life?'

The group remained quiet. They had never been asked a question like this.

'What about you, Hafizullah?' Insaan asked. 'If there was a school here that would teach you all the different types of dance in the world, would you go?'

When Hafizullah practised the art of dance, his whole body was liberated. He moved with passion and grace, and his eyes were aflame with joy. Faced with such a personal question in public, Hafizullah was hesitant to answer.

'Yes,' he said, eventually acknowledging a long-held desire.

'If the religious leaders opposed you, would you still go?' Insaan asked.

'Yes,' he said, with more confidence.

'But there is no such school here. Would you go if there was such a school in India?' Insaan asked.

'Yes,' he said defiantly.

Insaan knew that was what Hafizullah really wanted to do. But that would not make him an intelligent, successful person according to Afghan society. To be successful he needed to study too many irrelevant school subjects; most of what he would learn he would forget because it would not be very useful for everyday life. He needed to pass his high school exams and to graduate from university so he could get a high-paying and influential job. Then, very gradually, he would become the person that society expected him to be and he would bury everything that made him who he really was. Being successful and intelligent in Afghan society wouldn't help him to pursue his passions in life.

'How much we earn is determined by what value society places upon our profession. So why is it that teachers and farmers and social workers earn less than bankers? The farmer is doing the real work for society. We need the food the farmer produces.'

This struck a chord with the community members, most of whom were raised in agricultural areas by farmers.

'Will achieving status, wealth, power make you a successful individual? Will it help society? Or is it more important for us as a group to stand together to create alternatives, to ban weapons in our communities? To ban killing? To grow things in our gardens?'

KABUL, 2012

For Horse the years spent in community, maturing and learning about life, were formative. Horse remembered an evening when he and Insaan had walked together. They were side by side and it was a typical Kabul night, a little hazy from the pollution, which made the moon seem like a smudge in the sky.

'Do you know what causes an eclipse of the moon?' Insaan asked Horse.

Horse squinted at the dim crescent in the sky, but he did not know the answer.

'Some Afghans believe that eclipses happen when Afghan society has acted badly and sins have accumulated,' Horse said.

'Why don't you ask your teacher to explain it one day,' Insaan told him.

'I can't ask my science teacher because I'm afraid to embarrass him if he doesn't know the answer. Our teachers can get upset if we ask questions and they often use physical punishment or harsh words to scold us,' Horse said.

Insaan didn't understand how Afghan students could study science at school but they couldn't explain the science of everyday life. For the ordinary Afghan, science was still a discovery process. Insaan would always encourage Horse and the community members to use the internet to search for the answers to questions.

Horse had trouble expressing himself in these conversations. He grew up in an area where young people didn't ask and weren't asked questions. Now suddenly he was expected to contribute and participate in these lively discussions. He much preferred to play video games and joke around with Muslimyor and the others. When he felt the pressure to contribute something to the discussions, he usually parroted what Muslimyor said.

At a certain point, the community actively started to help Horse foster his own voice and encouraged him to think for himself. Insaan started to ask Horse questions first in discussion so he couldn't copy what Muslimyor said. These were steep learning curves for Horse, but those conversations were useful in encouraging him to think creatively. After two years in community, Horse started to develop his own opinions. The problem then became that he was so determined to have people hear his voice that he stopped listening to everyone else. Insaan encouraged him to work on his listening skills so he could feel comfortable speaking his mind, but not feel the need to voice it at every opportunity.

Most of what Horse learned in the community was about human values: what it meant to be a good human being; wanting for others what he wanted for himself. He even began to consider people from different religions as equal. He understood more how he should be relating with women, his own family and his future wife. He used to believe that women were less than men and he expected them to perform duties at home. Men presumed they could do whatever they needed to do to find a girlfriend or that they could treat women any way they wanted. He began to meet many women in his work, and this helped him to think about why he had those gender expectations. He was ashamed to say he used to hit his sisters if they didn't do work in the house. After spending time in the community he learned how to admit a mistake and he asked for their forgiveness.

Horse noticed that when he returned to his home in the mountains his ways of thinking about the world had become more and more different to his former peers. The clearest point of difference was his friends' views of people not like them. He tried to explain to them the concepts of 'humanity' and told them stories of Gandhi, Martin Luther King and

Rosa Parks. They were curious about these stories, but they remained suspicious of all foreigners. Horse thought they had legitimate reasons to be concerned. So many foreigners had deceived and were still deceiving the Afghan people; whether they were the international NGOs who gave people fish but didn't teach them how to fish, or the foreign powers who divided the people so they could rule. Horse knew it was difficult for rural villagers to differentiate who was well-intentioned and who was not.

Meanwhile the community members had joined a network of politically and socially conscious civil society groups in Kabul, performing regular actions and protests. After a politically tumultuous 2011 – which saw the Occupy Movement and the Arab Spring, with revolutions in Egypt and Tunisia – the volunteers felt part of a global awakening.

THE MOUNTAINS, 2012

Hafizullah trudged the quiet streets of town, dejected and bored. His feet were sore and the strap on his tray was chafing his neck. Ever since his friends had moved to Kabul, their social group had fallen apart. Insaan had started the exodus more than a year ago, and then Muslimyor, Horse, Asghar, Nadir and Arif had all followed him there to study.

The thought of all his friends studying in Kabul was completely demoralising. He desperately wanted to join them, but he knew there was nothing there for him. During the tent vigil, he had spoken with Insaan about returning to school. Although he should've been in the seventh grade, they decided he should restart school in the second grade.

He spent an entire year in the second grade, sitting a head and shoulders above all the other children in his class. By the end of the year, he still wasn't literate, his teachers were still beating him, and he was ashamed of his lack of progress. He returned to the seventh grade, but it became even worse.

'You will learn,' his teacher shouted at him, then launched into a torturous cane attack: stinging whips, ten times on the palm of his hand. On and on it went as Hafizullah tried to keep his hand upright. The berserk teacher then went to start on the back of his hand and Hafizullah told her to stop.

Instead the teacher took the cane and hit him on the cheek, which sparked a wildness in Hafizullah. He reacted instinctively, lashing out at her. His strike flicked her earlobe and, as if in slow motion, the lobe wiggled and jiggled as she shrieked in surprise. He fled.

After that drama, he started working again and vowed never to return to school.

One day Hafizullah received a phone call that left him agitated and excited.

'I heard you stopped going to school,' Insaan said.

'Yes,' Hafizullah said, not wanting to talk about it.

'Do you want to continue school? Would it be easier to do it in Kabul?' Insaan asked.

Hafizullah shook with dread at the thought, but deep down there must have been some desire to try again because after some pressure from Insaan he relented.

'I will talk to my father,' Hafizullah said.

At first Hafizullah avoided the idea. Thinking about his latest shameful episode at school left him stinging with embarrassment. But Insaan continued to encourage him and he eventually approached his father.

'You're not interested in school. You've already quit lots of times,' his father said. 'What will going to Kabul change? Where are you going to live? Who are you going to be with?'

Hafizullah explained about the group and Insaan. His father remembered Insaan; he had met him twice before. He also knew Muslimyor and Horse and this helped him to have confidence in what Hafizullah was proposing and the people with whom he would be staying. After much deliberation, he gave Hafizullah permission to leave home and move across the country to Kabul to study.

'I have spent all my life in war. I don't want you to have the same life. I want you to have a peaceful life.'

Hafizullah went to Kabul with the intention to study but he didn't have hope that he would learn. He predicted that he would fail, just as he had failed so many times before. This would be his last attempt at school – after that, he would accept that he could not learn, and he would spend his life working as a farmer like his father.

When fourteen-year-old Hafizullah arrived in Kabul he alighted at a bus stop where Muslimyor was waiting for him. When he entered the community house, he felt a little self-conscious: the country bumpkin coming to the Big Smoke for the first time. Muslimyor decided he should cut his hair to help him fit in.

The community had recently moved to a house that Muslimyor called the Human Rights Commission house. The community tried to move house regularly. If the neighbourhood or landlord became suspicious of the community's work or living arrangements, or if they noticed international guests staying with the community, they could cause trouble that would jeopardise the entire project. When they wanted to move house, they would walk the streets in the areas where they wanted to live and look for homemade posters placed in the windows or on the walls of houses. Property dealers charged a commission fee, so they preferred to rent directly from the owners.

Their new house was a narrow, two-storey building. On the ground floor there was a corridor that connected all the rooms and led out to a small concrete yard. The yard was encircled by a spiked fence, topped with hurricane wire. Hafizullah's home in the mountains didn't need this type of security and it made him feel nervous. In the corridor space, there were two wicker chairs where people usually sat and talked. Upstairs there was a cluttered kitchen full of dirty glasses, pots and pans.

Hafizullah was introduced to a young man named Paiman. It was the first time he had ever met a Pashtun, let alone been in the same house with one. Before that, his mental image of a Pashtun was of a savage: a wild marauding murderer. In his imagination, all Pashtuns were Talibs. Paiman smiled, offered his hand and introduced himself. The problem was that Paiman and the two other Pashtuns, Abdul and Baddar, couldn't speak very good Dari, and Hafizullah couldn't speak Pashto, so he couldn't understand anything they said.

When Hafizullah arrived in Kabul, there was no room in the house for him. There were sixteen people living there at the time, with four or five people in each room. So Hafizullah stayed with two other Hazaras, Nadir and Mirwais, in a room across the road from the main house. In that room, with his friend Nadir, he felt comfortable. But when he came to the main house he was forced to face the Pashtuns. Because of Hafizullah's inability to communicate with them, he avoided them, and he gave up trying to speak to them. It took many months for Hafizullah to recognise that Paiman was not that different from him, even though he was a Pashtun, and to be comfortable sitting in a room with him.

Arriving in Kabul, Hafizullah was overwhelmed by the amount of activity in the house. Everyone who lived in the community was busy with different projects, but there were also many young people who visited the house. Every room of the house was a hive of activity. One room was full of sewing machines and older women working as tailors. The women were taught how to sew so they could start a business by selling the clothes they made. The male volunteers never entered that room.

After a few days, Hafizullah was asked to join a meeting in the house – he'd never been in a meeting before. The community members were discussing what to do for a duvet project and who was responsible for household chores. Hafizullah was bewildered because up to that point in his life he had never done any housework. Now he was part of a cleaning roster – another first.

Muslimyor had volunteered to coordinate the duvet project for its first winter and Hafizullah was happy to participate in the distribution of the bedding. He felt proud to be part of a team of people who were helping others. He joined the community's cleaning campaigns where they cleaned the streets and unclogged the drains around their local area. The local municipality provided a few tools and workers to help them.

One morning the national news reported that US/NATO forces had attacked a village in Uruzgan province and killed two children who were grazing their cows in a field. Another meeting was held, and a decision was taken by the community that they would stage a protest.

Now much more savvy about publicity, the group hired two cows for their protest. They marched to the Human Rights Commission compound, leading the two cows, brandishing signs and chanting: 'We are those two Afghan children. Stop killing us.' It wasn't a long walk but locals were curious and surprised by the action; the media even turned up to televise the event.

Hafizullah arrived in Kabul during the long winter holidays, when the community ran all sorts of courses. And it was through these community classes, rather than through the formal education system, that he broke through the barrier and began to develop maths and literacy skills. With 64 per cent of the population illiterate, he was far from alone.[1]

In the classes he developed a rivalry, which motivated him to succeed. He saw that the girls were excelling at maths and literacy and he wanted to compete with them – or perhaps he didn't want to be seen as a failure in front of the opposite sex. He began to try, and he discovered that when he tried he could do just as well as them.

'I can learn. I am like everybody else.'

These mixed-gender classes were a new experience for Hafizullah. There were girls in his class at school, but they were separated by gender. He'd always been told he shouldn't mix with girls and he especially shouldn't be naughty with girls, so he tended to avoid them. It was during that first winter in Kabul he started to become more comfortable in the presence of women. He started to speak with women and work with them on different projects.

A turning point for Hafizullah was when Insaan taught him the English alphabet, but really it was a breakthrough in understanding phonics. 'You need to know what each of the letters sound like. You can't just look at the shape and think that the sound will come from the shape,' Insaan said. Once Hafizullah understood that, he learned to read very quickly and a whole world opened up before him. It wasn't long before he was reading for pleasure.

Despite all these positive developments, there were days when Hafizullah became discouraged and contemplated giving up and returning to the mountains. He was homesick and he couldn't believe he was progressing or would fit in. It was his friends in community who helped him to learn. The encouragement from Muslimyor, Horse and Insaan helped him to return to his books time and time again. Hafizullah learned a lot during that momentous winter, but most importantly he found encouragement, hope and self-belief.

At the end of that winter, he decided to make another attempt at school.

Chapter 15

The Student Becomes the Teacher

Hojar's life changed the day she met Insaan, although at the time she had no idea how significant this moment would prove to be. She was having dinner with her family and from below her window she heard a stranger's voice. She was immediately intrigued because the words were pronounced differently to people from her province and while there were often strangers in the nearby town, they rarely visited her village.

'It is Insaan,' her brothers said.

They had heard of him in town among their friends. When Insaan joined their family for dinner, Hojar and her siblings could hardly contain their excitement. He was wearing the Afghan *perahan tunban* but Hojar couldn't place his accent. During dinner that evening, Insaan spoke about the work he had undertaken with the youth in the community.

By the light of the *tandoor*, Insaan told stories of the volunteers making cell phone pouches for Pashtun youth in Kandahar. He spoke about peace treks and the freezing cold conditions at a tent vigil. Hojar already knew of the work the volunteers had completed with the peace park. She remembered how the ground had been dust and rocks and that she didn't think they could turn such a forbidding place into a green space. But they had defied her expectations, and to have this strange man in front of her telling such stories filled her with a sense of excitement. It was a feeling that did not leave her when Insaan departed that evening.

Over the next years, Hojar got to know Insaan very well. He would visit her village every week, but they rarely spoke. It wasn't socially acceptable for women to speak to men who weren't relatives. In the first few years of their acquaintance, whenever Hojar's mother invited Insaan for a meal in her house, Hojar would follow the necessary social customs of not sitting with Insaan and the men of the house during dinner, even though she wanted to join in the chatter about the activities of the group. Instead she was resigned to eavesdropping on their conversations. It wasn't hard in a small house with a loud and excitable Insaan leading the discussion.

In the years after Insaan's flight from the mountains, he maintained contact with Hojar's family and told them of his new life in Kabul and the resumption of his experiments in peace. One day Hojar received news that shook her.

'We are starting to recruit female volunteers. We are celebrating International Women's Day and we are going to give out scarves to all our female members. I have one for Hojar.'

If there are women involved in the group, surely I could join too, she thought.

Part of her insistence on attending school was to defy society's limitations on her. She wanted to be the first woman in her village to graduate from university. She realised that if she went to university in Kabul, she could also join Insaan and the other youth. But she didn't have the financial resources to pay the university tuition fees or to meet living costs in Kabul, nor did she have the support from her community and some members of her family. She was worried about the gossip in the village ruining her and her family's reputation. Instead Hojar studied at a local college for two years and qualified as a teacher.

It was not easy to find jobs after graduating from college: Hojar found that she either needed to know the right people or she was expected to offer bribes, neither of which were realistic options for her and her family. She was not optimistic she would ever be hired as a teacher, let alone get to university.

One day Insaan acted as an interpreter for a Skype conversation between Hojar and two women in England to discuss the advantages and disadvantages of higher education. Charlotte was a graduate from university and Jennifer was thirty-five years old and studying for a PhD, a feat Hojar found unbelievable. It was the first time she had spoken with women who had completed their university education and the exchange consolidated her conviction to continue her studies. Both of them said to her: 'We are with you. We support you.'

Hojar was buoyed by their encouragement. After speaking to Jennifer and Charlotte, Hojar thought, *I can do it too*. It was a chance study grant that made her once-impossible dream a reality. With financial support to attend university, she could then convince her family to allow her to move to Kabul.

KABUL, 2013

After that first winter in the community Hafizullah enrolled in school, determined to succeed. For the first time in his life he was excited to learn. Even though he still couldn't read fluently, if the teacher asked for volunteers to read, he would raise his hand every time. At first, the words wouldn't come out correctly or he didn't pronounce them well, so the teachers would sometimes tell him to sit down. But he refused to let this discourage him. When the teacher asked the class a question, he was the first to raise his hand and answer the question. After every lesson, the teachers would ask, 'Who has learned this lesson?' and Hafizullah would raise his hand. His straight-arm, raised-hand salute must have irritated his teachers, but he did not care. By the time he reached his first mid-year exams, he was still a very slow reader and his handwriting was poor, but he passed eight subjects out of sixteen. Several years later, in his final year exams he would only fail two.

When Hafizullah first arrived in community, the group actions were predominantly advocacy-based. The community wanted to clearly state their organisation's ideology, and when those views differed to societal norms they often manifested as protests. As the security situation in Afghanistan deteriorated and people became concerned for their safety, the community withdrew from protest actions and became more involved in constructive actions. The street school was their first practical step.

Even after years of US and NATO involvement in Afghanistan, the country's school system was broken. Almost half the schools supposedly built or opened in Afghanistan since the fall of the Taliban didn't actually have buildings. In those that did, students doubled up on seats and shared antiquated texts. Teachers were scarce, and less than a quarter of those teaching were considered qualified, even by Afghanistan's minimal standards. School enrolment figures determined how much money a school received from the government, but they didn't reveal the much lower numbers of attendance. No more than 10 per cent of students, mostly boys, finished high school. In 2012 only half of school-age children went to school at all. Of adult Afghan women, 75 per cent had never attended school and only 12 per cent could read. The community's school was the first step to rebuilding the country's future.[1]

One day Insaan approached Hafizullah and asked him if he would like to teach in the school.

'What would I teach?' Hafizullah asked Insaan.

'Dari,' Insaan said.

Hafizullah was astounded at the thought of teaching others, but his poor experiences in school motivated him to accept Insaan's daunting offer. He knew how the methods used in the formal school system didn't work for him, in particular the punishment, and so he wanted to offer the street kids a different way of learning.

The street kids attended Dari and mathematics classes as well as weekly lessons on nonviolence. The teachers tutored the children so they could catch up academically and return to school. The school's curriculum was designed not only to enable the street kids to become literate, but to nurture understanding, critical thinking, and compassion for the earth and the human family. The students learned about climate change, socio-economic inequalities and the negative effects of militarism and warfare.

Insaan liked to use symbolism, performance and action to teach the students, and early in the life of the school everyone participated in a piece of interactive, educational theatre.

In Afghanistan, like many countries around the world, it was customary for children to ask for toy guns as gifts, incorporating them into play. In the mountains where Hafizullah grew up, they used to play an Afghan version of tag called Taliban – a grim blurring of children's experiences of violence and their mimicking of it. The community hoped that if they could teach children to reject guns in all forms from an early age, they could instil a distrust of these killing-machines rather than a fascination.

The community and the street kids assembled in the Kabul peace park, dressed in black robes, each of them cradling a plastic gun. They dug small holes and placed the guns in their graves.

'Malala Yousafzai said, "With guns you can kill terrorists, with education you can kill terrorism,"' Insaan said to the crowd.

They then took up large rocks and hammers and physically destroyed the toy guns, burying the destroyed pieces.

'You can say no to violent practices,' Insaan said. 'We can bury these guns and then create something new in their place.

'Your beliefs become your thoughts. Your thoughts become your words, your words become your actions, your actions become your habits, your habits become your values, your values become your destiny.'

The community then dug up the polluting plastic from the ground and, in place of the smashed guns, they planted evergreen trees. They were replacing life-taking weapons with life-giving plants.

'These practices will die and in their place we will grow gardens,' Insaan said.

After planting the trees, the children removed their black robes. Passers-by and onlookers expressed curiosity and asked questions, but the learning and awareness-raising was principally for the students.

When Hafizullah began to teach the street kids mathematics and Dari, he saw himself at that same age wanting help. He wanted to show them that education wasn't humiliating, painful or frightening. When the street kids were naughty or didn't listen to him, he would shift disruptive students to different seats, rather than scold them or punish them. He realised it made him happy to watch young people learn.

These attempts to find alternatives to violence in the classroom were an educational process for Hafizullah. Growing up in the mountains he was often involved in fights with other young men. But from the time he moved to Kabul, he stopped this kind of behaviour. The community taught him that nonviolence was not just a set of theoretical values; it was a way of life to be practised and adhered to every day. After the first winter Hafizullah was familiar with the other community members but he wasn't friends with them yet. One year later there was a rearranging of the living quarters and he moved into a room with Paiman, the Pashtun, his friend.

Hafizullah's participation with and commitment to the community was increasing every year, but there was one particular action that positioned Hafizullah as one of the leaders of the community and endeared him to the street kids. He was going to lead a children's march to demand a school building.

KABUL, 2013-16

Musa sat at the edge of a dirty, litter-filled street, hidden amongst a forest of pants and burqas, ignored until some adult needed his labour. He kept his eyes downcast, looking for scuffed shoes; his tin of polishes and brushes sat heavily on his hip. He preferred to sit alone in the gutter rather than to roam the streets, where he risked bumping into gangs of street kids. A black loafer stopped in front of him, the heel of the right shoe positioned itself on the kerb at an angle. Musa got to work polishing and shining. He hated the smell of the polish that filled his nostrils when he worked, he hated the grease the polish left on his hands, but he knew the small payment he earned from each job might be the difference between his family eating and not eating.

Musa first started work when he was nine years old. His family of ten, which included five brothers and two sisters, needed to eat. And so, Musa became a boot polisher. After four years of working the street, he felt the family's dependence on his income weigh heavy on his small shoulders.

Halfway through Musa's job, a staff member from a nearby restaurant rushed onto the street, shouting and waving his fists at Musa, as if Musa was a rodent he needed to chase into the sewer. Musa picked up his tin and ran. He had learned not to argue with these men. One time he had been hit across the head so badly he began bleeding. Once he had escaped, he turned his attention to finding another spot, which was never a safe or easy task. Sure enough, it didn't take him long to turn a corner and run into a group of red-headed boys. They crowded around him, shoving him and taunting him.

'Shine my shoe, boy.'

'Does anyone have a dollar for the beggar?'

'Get outta here, this is our turf.'

He kept his head low and kept walking, enduring their pushes and their remarks. He knew that if he responded to them in any way, they might beat him. The street kids of Kabul worked in gangs that claimed territories. If a gang found him working in their area, they would threaten him with razor blades, fists or knives and force him to leave his spot. He knew that these gangsters were probably being threatened by other, older criminal gangs. He hated this rivalry among the street workers. He had never made a friend while working as a boot polisher because he was too scared to speak to anyone. He was lonely and discouraged by the work, but he felt like he didn't have any other choice. He had to go on.

Like most other street kids, Musa had stopped going to school when he started working. He'd found it hard to make friends there anyway and felt that the other students looked down on him, but he'd enjoyed learning. His reality now was a tough life on the street and strain at home. He was yearning for human connection. Perhaps that's why he was drawn to an unusual idea one of the other street kids mentioned to him.

'There is a community of young people who teach street kids in a school for free,' the boy said. 'I am learning to read and write. The teachers are friendly and they want more students. You should come.'

Musa decided to join the program, hoping it would be an opportunity to start learning again.

When he arrived at the community school for the first time, he saw crowds of young people busy in their work; he was greeted by smiling faces and warm handshakes. At first he was shy and unsure of himself, but in time he learned that there were people in the community who did not look down on him, and his self-confidence grew. He liked his teacher Hafizullah because he was a person with feelings. Musa felt like he cared for his students. Hafizullah taught Musa that there was no human being who was better than another. Though Musa was convinced that equality was important and had seen it being taught in the community, he didn't think it was common practice in Afghan society. Nonetheless, deep within him, he was gradually feeling like an equal to others despite their outward projection of superiority.

Over the next year, Musa continued to work on the street while studying at the street kid school with the community.

When Musa was fifteen, a tragic incident convinced his father to pull him out of work. Musa had been working in the canteen of a gymnasium. One morning he started his shift and he saw a kid that he knew, hanging dead from the ceiling of the gym. The boy was ten years old. Musa didn't know whether the boy had killed himself or been murdered. Images of the boy's bulging eyes and oddly twisted neck stayed in Musa's mind for months. Even a year later, when he was alone, Musa thought of the boy.

After that incident the gymnasium was closed for three months, during which time Musa's father decided Musa should enrol in school again.

With the assistance from the community teachers, Musa gave everything to his schoolwork. By the end of that year he was the top student in his class, and he had ambitions to study as a doctor. When he thought back to his nine-year-old self, working on the street, he wouldn't have dared to dream something so ridiculous. But now, aged sixteen, being a doctor didn't seem so farfetched. If he set his mind to his dream, and worked hard for it, he believed he could achieve it.

'Just wanting something itself is power,' he said quietly to Hafizullah, looking shyly at him.

KABUL, 2014

Hafizullah stood at the front of a crowd of more than eighty street kids brandishing protest signs: 'We don't want your charity!' and 'We want dignity!' He tried to suppress the fear that gripped his guts. Acts of violence were daily events in Afghanistan and being a part of a group like theirs increased their chance of being targeted. As the leader of this march he felt responsible for the lives of the children, his fellow volunteers and the civilian onlookers.

Up until that moment, he had been prepared to face whatever dangers might arise out of work with the community, whether that was trouble with the authorities, police harassment, false arrest or imprisonment, but he was not prepared for the ultimate sacrifice and was nervous about the event escalating.

In order to stay motivated, Hafizullah thought back to the reason why they had started this protest. There were now twenty-one students enrolled in the street kids program. They knew if they could get public funding for a larger school they could teach at least one hundred children. Hafizullah and the other community members planned to march through the streets of Kabul to the doors of the Afghan Independent Human Rights Commission, where they would deliver their request to the Department of Education to establish a school for the street kids.

The street kids were enthusiastic about the idea and they recruited their friends who worked on the streets to join them. Every day for a week before the walk, the volunteers went to the Community Centre and prepared the banners that the kids would hold.

Despite Hafizullah's fears, he couldn't help but feel energised by the excited chatter of the children who gathered before him. The kids, dressed in mismatched clothing of muddy tracksuit pants and skirts, gumboots and open-toed sandals, beanies and headscarves, huddled together for warmth on that bitter, wet winter's morning. Their colourful clothing gave the otherwise dreary day a touch of character. They looked up at Hafizullah with trust and expectation.

He knew these kids wanted to perform the march. He'd been that kid who had lost faith in the public education system after being mistreated by his teachers, that kid forced to skip school because he had to work to help his family eat. To him, *street kid* was a lived experience. He knew from his own experiences that these children needed to have a voice and they needed to know the system valued them. This was not just a request for a school; it was a demand for their humanity to be acknowledged.

'Never think that you can't study,' he said, through a megaphone, before they set off. 'Never let anyone tell you that you can only be a street kid. Better to walk the streets in dignity than work the streets in humiliation.'

'We are your children,' the children chanted back.

Hafizullah marched down the street, with the little kings and queens of the street behind him, peacefully protesting against the inequality of the violent global economy. And though they were just a small group of Afghan children, they did not march alone. They marched on behalf of the two million Afghan children who worked to supplement their families' incomes. They marched for the thousands of children who worked the streets of Kabul. They marched through the streets, despite the dangers. Shop owners stared at their strange procession and cars tooted their horns.

'We want to go to school,' they chanted.

Hafizullah spotted Fatima in a rabbit-eared pullover. Fatima, whose wish was to be a teacher, helped her father sell snow shovels instead of going to school. Here she was, walking tall, chanting: 'We don't want charity!' Her black eyes flashed with excitement beneath her headscarf. Over there was Iman, a slight ten-year-old boy, still with his shoe-shine bag sitting on his hip. Hafizullah remembered him making a school out of Lego and saying he wanted 'a safe place to study'.

Seeing Fatima and the other kids in full voice made Hafizullah feel proud that they understood they shouldn't have to work in the streets polishing boots or selling wares. They understood that they deserved a school. He was proud they believed their slogans and that onlookers were forced to recognise these children as more than waifs and scoundrels. He was proud of the children because they knew that after this protest they would have to return to work; but at least they could do this now.

'Education is the right of your children. Don't make us work in the street,' they chanted.

When they arrived at the Human Rights Commission offices, an official acknowledged the group and invited one of the volunteers inside to speak about their request. Hafizullah didn't expect a positive response to the protest from the government. He hoped that the kids understood this too. By being there, by showing up and asking for a school, they were asking the country to look after their children; they were telling the country they were not just a source of low-wage labour. As long as the children believed the words they were shouting it was a worthwhile activity. When the official emerged from the building, he explained to the street kids and the volunteers that their message had been delivered to the government – but there was no firm answer.

Despite being given what was essentially a negative response, the children marched triumphantly back through the streets to the Community Centre. When they arrived, they were elated to find the community members had arranged a party for them. They enjoyed drinks and cake while retelling stories of their bravery and audacity. For Hafizullah, all the stress and the nervousness evaporated once they made it to the safe walls of the Community Centre. They had completed the walk and they had not been targeted.

Chapter 16

Windows into Alternate Universes

KABUL, 2013

Hojar tucked her knees up to her stomach and buried herself under her blankets. The shadows crept in around her, advancing and retreating with every cloud that passed by the faint light of the moon. The shriek of an alley cat sent her further under the covers. Her dark imaginings conjured up armed thieves knocking down her door or perhaps a drug addict creeping in through her window. She didn't know what was possible in a city like Kabul. She had spent her whole life sleeping beside a fire alongside her siblings and her mother. This was the first time she had slept alone in her life. She eventually drifted off, dreaming of the mountains.

The next morning Hojar steeled herself for another challenging day. She stepped out her front door and was assaulted by honking horns, screeching tyres, street hawkers shouting profanities at each other and helicopters thundering overhead. She lifted her headscarf over her nose and mouth to block the smells of rotting sewage and rubbish and to prevent dust from coating her mouth. Faceless women in faded and stained burqas lay on the footpath like discarded handkerchiefs, scarred and knotted hands reaching out at her, desperate for a small offering of charity. Cripples and amputees wove through traffic, beating on windows, demanding cash; veterans of war indistinguishable from victims of war. Snotty-nosed children walked the streets, selling tea, polishing boots and avoiding rogue kicks from disgruntled pedestrians.

Hojar pulled her bag close to her, aware that pickpockets operated in the area, and crossed a bridge over a sunken corridor of rubbish, in fact a river. She tried to avert her eyes from the drug addicts who loitered below. Men and women were sprawled out lifeless in the rubbish. When she first saw the number of drug addicts and beggars on the streets, she couldn't understand why people weren't helping them. She thought their families had abandoned them to this miserable fate. Being confronted by it here brought her to tears.

She preferred to walk fast through the streets with her eyes lowered to the ground. This approach had its complications, though, and soon enough she had lost her way again. She had been in Kabul for several weeks already, but she still got lost. She stepped into a nearby shop to ask for directions, but her throat seemed to catch.

'Yes? What do you want?' the man behind the counter snapped at her.

She had learned not to trust shopkeepers after being cheated on prices numerous times. It was clear she was not from Kabul and people took advantage of that. She asked the shopkeeper for directions to the university and he pointed her down the road.

When Hojar first arrived in Kabul, she visited the community's Human Rights Commission house. The house reminded her of a disturbed ants' nest. There appeared to be people in every room doing things. She noticed the messy kitchen and yard, and how there were more people in the house than the space could accommodate. But she was also captivated by the people of different ethnic groups who were part of the community. She talked with the seamstresses about their lives and the group.

'These community members do have problems and arguments among themselves, but they are also a fine group of people and they are doing good work. If I had more time and did not have to do other work, I would spend more time with the community and I would ask my son to join the group because I see the value in the work they do,' one of the seamstresses told Hojar.

Hojar could see the potential of such work, but for the time being she was focused on enrolling in university and settling in to her new home. She concentrated on finding a well-respected but affordable university and she narrowed her options down to two. The one that ran a nursing course was too expensive for her, so instead she enrolled in journalism.

It had been a slow start to her life in tertiary education. The first few days at university she was a little unsure of the processes and how she should be learning. She discovered that the professors and the teachers wrote on the blackboard as if the students were in first grade at school. The teachers didn't give any printed notes, so the fifty students in the class had to frantically transcribe whatever the teacher had written on the blackboard. No reference notes were distributed and Hojar had no idea how they were going to be evaluated or tested at the end of the year.

When she arrived at class on her first day, she was pleased to see there were many female students. She later learned that of those women, only a few were from the provinces. The rest were from Kabul or were Afghans returning to the country from overseas.

That morning Hojar sat down next to a young woman who looked to be the same age as her. The woman smiled and introduced herself as Darya. Hojar thought that perhaps Darya could have been ethnically Sayyid from her physical appearance, but she didn't ask.

'Do you think we will learn some practical skills today?' Hojar asked in Dari and Darya laughed.

'I wonder if we will learn anything,' Darya replied, also in Dari.

At this point, most of the teaching had been theoretical but Hojar thought the information was ancient and irrelevant for a modern, technologically advanced world.

'Today we will learn about the telegraph,' the professor announced to the class, and Hojar and Darya shared pained looks.

After this first meeting Darya and Hojar became friends; they often walked to university or the bazaar together and Darya offered to guide Hojar around the city. One day Darya told Hojar that she had a Tajik mother and a Pashtun father. At first Hojar was stunned. Her childhood memories of Pashtun people were so contaminated by her father's death that she found it impossible to link this young woman with her nightmarish visions of the Taliban. Before she came to Kabul, she had heard stories of Insaan and the community members befriending Pashtun and Tajik people, and she doubted that it was possible. It was almost as if she didn't want to believe it. She thought that Pashtuns were not Muslims and she could never have imagined associating with such people.

With much discomfort, Hojar raised her attitudes towards Pashtun people with Darya and, to her surprise, Darya laughed heartily.

'Some of my relatives used to tell me I can't eat with Hazaras because Hazaras are *haram*,' Darya said. 'They said Hazaras are a pugnacious and warlike people who will find any opportunity to fight the Pashtun.'

This was exactly the same thing Hojar was told about the Pashtuns. Through her friendship with Darya, Hojar realised that her ethnicity had no impact on her personality or on their relationship. It was irrelevant.

Over the next few months, Hojar settled into life in Kabul with the help of her new friend. Unfortunately, her worst fears regarding her degree were confirmed. There was hardly any practical work. They didn't write articles or other forms of journalism and they didn't learn how to present news stories. They learned about the history of journalism, but not how to be a journalist. There were very few group discussions and those discussions were limited to the teacher and a few students who shared his opinions. Those students who had different views to the teacher and who spoke up too often would eventually be scolded by him.

One day the students were asked to make or edit a radio program and submit it, even though they had not been shown how.

'Perhaps you could teach us how to make a radio program first and then set it for homework?' Hojar suggested.

The teacher huffed out the indignant response, 'If you don't hand in your radio story in one week then you will fail the class.'

But Hojar had the last laugh. She didn't submit a radio story the next week and neither did the rest of the class. He couldn't fail the entire class, so the next week he recruited another tutor to teach them editing.

There were other, more concerning issues about the teacher that deepened Hojar's disillusionment with her university education. The teacher was Hazara and he knew Hojar had befriended Darya, a Pashtun. A few times he made discriminatory remarks about Pashtuns to Hojar and insisted she adopt those same views. On five occasions he walked out of the class when students disagreed with him. Once he remarked that Hojar's voluntary work with the community was useless and that she was stupid to do such work. Hojar did not judge him for his failings because she saw him as a product of a flawed system. She learned that this teacher had suffered greatly as a refugee in Iran, where he had finished his education. She theorised that he had become psychologically affected by his experiences there and was taking it out on the students. Perhaps her teachers were reflecting the way they were taught. They didn't know how to change the system because they didn't know how to change themselves.

While she tried to empathise with the teachers, this didn't stop her feeling dissatisfied with her tertiary education. If this was the education system, what was the future of journalism in Afghanistan going to be like? Journalists were supposed to keep the public informed. They were supposed to balance the power structures within a country by holding politicians and governments to account. By not producing talented journalists, Afghanistan was weakening an integral pillar of a just society. As it was, journalists in Afghanistan, particularly female ones, often encountered censorship, harassment and violence from government officials, police and other members of the Afghan National Security Forces (ANSF), government-allied warlords and militias, and insurgent groups like the Taliban. The government's failure to adequately investigate and prosecute threats and attacks against journalists had weakened press freedom in the country. Many of the existing media outlets were politically biased; owned or supported by political groups.[1]

Hojar often discussed these criticisms and concerns with her peers outside of class, but it was never acceptable to raise such ideas with her teachers. Despite her disappointment with her education, she felt she had no choice but to finish the degree. She had fought too hard for the opportunity to study to return to her village without graduating. She never felt like going to university wasn't worth the effort. She never doubted her path. But the university she imagined, a university with active discussion of ideas, a university that challenged notions and encouraged students to strive for greatness, was not the university she attended. Even so, at the end of her four years of study she became the first woman in her village to graduate and, more importantly, she felt as if she had paid tribute to her father.

For Hojar the community played the role in her life that she'd thought university would. It was through Insaan and the community that she started to contemplate radical thoughts, where she socialised with different people with different views. The community taught her how to interact with others, how to work in groups and with society. When she first moved to

Kabul, she didn't visit the community all that often. The live-in community members were all male, but there were female volunteers involved in the group and in some activities and causes. Hojar entered their world slowly, starting with events that were female-orientated like the community's celebration of International Women's Day. She participated in a few of the monthly calls as part of the World Peace Exchange program and then she became acquainted with the community's regular international guests like Mary. She enjoyed meeting the foreign female visitors and valued their stories, which acted as little windows into alternate universes of female liberty and autonomy.

As her visits to the community increased, she became more aware of the challenges they faced. She saw internal conflict in the house; arguments between housemates that could so easily boil over. She realised how some sectors of Afghanistan would consider this work controversial, and she worried that the group was susceptible to threats from the wider Afghan community and from within the community itself. She struggled with the very real risk of the work and the potential consequences versus its value. When she was introduced to the street kids program, she knew she wanted to be a part of the team. Ever since she had moved to Kabul and saw the way the children were living and working on the street, she had wanted to help them, but she didn't know how. The school gave her the opportunity to use her teaching skills for the betterment of their lives and that made the community work seem infinitely worthwhile, despite all the risks.

Even so, it wasn't until Hojar was offered a rare and never-dreamed-of invitation that she committed wholeheartedly to the cause. One day Insaan approached her and asked:

'Hojar, would you like to go to India?'

INDIA, 2014

The plane jolted forward suddenly, pushing Hojar's already pounding heart into her throat. *Was the plane breaking down? Maybe they were being attacked?* The plane stuttered again, and she realised that was the engine starting. Today was the first time she had been in an aeroplane and the first time she had ever left Afghanistan. Even though she was sitting in the plane, she couldn't believe it. She eased her grip on the arms of her chair and slowly sank back into her seat. She didn't want to draw attention to herself. She didn't want to give anyone an excuse to ask her to leave the plane.

Hojar was one of four female members of the community who had been invited to go to India by Mary Smith to study for two weeks at the Barefoot College in Rajasthan.[2] This global network of colleges based their educational philosophies on Gandhian principles, teaching poor communities to be self-reliant, to protect them from dependence and exploitation. Not only would this be a great opportunity for Hojar to further her education, she was also struck by a sensation that she'd never had the chance to entertain in her life: the thrill of wanderlust.

When the trip was first mooted, Hojar tried to contain her excitement, as she knew that the likelihood of her being allowed to travel was miniscule. According to Afghan Islamic tradition, there were many restrictions on women travelling. If a woman wanted to travel, the question would always be, why? If it could be done by a man, then let the man travel, not the woman.

This imbalance between male and female freedoms had governed Hojar's movements her entire life. It meant she could not see a male stranger unless there was a family member present; she couldn't leave her house and walk through her home village unless she was accompanied by a family member. Until she moved to Kabul, Hojar had spent most of her public life accompanied by a male member of the family. The burqa and the hijab sort of compensated for this rule. With the hijab the woman was covered and therefore was not seen by male strangers and that could make it less essential to have an escort. In Kabul Hojar did not have an escort, but Kabul was very different to anywhere else in Afghanistan. It was a bubble of relative liberalism. Maybe the cities of Herat or Mazar-i-Sharif could be considered similar but even they were more conservative than Kabul. Hojar remembered when she first returned home to her rural village after having moved to Kabul, she went into town with Muslimyor, forgetting they were not related. When she returned to her family home, her mother and brothers chastised her.

'This is not Kabul. You can't do this here.'

The female international members of the group told Hojar they would act as her escorts, because female escorts didn't have to be family members. However, even with this assurance Hojar was worried about how the members of her family's village would perceive her travelling abroad as a woman. Hojar discussed the trip with her mother, who allowed her to go as long as none of their relatives learned about it. Two of the female community members were not given permission to go by their families. Mina was allowed, but it was a long negotiation process before her father assented. Mary's invitation to the women was a bold act, but she saw potential in these four women. In each of them she saw the powerful combination of ability and enthusiasm. Hojar was forever grateful to Mary for believing in her.

When Hojar arrived in Delhi, she immediately began observing India and its society, comparing the country to Afghanistan. Delhi was much greener than Kabul. She saw homeless people in the streets and many poor communities, which showed her that India shared the problem of poverty with Afghanistan. Women in Delhi seemed open and free to move around the city and they didn't have the same restrictions as Afghan women. In Afghanistan there was only one religion, whereas in India there were many different religions and many different places of worship. In amongst these observations, she realised something significant: the anxiety of war she carried inside of her had disappeared. For the first time in her life she wasn't fearful of bombs going off. She hadn't even realised she was burdened by this anxiety until it was gone. Hojar and Mina discussed their initial impressions of India and they agreed that if they had the opportunity they would like to stay in India

Hojar and the group then took a train to Rajasthan and the Barefoot College. The college was solar-powered, they harvested rainwater from their roofs, and they had an organic farm. Barefoot encouraged opportunity and accessibility, taking students, primarily women, from the lowest strata of Indian society, the 'Untouchable' caste, and teaching them practical skills such as building and repairing water pumps or making solar lamps. Hojar noted that in the college the women were deliberately given more opportunities than the men. The classes did not require the students to be literate; the emphasis was on a person's ability to learn rather than their ability to read or write. They did their best to accommodate people, offering night classes for students who worked during the day.

'It is made by the poor, for the poor,' the teachers said.

At Barefoot, Hojar saw with her own eyes how aptitude could be just as valuable as a qualification. The local dentist was a woman who ran her dental clinic within the Barefoot College – she was half-literate and had never been to school. A French dentist had spent two years training her to perform almost all the necessary dental work for a small community. The college accountant was not fully literate, but he had learned how to enter data in a computer program, which meant he could manage all the college accounts. Hojar was excited by these two success stories and became convinced that the measure of a person's intelligence could exist outside of the traditional education system.

The trip to India was significant for her because she saw how close the aims and the vision of the Barefoot College were to that of her own community in Afghanistan. Barefoot was her utopia. The college had been established in the 1970s, which inspired Hojar because she knew that the work was not a one-off. It gave her hope that their Afghan experiments in peace could eventuate and last as long in a similar community.

While in India she had time to be a tourist. She visited Gandhi's ashram and, though she had learned about Gandhi and read his books, seeing the building where he lived helped her understand that his practice and philosophy of simplicity had actually happened.

At the end of the trip, Hojar and Mina attended a 'right to work, food and land' conference. Local Indian women organised the entire two-day conference and Hojar was inspired by these women, who were bringing progress to their communities. The conference organisers asked Hojar and Mina to say a few words.

'The human race is one family,' Hojar said to the crowd. 'We are all in this together, in this work, in this struggle. All human beings living under one blue sky.'

She didn't expect her message to be relevant, she didn't expect it would move people, but at the end of their speech the whole audience stood and cheered and began singing 'We shall overcome'. Never before had Hojar believed so strongly in humanity. She saw that to travel outside of Afghanistan was an education that most Afghans were denied. They would be able to visit countries that didn't have open warfare and they would see what could be possible at home. They could see the different ways women lived all over the world and implement these changes in their country.

In her last days before she returned to Afghanistan, Hojar tried to absorb all the scenes of India and preserve them in her mind. She was acutely aware that she might never get a chance to visit India again, that she might never get a chance to travel outside of Afghanistan again. Returning to Kabul, she felt like she was stepping back inside a dark house and someone was closing the door to the outside world.

War not only physically affected a person; it brought fear and it removed hope. In India Hojar could think more about life and she was not burdened by the regular reminders of war and the feelings associated with it. But she was still plagued by her worry for her friends and her family who were suffering in Afghanistan. She realised more deeply how difficult it was for people who lived in ongoing war. That made the return to Kabul and those unhappy feelings even heavier.

After her trip to India, the male live-in community approached her with a request. They wanted her to start a female live-in community.

Chapter 17

Even Our Mistakes are Progress

KABUL, 2014

Since the community began to ramp up their productivity, they were receiving more and more visitors, particularly at lunch time. There were regularly more than thirty people in the community expecting to be fed. They would have to split lunch into three rooms at times to fit everyone. Some mornings, live-in members would still be asleep when students began arriving for their activities. They'd have to clear away their sleeping gear each morning because their bedroom would be converted into a community centre. This meant there was a lot of extra work for the community but they were excited by the new projects and by meeting so many new people, so they tried to juggle their responsibilities. They could see the community growing in its scope and perhaps this motivated them to take on more than they could handle.

Abdul and Asghar entered the kitchen to check on the lunch preparations, but the kitchen was empty.

'Where is Baddar?' Abdul asked. 'He's supposed to be cooking.'

It was almost lunch time and Baddar, who was rostered to cook that day, was nowhere to be seen.

'Still asleep,' grunted Muslimyor, as he bustled past Abdul with a pot full of water ready to boil. 'We will have to cook for him.'

This was not the first time Baddar had slept in and skipped his household chores.

The rules of the community, which were crafted over many meetings, stipulated how a member could join the live-in community, included a written contract on participation in cooking and cleaning, and stated what conditions would prompt the community to ask a member to leave. It was agreed that failure to uphold the constitution would lead to removal from the community. All the community members signed this manifesto. But this didn't mean community members always behaved according to these agreements. In an all-male house, in a country where women were expected to perform household chores, it was not so surprising that most of the challenges in the community concerned cooking and cleaning. Some members resented having to do household chores. Some people didn't cook on the day they were supposed to cook, or if they cooked, they didn't clean up after they cooked. Some members refused to clean and others had to clean for them.

'I will help you cook,' Abdul said to Muslimyor.

'I don't want your oily Pakistani food,' Hamza said, entering the kitchen, glaring at Abdul.

'I'm not Pakistani,' Abdul said quietly.

'What did you say?' Hamza asked.

Since Abdul joined the community, he had been learning Dari, but none of the Pashto speakers could speak Dari well. It frustrated Abdul that the Pashtuns learned Dari but the others didn't learn Pashto. He saw it as an example of inequality in the community and thought it was insulting because it showed him the other community members didn't value the Pashto language.

'What did you say?' Hamza asked again.

'I'm not Pakistani,' Abdul said a little louder.

'You are a Pashtun, suicide bomber, warmonger,' Hamza said, walking right up to Abdul in a threatening manner. He was not angry; he was serious, matter of fact. Abdul was scared of Hamza. He had been warned by the other community members that he was a war veteran and could be unpredictable.

'Ignore him,' Asghar said.

It was not the first time Abdul had been accused of being a terrorist, a suicide bomber or a Talib purely because he was Pashtun – as though Pashtuns were the only ethnic group who had committed atrocities during the wars. Sometimes other Afghans believed that their ethnic groups were the only ones to suffer hardships. Such generalisations disregarded the suffering of Pashtuns and undermined the peace-building process. For him, the Taliban was not a *Pashtun movement*, it was *a movement of Pashtuns*. Before Abdul joined the community, he reacted badly to these comments, but he was learning to ignore the criticism.

'Yes, you're probably right,' Abdul said, then left the kitchen to avoid any further conflict.

Hamza wasn't always this aggressive. There were times when he was friendly and he would joke with Abdul. But Abdul was beginning to learn to avoid him when he went berserk. Hamza had been particularly confrontational ever since Abdul had cooked a traditional Pashtun meal, a dish of sticky rice with oil and milk and lentils from Paktia province, called *dandakai*. He learned the recipe from his mother. The rice was shaped in an oval on a large plate and everyone sat in a circle around the plate and ate using their hands. When Abdul cooked he used lots of oil and peppers to make it spicier, but the rest of the community weren't used to this style of cooking and they didn't like it. Nobody ate very much and since then Hamza had attacked him for his cooking.

'We've run out of bread,' Asghar called out. 'Can someone buy some more?'

Hafizullah rushed out the door.

The preparation of the meal was frantic but the younger members of the community banded together to make it happen, with some degree of resentment powering their activities. The trouble with the community's generous lunchtime gatherings was that the visitors were beginning to treat the community like a canteen. They would eat their food, socialise for a bit and then leave their plates for the live-in members to clean. The older members usually refused to clear up the visitors' mess, which meant the responsibilities fell upon the younger ones.

After the food was prepared Baddar strolled into the kitchen, still in his pyjamas, and served himself a plate of food. Abdul felt a rumble of discontent and spite in his belly, but he didn't say anything. No-one did. The community members did everything they could to avoid criticising each other. To criticise was disrespectful and offensive.

Sharing of household responsibilities became one of the biggest challenges to living in community. The older members of the community (aged eighteen and older) felt that the younger members should do more housework. They even demanded the younger members of the community complete menial tasks on their behalf, like fetch items for them. This was generally the custom in Afghan families – older people expected younger people to run errands for them – but this was not congruent with the community's philosophies of equality and fairness. As the pressure of preparing lunches and cleaning the house fell upon the young members of the community, they began to feel exploited. This created an atmosphere of resentment and bitterness in the house that was affecting their work in the projects and damaging the entire community vision. There was only so long this inequity could exist in the group.

The younger members of the community felt unable to say anything about the issue themselves, so they spoke to Insaan in private and asked him to raise the matter. Insaan chose that afternoon to hold a meeting.

'Everyone who is on the cooking and cleaning roster must do their jobs. It doesn't matter who you are, or how old you are. Otherwise this will cause problems,' Insaan said.

Arif didn't take the suggestion well, viewing it as a personal slight against him. He sulked for a number of days without doing his cleaning jobs and then finally he approached Insaan.

'These Hazara boys are complaining about the cooking and cleaning because I'm Tajik. This is ethnic discrimination,' he said.

Insaan tried to reason with him but he refused to budge. So Insaan held a meeting with the rest of the community to discuss Arif's concerns.

'I would like you to suggest some possible negotiation tactics,' Insaan said.

The community's answer was to assume his responsibilities to avoid confrontation.

'We will do his cooking and cleaning.'

Insaan was shocked and frustrated by their response and insisted Arif resume his responsibilities in the house. So Arif packed his bags and left. Four days later, Arif called Insaan and asked if he could return to the community.

'I will only agree to your return on the condition that you will not accuse people of ethnic discrimination to avoid fulfilling your cleaning and cooking responsibilities in the house,' Insaan said.

These could have been viewed as trivial arguments but they were important lessons in nonviolent negotiation for the experimental community. If their purpose in starting the community was to be a microcosm of Afghan society, they needed to develop their ability to give and deal with criticism, share responsibilities and effectively communicate between ethnic groups.

Arif returned to a warm and welcoming community. They understood that he was damaged, just as they were. They cared for him, just as they cared for all the community members. Each time a member left they continued to offer them opportunities for redemption and salvation.

KABUL, 2014

One day Arif brought a hookah pipe to the house and Hafizullah, Muslimyor, Horse and Asghar decided they would try tobacco for the first time. They knew that Insaan would be upset if he found them smoking, so they hid in one of the rooms in the basement where they stored the duvets. To double their daring, they smuggled energy drinks in as well. If they were going to get in trouble for smoking they may as well enjoy the thrill of a sugar high as well. There amongst the flammable fabric and bedding, they smoked the apple and pomegranate flavoured tobacco and drank Red Bull. They took turns to smoke, attempting to blow smoke rings into the air. Horse marvelled at the warmth that filled his lungs as he inhaled the sweet vapour. The water in the vase bubbled and the hot coals on top of the hookah glowed warmly when he sucked in through the pipe. He inhaled too deeply, and the warmth turned fire-like in his chest and he coughed violently, sending grey clouds tearing across his throat and out into the room. Muslimyor was mid-smoke, mouth full, when Insaan entered the room. The boys froze. The hookah vase stood boldly in the centre of the room. Hafizullah tried to slide his Red Bull can behind him. Then Muslimyor blew two perfect rings of smoke towards Insaan.

'Go upstairs,' Insaan said quietly and then he left, stiff-backed.

The young men were in a panic to clean up and in their haste hot ash from the hookah burned holes in the duvets. Hafizullah, Muslimyor and Asghar went upstairs to face Insaan's wrath, but Horse was too scared.

At the last second, he ran to his bed and pretended to go to sleep. Two minutes later, Hafizullah ran downstairs and dragged Horse out of his bed. It was quite late, but Insaan insisted they write an agreement with him that said:

We agree not to use the hookah when in community.

'I can't stop you from smoking in your own time, but I don't want you smoking in this house. I'm appealing to you as a brother to stop. Please. It hurts me.'

After that day, Horse vowed to never touch tobacco or drugs again.

When Horse was a young child, he marvelled at how the fathers of his friends were so caring towards their children. It seemed that these men were willing to lay down their lives for their offspring. Horse realised at a very early age that his father did not feel this way about his children. He cared more about himself than anyone else. When Horse was young, his father told the family he was leaving for Iran. He said he was going to work to pay off the family debt. Horse had not seen him since.

When he arrived in Iran, Horse's father met another woman and started another family there. He never sent any financial support to Horse's family. It was as if Horse and his siblings and his mother ceased to exist in his father's mind. Horse couldn't understand how his father planned to have another family when he couldn't look after his first one. Horse didn't understand how he could be a loving father to his new children, when he had failed so poorly with his first family. The only way Horse could come to terms with his own feelings of inadequacy and shame was to realise that his father didn't understand what the love of a father was.

After his father left, Horse worried about whether the family would become hungry, whether he would be able to have a good upbringing, whether he would have a chance to study and complete his education. Sometimes the worrying became so intense he cried. Horse was sure these fears contributed to his interest in joining the community. With Insaan and the community he could see the potential for a brighter future.

One evening when he was in Kabul, he approached Insaan and asked him for some time alone.

'Can you play the role of a parent to me?' Horse asked.

He tried to say it casually, as if it was no big deal, but halfway through he choked up and his eyes filled with tears.

'I will try to be there for you, Horse,' Insaan said. 'But I can't replace your father and I can't promise I will be a good guardian for you.'

Horse didn't know whether he actually wanted Insaan to replace his father or not, but he knew deep down that it was not possible anyway. He had asked Insaan the question because he needed friendship and he needed guidance. Insaan was a moral teacher to Horse, a teacher of the immaterial things. Horse wanted to be a better person and he thought Insaan could teach him how. But he was also lonely and trying to create a second family.

Horse wasn't the only community member who struggled with this unusual role Insaan held. The community members were like brothers and sisters and with that came sibling rivalry. As traumatised children, they needed attention and love and affection, but within the context of community they fought for it. This often led to feelings of inadequacy arising in the community members. They constantly needed reaffirmation that they would support each other.

One day Insaan was talking about how to deal with anger and how to support each other. He gave an example: 'Next time I am shouting, Muslimyor could sit by my side.'

What Insaan thought was an innocuous phrase caused division and insecurity in the group. First Asghar confronted him about his choice of Muslimyor to support him. Months later, Hafizullah mentioned it, and then Horse asked Insaan why he chose Muslimyor and not him. Insaan apologised numerous times, saying it was just an example, there was no 'choice', but the community members couldn't help but feel slighted.

Asghar was a sensitive young man but it was clear to Insaan he harboured his insecurities, like most young Afghans. He felt left alone after the death of his father and, like many fatherless children, he was looking for a figure to replace him. As their friendship developed over the years, when Asghar better understood the dynamics of their relationship, Insaan told him: 'I can't be your surrogate father.' Asghar accepted that verbally, but emotionally perhaps he didn't. Whenever he became upset, he would claim he was going to leave the community.

One time in the Parliament house he had one such episode. Insaan didn't know what triggered it, but over the course of the evening Asghar slid into a depressed mood and then he threw a tantrum.

'I want to go home. Tonight. Now.'

He began kicking the wall and shouting. The community tried to calm him down, but he couldn't calm down. It was late in the evening, and the entire community were involved. Asghar struggled out of Muslimyor's clutches and ran out the door, aiming for the bus stop to go home to the mountains that night. Muslimyor caught up with him about a kilometre from the house. With great difficulty he brought him back to the community. Throughout the incident Insaan kept his cool. He hugged him and said, 'Don't go. I don't want you to go. Going is not the solution. It doesn't solve the problem.'

But over time, Insaan's reactions became more short-tempered and less sensitive. One time, Insaan responded to one of Asghar's tantrums by saying, 'I am so tired. If you really want to go, you can go.'

The result was dramatic. Asghar became even angrier and he cried even louder. By the time he calmed down hours later, he said to Insaan, 'I'm sorry I sometimes put pressure on you. Can you accept me for who I am and never say go? No matter what I say, don't say go. I don't want to hear that. Even if I'm shouting at you to let me go, don't let me go.'

'I know that,' Insaan said. 'I'm trying my best. I care for you and I don't want you to feel as if you should leave, as if you are abandoned. I will be there for you as long as I'm still alive.'

Asghar needed to be cared for in a way that Insaan couldn't provide. Insaan couldn't be his father. After this incident their relationship became more and more difficult. Asghar looked for affirmation in everything Insaan said. Eventually Asghar started hanging out with a new group of friends who were richer than the other community members. They went out to restaurants and cafes and bought gifts for each other. Insaan supposed it was a form of teenage rebellion. When Asghar was offered the opportunity to study in Mongolia it came as a relief to both of them. Insaan hoped that Asghar would learn that he could survive on his own and that the distance would strengthen his relationships in Afghanistan.

Insaan felt like he had played various roles for each of the community members over the years, over and above that of teacher: a brother, a guardian, a father, an uncle. But part of him wondered if he was trying to fill a void in his own life. He didn't do it intentionally, because he never planned for this community to happen, but perhaps he was subconsciously trying to create a family for himself. Maybe this community filled that gap.

Insaan had had opportunities to get married but the timing had never been right. His first serious girlfriend had wanted to marry, but he'd thought they were too young, and he wanted to study. They broke up and she moved to Australia. Then, in his twenties and thirties, when he had finished his training and was in a better position to marry, he didn't meet anyone.

There were times when Insaan wondered if he had missed out on a key part of life by not having a family, but he was not inclined to dwell on regrets. The community had become his family and, as challenging as these relationships were to maintain, they were too precious to give up. He was stronger with them than without them.

AFTER I HAD lived with the community for a few weeks, I started to see cracks in the harmonious living and work arrangements. The polite behaviour reserved for international guests couldn't be sustained for such a long period of time. At the centre one day I saw two volunteers almost come to blows because one of them tripped the other. Another time, some tomfoolery between Horse and Muslimyor escalated into a physical fight.

And then, in the Peace House, I walked into an argument between Insaan and the community members. Insaan raged and shouting filled the small house, followed by the bangs of pots and pans. Then there was silence. I didn't know what had caused such an outburst, but it was out of place in a community that was usually at peace.

I asked Insaan about it the next day.

'That is my volcano,' Insaan said, looking ashamed. 'In community there is no pretence of moral sainthood. We are all flawed characters, just as Martin Luther King and Gandhi were. Do you remember I once told you that in attempting to work for peace, even our mistakes and flaws are progress? That's the point of experimentation. I have never described our community as a success. Our mistakes have been many, but nonviolence is an evolutionary process. It is an ideal we are working towards. The live-in community tried to make it work. Perhaps we took on too much. Because we just weren't coping.'

KABUL, 2014

One morning there was an unexpected knock on the front door. Insaan opened it to find a tramp-like character laden with bags on their doorstep.

'I have no place to stay in Kabul. I heard of your community from one of the volunteers. Can I stay with you?'

Although Soban had come to the community uninvited, the group agreed to allow him to stay temporarily. But Soban had a talent for squatting and none of the community members felt comfortable explicitly asking him to leave, so he stayed for longer than ever agreed upon. During that time his mental health deteriorated and his schizophrenia became apparent. One evening Soban and Arif had an argument in the kitchen that escalated to the point where Soban picked up a knife and Arif was wielding the lid of a pressure cooker. The other community members had to restrain the pair. The community later learned that Soban had been in a mental facility in Iran for two years prior to returning to Afghanistan.

While the community was establishing itself in Kabul, they had an open-door policy as a way to encourage young Afghans to join their group. Perhaps it was inevitable that a recruitment process that didn't vet members would attract some disturbed characters. But in a country like Afghanistan everyone had a story of trauma and suffering, so it was hard to distinguish between those who could control their trauma and those who couldn't. Indeed, with this mismatched collection of young people it was only a matter of time before they experienced conflict and misunderstanding.

As challenging as Soban's health was for the community to manage, his situation was not unique. Each person in community had their own way of manifesting their psychological challenges. Some people suffered from violent nightmares and shouted in their sleep. Muslimyor banged his head against the wall until he was restrained. Asghar punched holes in the walls and broke windows. Whenever Abdul became frustrated or angry he'd lose control of himself and he'd pick up things and throw them randomly across the room. Others had picked up knives. On a few occasions, Hafizullah worked himself into a powerful rage and it would take three community members to hold him down; afterwards he would recall nothing of the crisis. All of these reactions were triggered by minor, trivial incidents. That's why they were called triggers, because they activated a much larger reaction built up from accumulated stress, anger, sorrow, uncertainty and fear. Conflict in the house often acted as a trigger that led to many members questioning the community's worth and effectiveness.

The community members talked about preventing the outbursts, but sometimes that was not possible. When they were waking up to bomb blasts, they had to accept that some incidents were out of their control.

'Why am I like this?' Muslimyor asked Insaan one day. 'Why can't I control my anger?'

'It's not your fault,' Insaan said. 'You did not plan to be unwell. It is not irrational behaviour. This is how war has shaped you.'

To help the volunteers cope with their psychological challenges, Insaan invited two female Afghan psychologists to conduct regular trauma healing workshops.

When those manifestations happened, it stressed everyone in the community, but the fact that these reactions afflicted them all also built understanding between them. They realised that none of them were well and they supported each other through their outbursts. This didn't stop them from being upset by the fighting in the community though.

'Anywhere in the world, relationships will face challenges; even a husband and wife will fight,' Insaan said to the community during a peace circle one day. 'You should expect conflict but don't give up because of it. Fighting doesn't mean you've failed. It doesn't mean the value of love is any less because we succumbed to an argument. Be brave. Be vulnerable.'

In those community relationships there was healing. Those relationships showed Insaan that the community members needed to connect with and understand their anger, grief and injustice, so they could recognise the signs before an outburst was triggered. For someone whose father had been killed by another ethnic group, it took courage to face those feelings of revenge and hate and find another way to feel about it. But that change in heart could make a difference in whether or not that person found inner peace, individual peace, interracial peace or community peace. If humanity could devote as much time and effort to understanding their emotions and developing methods of nonviolence as they did in developing deadly weapons, the world would be a much safer place. While community demonstrated the power of relationships, Insaan also had to expect that not everyone could be saved.

Hamza looked more like a poet than a soldier. He was a skinny man, distinctly unmuscular, with narrow shoulders that curved in towards him as if he was constantly protecting himself. He wore John Lennon glasses, he grew a scraggly beard that gathered at his chin and his hair was a thick, dark mess of curls. Aged twenty, he had already served in the army for two years in Kandahar, one of the most dangerous provinces in Afghanistan.

It was during one of the community peace circles that Hamza first spoke about his experiences at war.

'I used to think that soldiers and wars were necessary. But when I joined the military, I saw the injuring and killing of my fellow soldiers and opponents like the Taliban and I questioned if my presence was necessary. Is it right to have a weapon?'

When Hamza spoke he looked past people, not at them, and absentmindedly stroked his beard as he dug through suppressed memories.

'I held a weapon before people I didn't know and who didn't know me. We weren't enemies, because we didn't even know one another. Even before greetings, we were supposed to kill one another. I concluded that I should leave the army and after that, I had a crisis. I was affected by the war. I felt alone. I drew away from my family. I didn't want to hurt them or trouble them.'

One evening Muslimyor woke up to find Hamza sleepwalking through the house, muttering in a panicked manner. When he woke him, Hamza told him: 'One morning in Kandahar, I woke up in a ditch full of corpses and I could smell the stench of death.' Another night, Hamza woke up in the middle of the night shouting, 'I'm a murderer.'

In Afghanistan there was little psychiatric help for anyone, let alone war veterans.[1] Almost every older person in Afghanistan was a war veteran, having lived through decades of conflict. They could have fought in a war either as part of the army or a militia group, or just local people picking up arms to defend their homes. The United States still had difficulty caring for its veterans from the Vietnam War. Afghanistan was an entire country traumatised.

One evening Arif approached Insaan, looking worried.

'Teacher, Hamza is asleep and next to him are two empty pill bottles.'

Insaan rushed into Hamza's room and shook him awake. Hamza opened his eyes halfway, and his head lolled to the side. The community hive sprang into action. Hafizullah hailed a cab off the street and Insaan and Arif carried Hamza out of the house. They rushed to the emergency department at the nearest hospital, where the healthcare workers put him on a drip, observed him for a couple of hours and then sent him home. War and healthcare were incompatible. War was incompatible with most basic human services. The community agreed to help Hamza pay for private consultations with a psychiatrist. They did their research and found one of the few psychiatrists available in Kabul.

'Do you think the visits to the psychiatrist have helped you?' Insaan asked him, after several months of treatment.

'I can't say I'm very well, but I am better than before,' he said. 'The effects of war still remain. Veterans who commit suicide are not cowardly. They are victims of war. They were persuaded to do things they didn't want to do. Even if they chose to do those things, aren't they allowed to regret their actions? Those veterans who commit suicide have a conscience. These thoughts afflict them day and night. That's why I wake up screaming. I feel ashamed. I regret what I did. It is not cowardly fear. After what I did, I felt like I no longer had the right to live. Life became meaningless.'

'Do you have a message for your friends?' Insaan asked Hamza, motioning to the silent community sitting in a circle before him.

'How I wish that every human in the world would just once sit down alone and ask themselves, what are we here for? How have we been deceived? How true to ourselves have we been? I was brought up under the government system and I was a captive to society and the media. Now, I am free,' Hamza said.

It wasn't long after this peace circle that Muslimyor found Hamza in his bunker-like bedroom in the basement of the house, curled up on his dirty mattress, semi-conscious, encircled by empty drug containers. Muslimyor rushed to get help. They sent Hamza to the hospital and after he was discharged he returned to his psychiatric treatment.

The day after Hamza's second suicide attempt, the community sat down to discuss his future in the house.

'What if he is successful next time?' Muslimyor asked.

The thought of finding Hamza's body in the basement conjured revulsion and anxiety in the community members. The reality of such a tragedy would be too traumatic and horrific to come to terms with.

'We would also be in trouble,' Arif said. 'It would bring attention to our group. The police would come and ask questions about our unconventional living arrangement.'

'Because Hamza is Hazara the Pashtuns and Tajiks might be falsely accused of having hurt him, of having poisoned him and using the suicide as an alibi,' Abdul said.

The group agreed that the continued presence of Hamza in the community was a threat to them all.

'Can we help you?' Insaan asked Hamza. 'We don't judge you for wanting to cope with your war trauma by attempting suicide, but it's not helping our community. Your suicide attempts traumatise us too.'

'I understand, teacher. I myself have doubted whether I can cope in such a community. But for the time being, I have nowhere else to go,' Hamza said to Insaan.

The trouble for the community was that every day a sick member of the community remained in the house it potentially brought them closer to disaster. While Hamza struggled with his recurring trauma, a psychiatrist from the United States, who had eighteen years' experience working with war veterans there, visited the community.

'This is a full-blown psychiatric ward,' he said to Insaan. 'How are you going to manage?'

Being asked that question allowed Insaan to reflect on his own mental health for the first time in years. He felt like he was a cartoon character carrying a tower of luggage in his arms, a tower that was perilously close to crashing to the ground. Over the years his suitcases of trauma were stacked on top of each other, suitcases upon suitcases upon suitcases. Never-addressed trauma was pushed aside to be dealt with at another time. And then he tripped, and it all crashed to the ground.

'I'm not managing.'

That was when the warden himself became a patient.

KABUL, 2014

As the oldest member of the community, Insaan felt like an outsider, or a neutral observer. He enjoyed watching the young men and the community develop. However, remaining neutral when the community was in turmoil was a fragile position that was bound to be tested.

The community members used Insaan's neutrality to turn him into a judge or arbitrator. They came to him with their complaints or arguments and all expected him to resolve the issue in their favour. Sometimes he received criticism for his handling of these disputes. He needed strength to cope with this role; he thought he could do it. But he didn't realise he was just not managing. The volcano started to rumble.

'Insaan, it is your fault that the young members of the community are discriminating against me,' Arif shouted at him.

'Why don't you support us enough?' Asghar said, with spite in his words.

'This community is a failure and it's your fault,' Hamza said.

Insaan sat still and smiled and said, 'Oh, okay. Yes, I am at fault for this. I accept that.'

But deep down he was not okay with these unfair accusations. He tried to suppress these negative emotions but that only made the pressure inside of him build up.

Tension grew in the house. Accusations were thrown between ethnic groups, accusations born from perceptions of injustice and unfair treatment from within the community. Their regular program of peace circles stopped working when they stopped listening to one another. There was too much pain, too much trauma, too much suspicion. Eventually the volcano erupted over some inconsequential teenage bickering.

Insaan's meltdowns began to take place every few months, when the stresses of community accumulated beyond his ability to cope. The shouting varied: sometimes it would just be a few moments, other times he wouldn't be able to calm down for hours.

Insaan realised that for the past decade he had been living in a state of high alert, of hypervigilance. He was only now starting to realise the physical, emotional and psychological impact. Suddenly, Insaan identified an ugliness inside of him and he didn't like it. This was not who he was, but it was who he had become. He was traumatised and needed to heal.

Insaan approached the community with his problem.

'I don't like this volcano in me. I detest it. I am not handling it. Can you help me?' he said to the community.

One of the Afghan psychologists who visited the group said, 'Afghans shout a lot because they have so much anger inside of them. One good way to stop the shouting is to put a pillow on Insaan's face and let him shout it out.'

Insaan was willing to try anything.

'Don't suffocate me, but put it there until I calm down,' he told the community.

There were not many times when the community smothered his trauma with a pillow but they often sat beside him while he raged.

Mary Smith had witnessed Insaan's struggle with the pressures of community life and she decided she needed to act.

'I think Insaan needs to extricate himself from the community and go see a counsellor,' Mary said to the community.

She was thinking the way Insaan used to think as a medical doctor: isolate the disease and cut it out. Remove Insaan from the stresses that cause the problem, remove Insaan from the community. But the community approach was different. All of them said things that surprised Insaan and Mary.

'Then shouldn't you make the same recommendation for all of us here?' Abdul said. 'Shouldn't I extricate myself as well?'

'Where are we supposed to extricate ourselves to?' Asghar asked.

'Does that mean we have no hope of healing while we are here in Afghanistan?' Muslimyor asked.

Mary tried to support her theory with an example of how to deal with this anger.

'Remember when we did our peer mediation class among the volunteers. We took a Coca-Cola bottle and shook it up so the gas was bubbling inside. I asked you what would happen if you opened the cap. Your response was that it would explode. The lesson was that if someone is acutely angry, you leave the person alone. You remove the bottle, isolate it, until the bottle calms down. Then you can think about opening the cap. Maybe Insaan should take breaks from the community more frequently.'

That was an idea Insaan supported. And then Hafizullah's wisdom came out.

'What I think Insaan needs is not for us to isolate him or leave him alone. What Insaan needs is for some of us to go around the bottle and with great skill slowly release the cap. He will not explode, he will calm down.'

'We are the ones who will make his healing work for him because it is from interacting with us and our society that Insaan is like this. It is here that we shall find the solutions to that problem,' Abdul said.

Insaan realised that the community was teaching him more about the power of human relationships than he'd ever known before. It was through community that he would heal, and, with the help of community, he was getting better.

Chapter 18

Humanising War, Not Normalising War

KABUL, 2016

Muslimyor's brother sat across from him on the floor of the Peace House, silently picking at his food. His eyes were cloudy and distant. How different their life paths had been, Muslimyor thought.

'Do you find it strange to stay in a community dedicated to non-violence?' Muslimyor asked him.

'If I had the same opportunities as you, maybe I would never have become a soldier,' his brother said.

His brother was in Kabul for one evening on his way to Kandahar. A year ago, his family had persuaded him to leave the Afghan national army and return to their home in the mountains. However, when he came back the family saw he was a changed man. He had been affected by his experiences in the army and would often lose his temper. After he had married, the family hoped he would be able to settle down, but he couldn't find any work and he returned to the only organisation hiring: the army. He was deployed to Kandahar.

'I already miss them,' he said to Muslimyor, referring to his wife and his newborn daughter.

He didn't eat much that evening, preoccupied with his own thoughts and fears. The next morning, Muslimyor accompanied him to his car. They hugged, and his brother gripped his arm and offered him a sad smile. That was the last time they saw each other. Muslimyor tried calling his brother several times in the next few months, but his calls never connected.

Eventually they received news that he had been killed by the Taliban. His bullet-riddled body was returned to Muslimyor's home. He'd been shot in the face, chest and back. He was only twenty-three years old.

KABUL, 2014

'Are human beings capable of abolishing war?' Insaan asked the community, and allowed them to engage in a heated discussion. Some had their doubts. Some argued war was necessary to control 'terrorists'.

Insaan thoughtfully thumbed a photo of himself with a group of fierce-looking bearded men, then passed it around the table. The community members' eyes widened, and they instinctively pushed it away from them.

'These are the Taliban,' they said, frightened and confused. 'Why are you in this photo?'

'When I was in Pakistan, I became friends with a Pakistani student,' Insaan said. 'One day he invited me to a family dinner. He made it clear that some of his brothers were members of the Taliban, but he wanted to introduce me to them because he liked me. I decided to go. I had already developed a friendship with this man and we were building trust, so I decided to trust him.'

The community members were shocked at Insaan's boldness. How could he even contemplate associating with the Taliban?

'When I arrived at the house, the family had prepared a delicious Pashtun meal, and we talked. The Taliban in the room told me they were waging a holy war – it was their religious obligation to fight against the infidels. "Why are you so angry?" I asked them. And they said, "Because we've had relatives killed in this war and we want to take revenge." They were scared of losing their religion. They believed foreigners were trying to impose their faith and way of life upon them. After the meal, they accompanied me home because the streets weren't safe. What can we learn from this story?'

The community sat in front of Insaan in silence. They were struggling with Insaan's attempt to understand people they considered enemies.

'Arash, why don't you tell your story?' Insaan said.

Arash was one of the street kids who attended the community's school. He was nervous about speaking in front of his teachers and the older community members but Insaan encouraged him to begin.

'When I was young, I didn't know that some of my relatives were involved with the Taliban. It was only after my father was killed by a suicide bomb attack in a mosque in Kabul that my grandmother and mother told me about his involvement in the group. My father became a Talib when we lived in the northern provinces of Afghanistan. We were poor and he joined the group to earn money to help feed his family. Two years ago, the Taliban attacked my family's village and killed one of my cousins. We left our village because it was too dangerous. I believe that the original intentions of the Talibs were to be good religious students but now I dislike their group. They claim to be an Islamic group, but they are a criminal group and that is what everybody recognises now. My opinion of my father hasn't changed because I understand my father's circumstances forced him to join the group.'

This was an important story for the group to hear, as it was easy to see all Talibs as 'wild beasts'. Many community members had relatives with extreme political or religious views, or relatives who had been forced into drastic measures to survive – this didn't make them evil people or enemies of the state.

'When I was a child, studying with the religious leaders of my village, I used to have fantasies of participating in a holy war in the name of Islam,' Horse said. 'If those thoughts had been allowed to grow I could have become a member of the Taliban.'

'Then you would be considered a terrorist and have to be killed,' Insaan said. 'But how would that create peace or understanding? Killing those labelled "terrorists" by waging war against them doesn't work – war and weapons don't heal the root causes of terrorism. If our brother or sister was violent, we wouldn't think of killing them to reform them. Those Taliban members shared their home with me, their meal with me and their holy war convictions. They trusted me because their relative invited me into their home. How can we achieve peace in Afghanistan if we hate and fear the Taliban? The key to peace in Afghanistan is in building relationships with the people we perceive to be our enemies.'

But Insaan knew this was easier to say than to do. Many of the community members had been victims of the Taliban.

'I don't think I can overcome this wish for revenge in my heart,' Hojar confessed. 'How can I forgive the killers of my father and embrace them as my brothers?'

'I feel your pain and I understand how much it hurts,' Insaan said. 'Gandhi said, "It is not nonviolence if we love merely those that love us. It is nonviolence only when we love those that hate us." Or in this case, those we hate. In place of war and revenge, we should perform acts of kindness.'

With this philosophy in mind, the community launched a new long-term campaign for the International Day of Peace in September. That year, the community committed to working towards a world without war.

THE DAY HOJAR'S father died, happiness disappeared from her life. Hojar lived in a small village of mudbrick homes in a wide valley that plateaued at intervals down to a river. She shared a house with her parents, her younger sister and four brothers; they all slept together in one room. Hojar often slept safely nestled in her father's protective embrace. The family were farmers, and Hojar dreaded the hard work of the planting season but looked forward to the harvest.

During the summer the family would sleep outside by the river. She would talk late into the night with her father before falling asleep to the sounds of the river splashing on rocks.

'Why are those stars a little bigger than the others?' she asked her father.

'The star that you think is the biggest belongs to you,' he replied.

She was happy back then, lying in the summer grass looking up at the stars, not knowing this would be as good as life would get.

Hojar's memories began with the Taliban and war. When she was six years old, the security situation in her province became intolerable. The Taliban invaded her province and the local men joined militia groups to fight them. Her family would go to sleep with their shoes on in case they needed to escape in the dark of the night. Gunfights were common and the family could only cower inside their house as bullets flew past the windows.

One evening it became too dangerous to remain in their home and, like many, they fled to the mountains. Her father loaded their small amount of provisions onto the family donkey and when there was a lull in the shooting they escaped into the night. Her youngest brother, Jumal, was just a baby so everyone took turns to carry him. Hojar carried him with her hands behind her back. Jumal was heavy and the ground was difficult to navigate in the dark, but he was the most precious of cargo.

That night they dodged the bombs that were falling around them, deafening explosions of dirt and trees and rock. Whenever they heard planes passing, they hid in ditches or under big trees. When they reached their destination at the skirt of the mountain, the sounds of bombs and gunfire had ceased. They were safe.

There were many other families from nearby villages gathered there. There was a spring and a stream so the people could cook their meals at night, but during the daylight hours they hid amongst the cliffs further up the mountainside. They didn't think the Taliban would come that far up the mountain, but they felt safer in the cliffs hidden from view. Here they waited for the fighting to settle down.

A couple of nights later, Hojar overheard the adults discussing in worried whispers how they had seen smoke and fire in the nearby villages.

'The Taliban are coming,' one man said.

The next morning, Hojar's family prepared their donkey to head up the mountain to the cliffs. Three of Hojar's brothers left first and then Hojar, her sister, Jumal and her father followed not long after.

'You go on ahead,' Hojar's mother said. 'Once the bread is cooked, I will catch you up.'

Halfway up the mountain, fighting started and bullets began to fly. The crack of gunfire followed Hojar and her family as they scrambled up the slope. Her father led them to a narrow crack in the mountain and said: 'Get in. Stay here.' The three other boys were nowhere to be seen. Her father sat in the front of the cave protecting the children, waiting for Hojar's mother to arrive. Many women passed by, the fighting was becoming more intense and Hojar was scared for her mother. But her mother appeared not long after, her haggard eyes brightening briefly upon seeing them. The five of them left the cave and gathered with a large group of villagers in the shadow of a boulder at the cliff they once thought was safe. Two of the men had been wounded. Then the Taliban came.

They were tall men with thick beards, dressed in traditional Afghan clothes, their heads wrapped in turbans, weapons in their hands. Their eyes were painted in black plant dye called *surma,* which illuminated their stares. One of the Talibs looked at Hojar and she dropped her gaze, staring at his bare ankles where the cuffs of his pants ended abruptly. Those hairy brown ankles didn't look so different to those of her father, she thought.

The Taliban took her father and the two injured men away.

'To talk to the mullah,' the Talibs said.

The terrified women were ordered to leave; they didn't protest, they didn't even question where the Talibs were taking the men. Shortly after that, from the direction where they had taken her father, Hojar heard gunshots. She felt her heart stutter, there was a roaring in her ears, and she was certain the Talibs had executed her father.

Her mother found Hojar's eleven-year-old brother Mahdi further up the mountain trail with the donkey. Her other two brothers, Ali and Musharat, had disappeared. They decided to return to the skirt of the mountain where they could at least cook some dinner. It was late in the afternoon and the sun would soon set. The gunfire had stopped but the mountainside looked different. The colour had faded out of it, like a dress that had lost its dye. Hojar's mother's legs gave way and she collapsed to the ground.

When they limped into the camp, there were other women and children present but no men. They'd all been killed.

The women were verging on hysteria. The loss and grief were too raw to comprehend, too sudden. Nobody knew what to do. Maybe they would be killed next. A very tall, powerful-looking Talib arrived on a horse. He assured the women and the children that he was also a Muslim and that he would not hurt them. The women decided amongst themselves that they were probably not going to be killed that evening.

Hojar's mother held out hope that her husband was alive. Even though it was late in the day, she wanted to find him, so Hojar and her mother walked back up the mountain. Hojar was hungry, she was frightened, she was feeling very weak; when it started to rain, and the light started to fade, their miserable, desperate death march ended. They had not found her father's body, but they knew they hadn't walked far enough into the mountains. The next day Hojar and her mother resumed the search, returning to where the men had been led away. Nearby they found the tossed-up soil of shallow graves and they used their hands to dig, until slowly the body of her father was revealed.

'Thank you, Papa,' she whispered through sobs. 'Thank you.'

Hojar and her mother had lost hope that her brothers had survived. Even if they had escaped the Taliban, they would die from hunger in the mountains. For weeks they waited on the mountain, asking if anyone had seen them; eventually it began to circulate that the boys too had been killed by the Taliban.

More weeks passed, then a villager told them the boys had been seen; it was barely more than a rumour and they didn't dare believe the villager. Forty days later, one of her uncles returned from across the mountains with Musharat and Ali.

During the years of Taliban control, Hojar's family was displaced from their home by violence over and over again. When news finally came that the Taliban had been defeated and there were no more Talibs in the province, the family dared to hope for peace. And a faint crack of light appeared in Hojar's long darkness.

SAEED AND I sat amongst educated, affluent Afghans at the launch of a book of poetry in the garden of an archaic building, hosted by the Afghanistan branch of PEN International.[1] At 30 years of age, Saeed was older than most of the other community members. He was a writer and an academic who ran his own private cultural organisation that provided young Afghans with a safe space in Kabul to explore the arts.

Many of the attendees were dressed ostentatiously, including the poet, who wore a traditional coat of purple silk called a *chapan*. The Afghan love of poetry, folk songs and proverbs dated back millennia. Poetry was taught in schools, even in the madrassas. Afghans celebrated winter solstice night with readings from the thousand-year-old epic poem *Shahnameh* (Book of Kings) by the Persian poet Ferdowsi, which was widely hailed in Afghanistan as a literary masterpiece. There were poetry festivals held across the country, with the two most well-known being in Nangarhar and Kandahar, called Narenj Gul (Orange Blossom) and Anaar Gul (Pomegranate Blossom). The most famous Afghan poets were treated like celebrities.[2] This love of poetry was shared across ethnic and political divides. Each language group celebrated their own writers, but all Afghans appreciated the works of the ancient Persian poets like Hafiz, Rumi and Saadi.[3]

'Even uneducated or illiterate Afghans can enjoy and participate in poetry and music,' Saeed said.

Writing poetry was often taboo for women; however, many were writing despite the dangers. The following landay was written by a Pashtun poet about child marriage.

Making love to an old man

Is like fucking a shrivelled cornstalk blackened by mould.[4]

On the stage in front of us, poets discussed the influence of the American invasion on Afghan poetry, affecting Persian accents to sound more educated. Prior to the American invasion poets used a mystical, sufi style of writing like that of Jalaluddin Rumi. Many of Afghanistan's most famous poets, artists and musicians were Sufis, followers of a form of Islamic mysticism that sought the truth of divine love and knowledge through intimate relationships with God. Conservative, fundamentalist Islamic groups like the Taliban and the Islamic State claimed followers of Sufism were idolaters and pagans, and targeted Sufis with attacks and killings.[5] The host lamented that, post 2001, the younger generation of poets were challenging traditional Afghan values and morals, writing about cigarettes, cafes, intoxication, sexuality and infidelity. Amongst this new age, bohemian self-expression was the pervasive taint of war.

'Every artist tries to express their own ideas related to peace and war and politics. There is a hopelessness in our art because of the war; because of the bleak future of the country,' Saeed said. 'Even members of the Taliban write poetry.'

I was shocked to think that the Taliban would enjoy poetry and then I immediately asked myself, *why shouldn't they?*

'Many of them are Afghans, just like us. They were also raised with poetry and literature,' Saeed said.

The Taliban's Cultural Committee produced official works of propaganda on their website, but many of the individual members also wrote their own poems unaffiliated with the party line. The content of those individuals' poems was often almost completely separate from, or a contradiction of, the religious and political ideologies of the Taliban.

The pre-2001 Taliban regime's ban on cultural activities such as music, television, cinema and art had thrown Afghanistan into a cultural depression from which it was still recovering, almost two decades later. And yet, individual Talibs were writing poems that touched upon themes of love, religion, nationalism, war, suffering and even nonviolence. Many of the poems spoke of a simple, rural Afghan lifestyle full of natural splendour, which was destroyed by the heavy weaponry of foreign forces. Some of the writers criticised the occupation of their lands by foreign soldiers and corrupt NGOs. Others lamented the loss of humanity in Afghans.

These poems illustrated how important the arts could be in building a peaceful future. With a few beautiful and well-crafted lines, I was taken past the Talibs as soldiers or 'terrorists' or religious extremists and could see their human qualities.

> A small house
> I had from father and grandfather,
> In which I knew happiness,
> My beloved and I would live there.
> They were great beauteous times;
> We would sacrifice ourselves for each other.
> But suddenly a guest came;
> I let him be for two days.
> But after these two days passed,
> The guest became the host.
> He told me, 'You came today.
> Be careful not to return tomorrow.'

Najibullah Akrami, *Poem*[6]

KABUL, 2014

Insaan, Asghar and Muslimyor sat on the floor of a hotel room. In front of them sat Owen, a handsome young American, dressed in traditional Afghan clothing. Owen was a US veteran of the war in Afghanistan and he was in the country with a small group of other veterans seeking forgiveness from Afghans for their part in the invasion.

'I went to Afghanistan to serve my country but really I was just a poor farmer being sent to kill poor farmers while people in the world were starving,' Owen said.

When Owen finished his tours and returned to the United States, he searched for salvation. He left the army, became a conscientious objector and joined the international organisation Veterans for Peace. Sadly, like many veterans of war, he turned to drugs and alcohol, and became homeless.

'We had been sold a lie,' he said. 'And we had to lie to ourselves to convince us what we were doing was right. We had to convince ourselves the Afghan farmer was the enemy.'

'Before soldiers go anywhere to fight wars, they should be made to learn about the people they are fighting against,' Asghar said. 'Maybe they would learn that those people could be their brothers and sisters.'

'Words cannot express the true depth of my feelings, but I need to try to convey my shame,' Owen said to them. 'I still suffer from nightmares about what I did here. I want to ask for your forgiveness.'

Before he left that evening, he played the banjo and sang. At the end of the song he screamed. He said he had to empty the grief and negative energy that he kept inside of him, but that didn't make it any easier for Insaan, Asghar and Muslimyor to hear.

When Owen returned to the States, he was determined to spread a message of peace and reconciliation. He kept in touch with the community, maintaining their friendship by email.

Owen took his own life shortly after President Obama announced the new US military mission against ISIS in Iraq and Syria. He was thirty-two years old. When the community heard the news, Muslimyor pulled his blanket over his face and refused to come out for the rest of the evening.

KABUL, 2014

Paiman was squashed into the back seat of a taxi alongside Hafizullah and Insaan; a bundle of kites poked their faces. It was the first day of the Persian New Year, and they were driving to a hilltop overlooking Kabul, with a wish for freedom from US and NATO drone attacks. On the way to the hilltop they passed the infamous Ghazi football stadium, where the Taliban held public executions during their reign in the 1990s. This was a place where women in pale blue burqas were stoned to death; a place where people were hanged to the fanatical cries of 'Allah Akbar' – 'God is great'. Although the horrors of that giant graveyard were from an era that pre-dated Paiman and most of the community members, the legacy was still felt by the children of the next generations. People said that the stadium was haunted and Paiman had heard that so much blood had been spilled in the stadium that grass could not grow there anymore. Now the stadium was adorned with new portraits of this government's war heroes and martyrs, the most prominent banner belonging to the Lion of Panjshir, Ahmad Shah Massoud.[7]

In the car with Paiman and the others was Hadi, a nine-year-old with spiked hair and a blue scarf wrapped tightly around his neck. Hadi never knew his father.

'My father was killed by a computer,' he told Paiman.

Hadi held a homemade banner to his chest that read: 'Fly kites, not drones!' After suffering through years of attacks by drones, the children in rural villages like the one Paiman grew up in were too afraid to fly kites because of the threat of being struck by missiles. They had learned to fear blue skies because clear, bright days were ideal for weaponised drones to see people on the ground. In light of Hadi's story, and on behalf of all Afghans, the volunteers decided to fly kites as a demonstration against the indiscriminate killings of Afghan families and to honour the deaths of their loved ones.

In the two years since Paiman joined the community his life had changed completely. He became an advocate for ethnic equality and would tell people that everyone was a human being and that they could mix and be friends with people from different ethnic groups and nationalities. He became a firm believer in the collective humanity of all citizens of the world. Since Paiman joined the community he became involved in many protests and actions, but this particular kite demonstration was personal.

It was 2007 when his brother-in-law was killed. Paiman was in the tenth grade and in his district there was fighting between United States and NATO forces and the Taliban. The local people heard that the United States was using special planes that were controlled and directed by computers to bomb areas of Pakistan, but the people weren't sure whether those planes would be used in Afghanistan. These drones didn't sound believable to Paiman and his family, but then rumours of sightings started to spread around the villages and then drones began to appear. They would arrive at dusk every day and hover in the sky until the next morning. At night they could be identified by two lights, one blue, the other red, on the wings of the plane. During the day the drones weren't easily spotted but their bumblebee buzzing quickly became familiar to the villagers and they soon learned to fear them. When the drones were about to drop bombs, they hovered a little lower in the sky and the buzzing sound filled a person's ears, scaring everyone on the ground.

One evening Paiman's brother-in-law and four friends worked together in the fields and talked as they irrigated the land. The next minute they were dead, incinerated in a drone strike operated by a pilot thousands of miles away. Paiman's brother-in-law was a friendly young man with his life ahead of him. He was a twenty-year-old student, a husband and a father to a newborn son. He was not a Talib soldier; he was not armed.

The next morning foreign NATO soldiers apologised to the villagers and offered compensation, as if the pain of losing loved ones could be assuaged by money. For the villagers, this demonstrated the foreign invaders' lack of empathy for and understanding of the Afghan people. If these soldiers' loved ones were unjustly killed would they feel 'compensated' by cash? The villagers refused the money. They wanted to know who was responsible for the strike and how they would be brought to justice.

Stricken with grief and anger for his murdered relative, Paiman expected that the media would report the international forces' version of events: according to the media, those bombings killed Taliban terrorists. No-one would be held accountable for their actions in the courts. The people in the village believed those who were directly responsible for the killings should be killed in revenge; without a person to blame, their anger was directed towards the juggernaut that inflicted the pain on their families and denied them justice.

The United States justified drone attacks because it meant they did not have to risk their own troops' lives. Use of drones absolved those responsible from guilt and distanced them from punishment. Paiman wondered if the people who operated these machines understood the trauma they caused by pressing that deadly button. He wondered if they cared. But perhaps that was unfair, because Paiman acknowledged that there was a big difference between the soldier who killed and the political and military elite who ordered him to do so. Soldiers were the tools in the hands of the elite who used war to divide and control people.

Drones called 'Reapers' and 'Predators' became a part of daily life for the people of Paiman's province. Village gossip turned into updates on drone attacks. Paiman's family didn't use lights at night, fearing becoming a target. The presence of drones in the area had a psychological effect on everyone, especially the children.

Drones were formerly used as spy planes. In 2000 the United States became the first country to successfully fit drones with missiles. There were no international laws and regulations to control the use of these drones, which allowed the United States to conduct operations in countries with which it was not technically at war. Soon the United States was using drones in at least seven countries including Pakistan, Iraq, Iran, Yemen and Somalia. The kill radius of a drone missile, known as a Hellfire anti-tank missile, was 15 metres and the established procedure for drone operations was to knowingly forfeit the lives of nearby civilians in order to assassinate someone on a 'kill list'.[8] Drone operators described children as 'fun-size terrorists' and 'tits' (terrorists in training) and used mottos to justify killing children like 'cut the grass before it grows too tall'.[9]

The Nobel Peace Prize winner Barack Obama ordered ten times more airstrikes in the US covert war on terror than his predecessor, George W Bush.[10] His administration used 'signature strikes' upon suspects whose identities were unknown but whose behaviour appeared suspicious, and 'double-tap strikes', where one strike was launched followed by a second strike hitting those people who responded, often killing civilians or rescue workers.[11] Paiman suspected his brother-in-law was killed by a 'signature strike'.

It was clear to Paiman that indiscriminate killings by drones contributed to opposition against US and NATO forces. There were hundreds of families in Afghanistan and Pakistan who were feeling the same anger and desire for revenge as Paiman's family. Many Afghans who had no particular ill-feeling for foreigners or US and NATO forces could be radicalised after their family members were murdered by drone strikes. This was a war on terror, but all it was creating was more terror.

When Paiman and the volunteers arrived at the dusty, deserted hilltop, a few lone kites battled the winds. Children played cricket amongst gravestones. Street kids begged for money to help their starving families. A young boy selling kites and rolls of twine sat on his stool, bored and glum. The view of Kabul was hazy and polluted. Wind threw dust into people's faces. This used to be a popular location for families who wanted to fly kites.

Thanks to the networking of internationals who had befriended the community, the volunteers were joined in action by over thirty peace groups in the UK, United States and Europe, all of which were holding kite-making workshops and kite-flying days in solidarity with their Afghan brothers and sisters. Although the people holding the strings were in very different circumstances, when they looked to the sky they could share the same vision of a drone-free future.

The wind picked up, and the storm clouds let go of their heavy burden. The rain fell, turning the hilltop into mud and puddles. These homemade plastic kites looked flimsy, but their flexible frames rode the wild weather like wheeling birds. When Paiman was a child, he used to fly kites on the Persian New Year with his friends and family. Now, aged twenty, he was flying one as part of a political protest. To be pulling the strings again, finding currents of air to lift the kite higher and higher, made him feel light and free.

AFGHANS CELEBRATED THE Persian New Year, or Nowruz, around March every year. It was a time to be with family and loved ones, and the community members who lived outside of Kabul took this opportunity to return home and visit their relatives. I spent Nowruz in Kabul with Insaan and Horse, visiting their friends' houses and welcoming guests of our own to the Peace House. There was a joyful, festive atmosphere among the people on the street that I hadn't seen before. Everyone was smiling and waving; little children were dressed in traditional outfits. Even Insaan seemed to forgo his usual cautiousness in public. I imagined this was what peace could look like.

Seventeen years after the US invasion, the future of political peace in Afghanistan rested upon unreliable negotiations between the government and the Taliban and other armed opposition groups. Close to forty years of conflict and corruption had damaged the country almost beyond repair and engaging in peace negotiations was like trying to build a house on shifting sands.

In 2014 the United States and its allies began to withdraw combat forces from Afghanistan. That same year, the Taliban, local warlords and other armed groups escalated hostilities. The Taliban sought a return to power and the removal of the remaining international forces, although it was unclear what a Taliban government would look like or if they would be willing to participate in the current political system. If they returned to power would they resume their persecution of women or would they follow a more moderate agenda? The corruption in the Afghan government and the economic failure of the nation over the past years had left many Afghans disillusioned with the liberal Western democracy that was supposed to revive the nation. The government and international forces' failure to protect Afghan citizens from the corruption and violence perpetrated by the warlord groups had allowed the Taliban to regain influence, even outside its traditional Pashtun heartland. They were even recruiting non-Pashtun fighters and becoming a multi-ethnic organisation.[12]

In addition to the Taliban, the country's security situation was also threatened by other loosely allied groups such as the Haqqani Network, al-Qaeda and affiliated groups, and IS-KP. The Haqqani Network was an Afghan insurgent group which formed during the Soviet invasion and was originally financially supported by the CIA. They allied themselves with the Taliban after the Taliban came to power in 1996, however, during the US invasion, they relocated their operations to Pakistan where they were supported by Pakistan's ISI. The network was linked with al-Qaeda, deploying and supporting foreign fighters in Afghanistan, and they remained one of the most potent dangers to peace in Afghanistan, capable of arranging high-profile attacks in Kabul. While Pakistan funded and protected insurgency groups like the Haqqani Network, peace would be difficult to negotiate.[13]

While the Haqqani Network shared similar goals for the future of Afghanistan with the Taliban, both al-Qaeda and the Islamic State were foreign organisations with global aims. Most al-Qaeda forces had been driven out of Afghanistan by international counter-terrorism operations. However, they continued to organise other forces and attacks in Afghanistan and, while the country remained at war, al-Qaeda could always establish itself in remote areas as it had done previously.[14]

The presence of the Islamic State in Afghanistan further complicated peace negotiations. The Islamic State originally formed in Iraq in 2006 as an alliance of Sunni insurgent groups that opposed the US invasion and wanted to create a Sunni caliphate in Iraq. The IS-KP was a branch of the Islamic State, which was primarily active in Afghanistan and Pakistan.[15] The 'KP' in the title refers to Khorasan province, a region that is now north-eastern Iran, Afghanistan north of the Hindu Kush and parts of Central Asia. The IS-KP established itself in Afghanistan in 2015, and by the end of 2016 it had increased its presence across most regions of the country. The majority of the IS-KP members operating in Afghanistan were foreign fighters, particularly from Pakistan, and Taliban defectors.[16] It was widely reported that the group's brutal methods, such as beheadings and public executions of civilians, had made the group unpopular throughout Afghanistan.[17] Despite that, the IS-KP continued to compete with the Taliban, trying to affirm itself as the only legitimate jihadi force in the region. It targeted Afghan government and international forces in the region, continuing to claim responsibility for bombings in Afghanistan.[18]

As the Taliban and other opposition groups grew in power and influence, the nation's security deteriorated. However, neither the government nor any of the opposition forces had proven themselves strong enough to win the war. Without a peace process, the most likely outcome would be ongoing war.

Since the US invasion, there had been numerous efforts to engage in peace talks. Unfortunately, these negotiations were undermined by the constantly changing state of the military intervention, which resulted in contradictory and confusing approaches from Washington, Kabul and the Taliban.[19] There was consensus among experts that the best way forward was an Afghan-owned and led peace process; however, the specifics of what that peace would look like and how it would be achieved were in dispute.[20] For example, in 2016, the Afghan National Unity Government signed a peace agreement with the notorious warlord Gulbuddin Hekmatyar, the 'Butcher of Kabul', and his Hezb-i-Islami militia. The deal was considered controversial and sparked heated public debate about war crimes and reconciliation, but it was the first significant peace agreement with an insurgent.

The Afghan government's reliance on the United States appeared to be a significant stumbling block in peace negotiations. A bilateral security agreement between the United States and Afghanistan allowed more than 12,000 foreign military personnel, which included 9800 US troops, to remain to assist Afghan troops. In addition to that, more than 26,000 private contractors were employed in Afghanistan.[21] In 2018 Ashraf Ghani admitted that the United States bankrolled 90 per cent of Afghanistan's defence budget of approximately US$4 billion a year and that, without this support, the Afghan army would collapse within six months.[22] With this financial dependence in mind, the Taliban's hope for the withdrawal of the remaining international forces seemed unlikely.

Prospects for peace were further hampered when President Trump deployed 3000 more American troops to Afghanistan in 2017, a reversal on his pre-election Tweets that criticised the US presence in Afghanistan.[23] Since then, the United States significantly increased the number of airstrikes, bombings, and missiles dropped on the country.[24] Some 4361 bombs were dropped on Afghanistan in 2017, including the 11-tonne Massive Ordnance Air Blast bomb, which was nicknamed the 'Mother of All Bombs'.[25]

It made me think of Muslimyor's response to my question about the possibility of peace in Afghanistan.

'Foreign nations have their own agendas in Afghanistan.'

The truth was the world's superpowers still had vested interests in the country. A US Geological Survey study in 2010 estimated that untapped Afghan minerals were worth from $1–3 trillion. China Metallurgical Group Corp controlled the world's largest untapped copper deposits, a

$3 billion mine at Mes Aynak in Logar province, although operations had not yet commenced due to security concerns.[26] In recent years, Erik Prince, the founder of the private military company Blackwater (now known as Academi) and more recently the chairman of logistics firm Frontier Services Group, had been trying to convince the US government to privatise the Afghan war and exploit the country's minerals.[27]

Afghanistan remained a field of war where the US could trial its military hardware; where weapons manufacturers and private security companies profited from the misery of the Afghan people. The increase in troop numbers and airstrikes were hardly attempts to win the war in Afghanistan, as Trump claimed.[28] Before President Obama announced its withdrawal, the United States maintained an estimated force of 140,000 troops in Afghanistan. Rather, Trump's decision indicated that the US cared more about maintaining its strategic presence in the region than negotiating peace in Afghanistan.

Considering how fragile and unreliable these peace negotiations were, was it so unrealistic for Insaan and the volunteers to seek alternative roads to peace? Negotiating peace in Afghanistan would be an exercise in trust and compromise. In order to end the conflict, people would have to shake hands with their enemies. What better way to approach that process than through Insaan and the community's philosophy: to start with the nation's inner peace and work their way outwards.

Chapter 19

Part of a Great Human Family

KABUL, 2014

Soban was a stirrer who liked to antagonise the other community members. One night, as the community were enjoying dinner, Soban announced: 'Why should we say our prayers?'

That was too much for Muslimyor, who was young and religiously conservative and wouldn't compromise on his faith, with prayer being one of the five main pillars of Islam. He took these attacks on his religion personally. 'I can't cope with this,' he shouted, tears running down his face, and stormed out of the room.

This was not the first time Muslimyor had been upset by the actions of people in the community, especially Soban, but this was the incident that broke Muslimyor's resilience.

Muslimyor was tired of community life and the conflicts between community members. There were mundane arguments over how to clean the teapot; whether they should use more oil or less oil in the cooking; whether they should sweep their own rooms every day. Some of the community members preferred to be loud and rowdy and some preferred to be quieter. Conversations with Hamza were usually intense and could be heated. The challenge for Muslimyor and the other community members was that this was the first time they had ever lived in a shared environment such as this.

Muslimyor found it difficult to resolve these issues because most Afghans weren't in the habit of talking about problems openly and honestly, certainly not criticising one's elders. He was fearful that if he pointed out unfinished work, community members might get angry at him. The fear of a bad reaction would grip him for weeks.

One day, money was stolen from Insaan. The community knew who committed the crime, but they didn't want to accuse the person of having stolen it. They held a meeting and announced to all the volunteers in the group, 'If anyone knows what happened to the money and is able to return it, please leave the money in this spot.' The money was returned anonymously but the group wanted closure, so they held another meeting to agree on a narrative that would resolve the issue. They decided that the volunteer liked the group and Insaan so much that he was generous enough to pay the money out of his own pocket. It was a uniquely Afghan way of dealing with a crime.

Organising action on behalf of the community also had its pitfalls. There were those who preferred to engage with concepts and ideas as opposed to those who liked action. There were those who liked to be at the centre of attention, compared to those who preferred to work behind the scenes. There were those who tended to talk less but do more versus those who talked more than they did. Some community members proved themselves to be more reliable than others. This created perceptions of who was better or worse, and it bred jealousy and distrust. Fear of open criticism made community operations a delicate haggling process.

The responsibilities of the community projects weighed heavy upon Muslimyor's shoulders. He was making decisions and in charge of some projects – yet he often felt filled with self-doubt. To make matters more stressful, his family were experiencing difficulties at home. They were a big extended family of his parents, his siblings, his older brothers' wives, even their grandfather, all living under one roof. Personality clashes in the family had resulted in family members deciding to live in separate houses, as neighbours rather than family. Muslimyor's father and mother were left alone with just his younger brother in their house.

Winter was almost over, the duvet project was coming to an end, and, with spring around the corner, Muslimyor decided he needed to go home and support his parents. He didn't know if he would return. The community feared the worst.

When Horse learned Muslimyor was leaving, he was devastated. He didn't want to live in the community without his best friend, although he never admitted that to anyone else in the community. Despite the community members making assurances that they would stand by one another, Horse approached Insaan and talked to him about also leaving the community.

'Why don't you think about it? You don't want to rush into a decision,' Insaan said, fully understanding Horse's transparent motivations.

Horse had already been thinking of returning home to support his struggling family. Horse's eldest brother was unable to find work to pay off his marriage debt and so the family were surviving on his mother's income from washing clothes. His brother's new wife had moved into the family house, but she had clashed with Horse's mother and the couple had moved into a room behind the house. Horse's mother now felt alone in her own home.

When Muslimyor completed his school transfer papers, it was clear no-one was going to be able to persuade him to stay. A week after Muslimyor left, Horse completed his own school transfer papers in secret, not wanting to tell the community he was leaving until the last moment. Two people leaving the community in the same week was a crippling blow to the other community members, especially to Asghar and Hafizullah.

After Horse and Muslimyor returned to the mountains, they called the community every two weeks, catching up on news and staying involved with the work. Horse still agonised over his broken agreement with the community. He vowed that when his mother's situation became manageable then he would return.

Their absence in the community was keenly felt by Hafizullah, who desperately missed his friends. He had come to Kabul at their request and now he didn't know if they would ever return. Hafizullah didn't feel betrayed – he accepted their explanations – but this didn't help to ease his sadness.

Insaan saw his despair and tried to reassure him. 'Missing people is awful,' he said. 'It's a bittersweet feeling, but it's also a privilege. It's one of the most beautiful emotions a person can feel. Because the more of the human family you discover, the more people you love, the more you will miss them and the more you ought to miss them. And you will learn in this great human family, we are all part of one another.'

For Muslimyor, the break provided him with a chance to reflect on what the community meant to him. He had been with Insaan and the community for many years. He learned about values such as truth and love, but he had his doubts. Were these ideas of peace realistic? Or was this group just a way to expend the energies of the youth? But he knew that when they worked together, ethnicity or religious sect became irrelevant – he'd lived it in the community. What was important was cooperation and generosity. What was important was helping the poor and vulnerable.

By the time Muslimyor and Horse returned, the community had changed dramatically. Just when the group looked like it was breaking apart, they decided to create a female community.

KABUL, 2015

It was nine o'clock at night and Yalda was missing. Hojar had tried calling Yalda several times but her phone was off. It wasn't the first time Yalda had disappeared, unreachable, but it didn't make it any easier to cope with her unpredictability. Hojar had no way of knowing where Yalda was, who she was with, and if she was safe or not. The unofficial curfew of nightfall usually regulated most people's behaviour, but Yalda could be a law unto herself.

'What do we do?' Rahela fretted.

'We pray for her return,' Hojar said.

It had taken Hojar time to prepare herself for the challenge of starting a female live-in community. The philosophy was that if she could establish a female community similar to the male community there would be, on a physical level, a clearer representation of their equality and their partnership to address ethnic divisions. They would be able to strengthen one another by sharing the burden of the work. While Hojar appreciated the theoretical positives of such a community, she had seen how difficult making a success of the male community could be, and she was wary of putting that kind of pressure on herself. It was during troublesome nights such as this that Hojar thought of the advice Insaan had given her before she committed to the project.

'You will be faced with the same challenges that I have faced, and you will try to place the burden on your shoulders, but they are not problems that are within your control.'

'I'll take up the challenge,' she said to Insaan, resolute and determined in her mission.

It was very hard to find women from any ethnic group whose family would allow them to live with strangers outside of their family home. A family from Kabul would never allow their daughter to live in a share house in Kabul. So Hojar was limited to asking women from rural provinces who had come to the city to study. Rahela, Yalda and Hojar were the only three who volunteered, and they were all Hazara.

The three of them decided to start the experiment anyway, despite the lack of ethnic diversity, with the hope that over time they could inspire other women to join their community. They adopted the agreements of behaviour and participation made by the male community and settled into their different routines. Each of the women had their own habits, personalities and approach to living. Rahela was generally a quiet person who didn't like crowds. One of her legs was weaker and a little shorter than the other and when she walked long distances on the street she would tire easily. She was comfortable being on her own, working around the house. Like all Afghan women, she participated in the cleaning, cooking and gardening.

When Yalda joined the community, she confessed to Hojar and Rahela, 'I need a space to heal.'

Over time in community Yalda slowly revealed how significant her psychological problems were. Though each of them had suffered their own individual traumas, Yalda had been swept up in one shocking event that still haunted her.

'Fatimah was a friend of mine. She was a very sweet girl,' Yalda once told them.

'What happened to her?' Hojar asked.

'We were travelling by bus from Kabul to Herat and she carried her identification papers. I don't know why she did that.'

Afghans knew not to carry any identification papers when travelling across the country, especially identification papers from a government office or international organisation.

'The bus was stopped by thieves or militia or Taliban. It doesn't matter who. They stopped the bus and they unloaded the passengers and they checked our papers.

'I begged them not to kill her, but they did. They cut her head off in front of me.'

Such horrors were beyond comprehension for the other women. There were days when Yalda suffered physical pains that would not go away, no matter what painkillers or medication she was prescribed. The days in which she was like this, Hojar and Rahela could not do anything to comfort her. All they could do was stay with her, without knowing when or how she would calm down. There were also days when she would not eat, when she could not sleep at night, or when she disappeared entirely. And on nights like this, her trauma affected the whole community.

The door banged open and in strode a very tall, elegantly dressed woman of regal bearing. She had high, defined cheekbones and emerald eyes that gave her an almost haughty look. This evening, Yalda looked haggard. The corners of her eyes were red and strained. The mischievous twinkle in her eyes was dull. Her usually powerful voice faltered, and she collapsed to the floor. Hojar and Rahela sprang across the room to comfort her.

'Where were you?' Rahela asked.

'With Pelabo,' she whispered.

Yalda not only had historical traumas to overcome, but she had fallen in love with Pelabo, a young Pashtun man. It was a romance that divided their families, who disapproved of an interethnic relationship. But neither Yalda nor Pelabo were willing to give up their love for each other.

Their little female community of three stayed together for one year. They lived in a quiet two-storey mudbrick home with a very small kitchen. They had a garden where they grew vegetables and plants and there was a well in the yard from which they drew water. They lived in a residential area filled with families, so the three women pretended to be related to each other in order to avoid attention. However, in that close-knit, high-density community everyone knew each other, and their neighbours grew suspicious of the unusual activities at the house.

The controversy reached its peak when the neighbours noticed female international guests were visiting the community. Rumours and gossip spread. A neighbour asked Hojar if their strange guests were family members. There were times when some neighbours followed them to see what they were doing. One neighbour openly asked why international visitors were coming to stay with them. The owner of the house made impromptu checks to try and catch the girls out. Because he had keys, he could open their front door and access the yard without their permission or knowledge.

Mary Smith visited the community on a few occasions. She became like a mother to Hojar, offering advice and teachings. During one of her stays, they told her that if the owner entered the yard she would have to hide herself. One day there was a knock on the door, and Mary immediately closed the door to her room and lay under a blanket. It turned out their unexpected guest was Rahela and they laughed about how Mary tried to disappear herself.

During that time, Yalda and Pelabo became engaged and Yalda decided she wanted to live with her future in-laws. Hojar believed that Yalda found healing in the community. Living in a community gave her the space to share her stories and express her trauma. But community could not cure Yalda of all her demons and it was clear that she was not coping with the multitude of stresses in her life. After Yalda's announcement, Rahela explained that she also wanted to leave the community. She was going to graduate from university the next year and there were plans for her to be married, so she felt social pressure to leave the community and return to live with her family. Truth be told, Hojar was also, gradually, becoming so stressed that she couldn't cope with community life. And so, the female community decided to naturally part ways without ill will.

While Yalda left the live-in community, she remained a member of the wider group. A few months after Rahela left the community, she moved to Canada. Before she left she visited Hojar one more time.

'I'll only be there for two years,' Rahela said. 'I'm going to get an operation on my leg.'

Although she used words that portrayed excitement, Hojar wasn't sure if she was actually happy with the move. Hojar acknowledged that in terms of security Canada was a much better place, but Rahela's mother and her family members were going to remain in Afghanistan. A lot of young Afghans, like those undergraduates she met at university, seemed to prefer the idea of life in another country. Hojar understood the desire to leave. She understood how and why people felt tired of life in Afghanistan. She thought it was a legitimate right to want a safer life and she could understand how people might imagine that life in other countries would make them happy, but she also predicted that if she went to another country there would be numerous unforeseen challenges to resettling. There would be cultural and language barriers, society might not be so accepting of Afghans and she wouldn't have the same social and familial networks to support her as she did in Kabul. Rather than feed this desire to search for a safer life, Hojar felt a responsibility to work for the betterment of her country. She didn't want future generations to look back on this era and say that her generation was selfish and didn't try to effect change.

After Rahela left Afghanistan, Hojar stopped hearing from her. Hojar heard from mutual friends that Rahela had cut off contact with her friends in Afghanistan. Despite their lack of contact, Hojar was confident that Rahela had not forgotten their friendship. Hojar was satisfied with the female community experiment. It brought the three of them closer together in the embrace of working for a common purpose. They learned to understand each other and dealt with their past traumas and the challenges of living in community by sharing experiences. She felt confident that, though Rahela had gone to Canada, she would take the community philosophy with her. Rahela's parting gift to the community was introducing her brother to the group, so the connection with the community carried on.

WHEN THE MALE LIVE-IN community collapsed in 2015, the group didn't part ways amicably. It imploded. The challenges among the community were numerous and constant. Each member struggled with their own individual historical traumas, wounds that were reopened with every attack in Kabul. This jeopardised the development of relationships and trust in a community where there were already frequent arguments around domestic concerns. The arguments over household responsibilities drew battle lines in the house between young and old. Soon, the older members of the community stopped participating in community activities. It became apparent that they were enjoying the benefits of the house, the free food and accommodation, without assuming any of the responsibilities expected to maintain the community.

Eventually the younger members of the community found the inequalities within the community had become unbearable. After much deliberation amongst themselves and Insaan, they decided to host a meeting in which they would express their views. This was a major step for a community that tried to avoid conflict or criticism. They were essentially challenging the cultural hierarchy of age. But if they could not address this issue within their own experimental community, how could they hope to communicate revolutionary ideas of peace to the greater Afghan society?

When confronted with their past behaviour, the older members of the community refused to acknowledge any wrongdoing. They accused Insaan of bias and discrimination. They did not commit to changing their behaviour because they believed they hadn't done anything wrong.

'We think the older members of the community who are not willing to do actual work should separate from the main community,' Abdul said.

Immediately the older members of the community became even more defensive and aggressive.

'Why should we leave the community? The resources are there for us as well. We have the right to room and board.'

When Insaan first accepted funds from an international organisation he dreaded the corruptive power of money. It appeared his worst fears had been realised. These young men had developed a sense of entitlement to the community privileges and assumed that once they had joined the community they were there for good. The minute their source of free accommodation and food was withdrawn they panicked.

The younger members of the community realised that in order to negotiate the separation they would have to reword the conditions. Instead of the older members being asked to leave the community, the younger members said they were opting out. The younger community members began searching for a new house to move into. As the community divided and fell apart, many of the older members of the community decided to leave on their own terms. But they didn't go quietly – instead they left an enormous exit wound.

The first act of retaliation came from Zilal. In the weeks leading up to the date of separation, the date Insaan and the younger community members would move house, Insaan discovered Zilal was stealing money and items from the community and its members. The community agreed that Insaan should arrange a one-on-one meeting with Zilal to resolve the issue peacefully. However, when Insaan approached him, Zilal refused to acknowledge he had committed any such crime. The next day he left the community without a trace.

Insaan suggested the best way forward would be to forgive Zilal and forget the crimes he had committed. Some of the volunteers grew frustrated with Insaan's insistence on nonviolent methods.

'Why don't we do it the Afghan way?' they said.

The implication was to use violence, a notion Insaan explicitly refused to accept.

'At least contact the police,' they said.

'Do you think the police will resolve this matter peacefully?' Insaan asked.

It was agreed that involving the police would make the community complicit in any resulting violence.

'We can forgive but we shouldn't be weak,' a community member said.

These were trying times for the community. Their core philosophy was being questioned and challenged by their own members. Zilal did not return their money, but they stayed true to their principles of nonviolence and chose forgiveness instead of a violent reaction to his crimes.

The second act of retaliation was much more personal. One day, when all the other community members were away from the house, Mirwais found Insaan alone in the basement. He stopped at the entrance to the stairwell, blocking Insaan's only exit.

'Take me with you,' Mirwais said.

Insaan looked up at Mirwais in surprise. His face was contorted, a transparent reflection of an inner struggle.

'This is a community. I can't make that decision on behalf of everyone,' Insaan said.

Mirwais advanced towards Insaan in a threatening manner and Insaan feared things were about to get violent.

'Let's settle this matter right here,' Mirwais said, his voice taking on a dangerous tone.

A horrible thought passed through Insaan's mind: no-one outside the house could hear shouts from the basement. To be turned on by one of his own left Insaan feeling paralysed. Insaan's heartbeat accelerated dramatically, but he remained calm and disconnected from the threat, as if this situation had nothing to do with him and they were speaking to another man in the room.

Insaan braced himself for an attack but instead Mirwais picked up his phone and said he would call the police. Insaan was stunned by this move. There was no way of knowing what he might accuse him of and what the police would do when they arrived.

Insaan could feel his world seesawing. All that he had worked for – the community and their projects, the years he had invested in Afghanistan and the peace movement – it was all on the brink of destruction, being brought down from the inside by this desperate young man. Insaan was shaking uncontrollably, his knees wobbled and his body trembled. It was all happening so fast. He just needed Mirwais to calm down.

'This is not useful at all. You are using very threatening words,' Insaan said, attempting to engage him in dialogue.

The tension in the basement boiled and expanded and contracted.

'Insaan, you should know better than this. In Afghanistan, using threatening words is not violent. Don't you know what killing is?' Mirwais said.

'I know what killing is,' Insaan said. 'But right now, you should not be lashing out at me. It doesn't help the situation. This is not the community philosophy.'

Just as the stand-off seemed ready to escalate, the front door banged open. Muslimyor and Horse had returned home from school. Mirwais looked at Insaan, like a desperate kid, and then he ran out of the house, never to return.

It was difficult to see how Mirwais thought this act of aggression would work with the community in the long term, but Insaan saw a scared young man who was losing his home and his friends. He was losing a safe environment and being thrust back into the cut-throat Kabul city life.

The third act of retaliation came from Hamza. A year after he had disappeared from community life, he sent Insaan an email that brought fear, anxiety and uncertainty roaring back into their lives.

'I want money to help me with my university education. I will report you to the police if you don't help me.'

Hamza's poor mental health had already been the cause of drama and tension in the house, but the threat implicit in the email was out of the blue. Insaan didn't want to think about the impact of such a vengeful tip-off.

Soon after, Hamza returned to the community, confronting Insaan when he was alone in the yard. Hamza was clearly agitated, and he moved around with a strange jitteriness, eyes darting to and fro.

'If you haven't got the money, I'm going to get the police.'

Insaan tried to reason with Hamza.

'I don't have the amount of money you are asking for. Search me and take whatever I have on me,' he said.

But Hamza was not listening. 'I will shut down this group,' he said, pacing and slapping his legs, working himself into a state. Then he snatched a piece of broken glass from the ground and placed it against his own wrist. He pleaded with Insaan, distressed, tears in his eyes.

'I need this money.'

Then, before Insaan could react, Hamza slashed at his wrist and slumped to the ground, deflated. Luckily the cut was shallow and not life-threatening, but Insaan washed the wound and bandaged it nonetheless, gently talking to Hamza as the crisis seemed to pass.

'This is not helpful,' Insaan said. 'You're hurting yourself. It can't be resolved like this. We love you, but we don't love what you are doing.'

Insaan sat in the yard with Hamza until quite late, allowing the young man to slowly calm down. Eventually Hamza left without saying anything more. It was the last Insaan and the community saw of him. They later found out he had fled to Europe seeking asylum.

INSAAN STRODE ALONG the mountain path sucking the fresh, cold air deep into his lungs. He stood high above Kabul, looking down upon its blanket of smog. By 2015, after four years in the city, he still found peace of mind in the mountains.

'Is the mountain a living or non-living thing?' he asked the young community members who had accompanied him on the walk.

They passed dormant shrubs and freshly dug graves; the mountain peaks loomed above them.

'The mountains are alive,' Horse said.

'If anyone is drowning with too many thoughts, they should allow nature to calm them,' Abdul reflected.

Insaan found it hard not to feel a sense of failure when thinking of the ex–community members. He had devoted time, energy and emotion into nurturing their humanitarian spirit, into educating them in the philosophies of nonviolence. It was painful to watch those community members abandon the community so dramatically. Their reactions were a product of an Afghan society that had adopted violence as the immediate response to disagreement. These threats showed the community just how difficult it would be for Afghan society to achieve peace.

Many of the members had questioned whether the work was worth the risk, but they found strength in their adherence to their principles of nonviolence. The group were learning through experience how to speak consistently and firmly with troubled people and to negotiate threats.

Insaan was dragged away from his thoughts by the impact of snow on the back of his neck. Suddenly the air was patterned by soft balls of powder, and merry laughter raised their spirits: the mountain had revived them.

Out of the ruins of the larger live-in community, the younger men banded together, united in their determination to continue their work and learn from their failures rather than be demoralised by them. They realised it was time to shift the focus of the community away from their living arrangements to a neutral setting. A community centre.

Chapter 20

A New Direction
for the Community

KABUL, 2015

In the garden of a shabby-looking building with a distressed facade, a large green, blue, red and yellow circus tent had been pitched. Inside the tent, a carnival atmosphere was brewing. At the front there was a stage decorated with rugs, ribbons and balloons. Facing this were rows of chairs occupied by a diverse group of people differing in age, gender, ethnicity, religious sect and nationality. The first rows were reserved for special guests: elders in suits with slick hair, members of civil society groups wearing elegant hijabs, and dignified religious figures. Mary Smith sat next to Insaan, beaming with pride. Behind the dignitaries sat the community members, university students, street kids, and their family members, dressed in their finest attire, all restless with excitement. The tent was so full, people stood around the outer edges trying to peer in. All were gathered to celebrate the opening of the new community centre.

Muslimyor and Hafizullah acted out a theatrical scene on stage as part of the afternoon's entertainment. Muslimyor's caricature of a frail old man had the younger members of the crowd laughing uproariously. The greedy old geriatric was trying to sell his daughter to the highest bidder, which happened to be the lecherous Hafizullah who coveted the pretty bachelorette with overt smacking of his lips. The moral of the skit was to discourage the selling of daughters like cattle. This was followed by poetry readings from community members and then Insaan addressed the crowd.

'A better world is not only possible; it is being built right now. If you have pain or mistrust in your heart, befriend someone from another ethnic group today. If you've made a mistake, ask for forgiveness. Reconcile with a handshake or an embrace. That is the love that opens the borders in our hearts. That same love will open the borders in our minds. With that same love don't think of others as Sunni or Shia, just think of them as Muslims.'

'They're humans,' the crowd responded.

The opening of the Community Centre was a pivotal moment for Insaan and the community. It was a necessary and important transition from the chaotic and self-destructive live-in community to a more structured and inclusive program based at this shared day centre. It precipitated a surge in participation from those volunteers who had never lived in community. Suddenly they were becoming involved in the activities every week. Those volunteers felt more connected with the work and began to describe the community as their family. After the transition to the centre, the group was no longer embroiled in the domestic challenges of the live-in community and any sense of proprietorial ownership of the work seemed to have been eradicated, allowing space for the new volunteers.

The members of the live-in community who had family in Kabul, such as Abdul, returned to their homes. The Stalwarts from the mountains and Insaan had no family in Kabul to whom they could return, so they rented a house together. This arrangement became known as the Peace House. Responsibility to host the community's international visitors was transferred to the new Peace House.

After the centre opened, the community work began to develop along clearer and better-defined lines. The teams began to be grouped in three broad areas targeting a green, equal and nonviolent world. They started regular coordinator meetings at the centre. As the community grew and the coordinators became more influential and invested in the work, they incorporated the system of consensual decision-making.

The community's interest in issues that affected humanity and the world encouraged Insaan to formalise his education sessions in community and soon he was hosting regular classes called relational learning circles. In the next years they wanted to embed this way of learning through relationships and stories, and creative, radical, grassroots-based thinking. They continued to develop partnerships locally and internationally to widen their scope and there were plans afoot to establish an institute of nonviolence at a local university.

As activities developed around the Community Centre, Insaan realised this was a more replicable model for the rest of the country than living together across ethnic and religious divides had been. Afghans could learn to incorporate the group's philosophies into everyday practices, such as in social situations or at places of work. If people intentionally worked at those issues that divided them, if they learned practical ways of being nonviolent, there was a potential for the community's work to grow into a national movement.

I SAT WITH Insaan, Hojar and the Stalwarts on the floor of the Community Centre sharing a final meal of bean stew and bread before I returned to Australia. Warmth emanated from the *bukhari*, my close friend during the cold days and nights in Kabul. Now that I had heard the community's remarkable story in full, the challenges seemed far greater than I had ever imagined. But that hadn't dulled the community's ambition. These volunteers were children of the post-9/11 world. They lived in a wasteland of warfare; their country was on the verge of economic destruction, hounded for resources by a predatory international community; and the effects of climate change were only going to worsen in their lifetime. Instead of seeing the future as hopeless, the volunteers assumed the responsibility to fix the world one small act at a time. If their generation didn't, who would?

When I looked at Muslimyor, I tried to imagine him as a young boy with his gangster moves, trudging along the shale slopes, gathering firewood for his family. I marvelled at his transformation into the leader I had befriended. When I first asked him about any low points in the community, a pained look twisted his face, as if my question dredged up unpleasant memories. None of the Stalwarts, nor Insaan, wanted to be seen as criticising their friends and former community members. In a country where blood feuds between families prolonged conflict for decades, the community didn't want to breathe new life into past disputes. But they accepted that these stories were an important part of their history that could not be ignored, and so they faced their fears and opened up to me.

Muslimyor had been so scared by the threats and disheartened by the breakdown of the live-in community that he had contemplated quitting the group altogether. Through studying the lives of figures like Gandhi and Martin Luther King, and discussing within the community the problems that they faced, he began to understand that the community was engaged in a long-term struggle and in that struggle there were bound to be difficulties, including betrayal.

'I learned from Gandhi that a successful person falls but gets up again. The successful person will never give up,' Muslimyor said.

Muslimyor had found the transition of activities and focus from the live-in community to the Community Centre difficult at first. He struggled with feelings of ownership and how to balance his feelings towards new community members. Eventually he was able to acknowledge the newer volunteers' role was necessary to grow the work and was an equal contribution in the development of the community. The original members could not allow the work to stagnate. In undertaking the work with the community, he was gradually finding what he thought was the meaning of life. He was learning how to be humane to others, how to empathise, and how to become part of a community and a society. He was nurturing the practice of humanity.

Then there was Horse. When he first met Insaan and joined the group, all he wanted was to make new friends. He had matured from a boy trying to find himself and make sense of the world into a steady and reliable community member. He had shown courage, persistence and kindness to volunteer his time to organise the first food cooperative in Afghanistan, battling Kabul's 'corruption tsunami', as Insaan called it. Along the way, he'd emerged from Muslimyor's shadow and found his own strong voice.

'I have learned the value of humanity and I have learned how to coexist with other people in society. I feel like I have a better understanding of myself, other human beings and the world. And most importantly, I have made friends,' he said.

Horse felt that if he continued with this line of work his life would be full of meaning. He was too young to think deeply about his future with the community and his life goals and plans, but he was determined to lift himself and his family out of the cycle of poverty. Life would change, especially when he married and had a family, and then he would have to reconsider his priorities.

'I can't imagine where or how I will meet my wife. Perhaps I will meet her at university,' he said.

That sweet boy who loved romance films was always wondering about love.

Hafizullah didn't know if he would continue to be involved in the struggle, but regardless of where their futures would take them, he felt that the sense of family ties among the Stalwarts would always be there. His personal wish was to study dancing at college or university, but this was not possible in Afghanistan. There was no school for dance in the entire country. If he wanted to pursue such an education, he would need to go abroad. To even have the ambition of completing his education was a miracle for Hafizullah and he had the community to thank for that. Now he was literate; he had just finished reading *All Men Are Brothers* by Gandhi and a book by an Afghan writer on violence against women. He could also use the internet – it turned out he had a great appetite for knowledge, which promised him an exciting life of learning. Hafizullah didn't associate his memories of illiteracy and his troubles at school with shame. Remembering those days gave him hope to achieve the seemingly impossible.

When Hafizullah thought back to before he met Insaan, he was amazed at the change in his character and life philosophies. Previously he would never have sat with foreigners; interaction with people who didn't share the Islamic faith was forbidden. Nowadays, he felt at ease socially, in the community and in wider society. He could sit down in a group of strangers to discuss social and political issues. He didn't think of his generation as the future of Afghanistan. It would be the next generation who would bring a seismic shift to Afghanistan's fortunes. He just hoped he could help build the foundations for peace.

Perhaps I reserved my greatest admiration for Hojar. From a very young age she refused to submit to society's expectations, despite the many pressures to do so. She avoided telling people about the work she did because misunderstandings could endanger her life – she was fearful of harassment or targeted violence from strangers, but also from her own relatives. At some point she realised she desired freedom more than she feared persecution, joining the community to be an instigator for change. She believed the community could change society, as long as the Afghan people had the resolve to accommodate the changes.

'The biggest impediment to our work is society itself,' she said. 'To overcome that barrier, the individual needs to change their way of thinking. Otherwise they will be trapped in what society expects them to do. If I hadn't taken the risk to leave the mountains and move to Kabul perhaps I would never have engaged in this struggle.'

In her home province she assumed a solemn demeanour because girls were discouraged from laughing aloud. She found these expectations hampered and restricted her personality and her identity. When she moved to Kabul she felt there was a space for her to discover laughter and happiness; she felt like she could truly be herself.

Hojar worried about Insaan. She worried about what might happen if he was no longer around. His energy, his encouragement and his love were invaluable to the community. However, if something did happen to him, she was determined to face the challenge of continuing the work in his absence.

'Insaan has taken the first steps and he has left footprints for the community to follow in,' she said. 'And that's what we will endeavour to do.'

Despite all the hardships of Afghanistan, there were happy stories. One beautiful spring day, the community members filled a bus and travelled to a small village to celebrate the wedding of Hojar's Hazara former housemate, Yalda, and her Pashtun fiancé, Pelabo. The seemingly doomed love affair had officially been accepted by their families. Hojar and the female community members from Kabul sat with the female relatives of the bride and groom in a large tent, with brightly decorated gowns, fashionable hairdos and cosmetics; young and not so young women took turns dancing and singing. Hojar marvelled at this marriage across ethnic boundaries and saw it as a step forward.

Hojar thought her father would be proud of her. He was a peaceful man who wanted a better life for his family. 'Perhaps his death was my greatest motivator to continue the work with the community. I don't want any girl or boy to experience the pain and loss I felt.'

She looked up at me and smiled. It was a humble expression of defiance. As if to say, 'This is who I am. The real me.'

When I left Insaan and the Stalwarts that day I knew there was a high likelihood I might never see them again. I had grown fond of these inspirational young peace activists and in them I saw the real success of the community. With a nurturing hand, Insaan had shaped their intellectual, philosophical and emotional growth from children of the mountains into humanists. The constructive actions and projects of the community were a manifestation of this education, but I felt their transformative individual stories had the most power to spread peace. They were the future of Afghanistan and shone a light for the rest of the country to follow.

WHEN INSAAN WAS in high school, his classmates used to describe him as being wooden and impersonal.

'You are always asking what objective there is to a meeting, an activity or an event.'

He realised his relationships were more objective than they were relational.

During those long nights in the mountains, he dwelled on the worthwhile human struggle – but he often felt overwhelmed. He cried at night because he didn't want other people to see his emotions. He thought he had grown up and moved past the age of crying. As a young person, he thought emotional people were weak.

Perhaps he inherited this aversion to crying from his mother, a stoic woman who never shed a tear in front of him. Even when he left the family home for Pakistan she didn't cry. She said goodbye and slipped a handwritten note into his pocket. When Insaan read the note, he cried because he knew she was releasing him.

'My little treasure, I am behind you all the way.'

He now realised she had been crying on the inside.

In community, Insaan became raw. He couldn't hide his emotions. He became vulnerable. His flaws were seen. His anger was clear. There were times when he hated himself for it. *How ugly I have become.* Insaan had been to the depths of despair and he had considered giving up. But at the same time, he became in touch with his feelings. He found the darkest parts of himself and he came back to love.

When the live-in community disbanded, all their work appeared lost. But the community evolved; the strength of the community remained. Insaan reflected on the process of growth: of pruning, of reforming, individually and as a group. At times that process involved taking two steps forward and one step back. Humans were as much people of emotion as they were of reason, he thought, they were not mutually exclusive. Humans could not be reasonable people if they were not in touch or at peace with their emotional selves and the emotional lives of other people. Perhaps the distrust between tribes, between Pakistan, Afghanistan, Iran, Russia and the United States, could not be overcome through logic or traditional application of diplomacy. Perhaps the people who sat down at the negotiating table needed to acknowledge they were influenced by their own emotions or psychological scars.

When Insaan first left his home, he wanted to save the world, but he'd since learned that individuals couldn't do that. He'd moved far away from seeking contentment from success, influence or wealth. For Insaan, inner happiness, joy, contentment, or even peace, was doing what you wanted to do. Working with community was what he wanted to do.

Insaan thought that the indomitable strength of love was mysterious, that its strength might not be scientifically proven yet, but it could be proven sociologically. Roosevelt spoke of it when he said the science of human relationships would save mankind.[1] That atomic fusion of love in relationships was one of the most powerful values of life. Humanity's organisational constructs would come and go – economic, political and military structures would rise and fall – but our pursuit of love was everlasting. Insaan believed the key to humanity's survival was if we could understand and harness that power.

Insaan hoped that our evolution as humans would see us embody love of ourselves and of our Mother Earth. We needed to learn how to lead our lives without undermining the world around us and our very existence. We needed to reclaim our place in the universe and return to a state of interconnectedness.

Insaan's thoughts often turned to Amaan, the little boy he had befriended in Pakistan all those years ago. Insaan hoped Amaan was still alive. If he was, he'd be nearly thirty. Anything could have happened to him – he could have become radicalised, he could have become a Talib.

But Insaan knew that such a path was not taken because someone was inherently evil but because they were a victim of war. They'd all been children of war.

Insaan's journey started with a personal connection between a young doctor wanting to save the world and a child trying to live a life safe from violence. Ever since Insaan had met Amaan he had been on a mission to better the lives of all children through the abolition of war. Insaan wished he could find Amaan, to apologise for not doing more and to wish him well in life. Insaan still wanted to see Amaan smile – and not just for the camera.

EPILOGUE

A year after my visit, Horse and his family left for Iran. They were going to join Horse's father there, despite a ten-year absence and a second family. Until that point, Horse had been focused on his education: he'd recently won a scholarship to a private school and was well on his dream path to university. I wondered what would become of that dream now.

Insaan and the Stalwarts gave Horse two photos of the community and some notebooks to document his experiences ahead. I imagine it was a difficult farewell, as nobody knew what would happen to Horse and his family once they committed to crossing borders. Muslimyor sobbed for his childhood friend.

Horse and his family took a bus to Nimruz, a province in the southwest corner of Afghanistan. From there they engaged people smugglers to take them to Iran. They joined the 65 million displaced and frightened refugees of the world. Horse the Refugee was now a potential terrorist, a queue jumper, an economic migrant, a burden on society. Horse the Refugee was turning his back on the future he had been striving towards.

Nadir married, and Asghar completed his first year at university in Mongolia and was offered an ongoing scholarship to study there. Abdul moved to India to further his higher education; while he was there, two of his children died due to illness. Hojar faced family and societal pressures to return home and be matched to a good suitor.

Hafizullah remained in Kabul to take his college entrance exams, but after that his future was uncertain.

Muslimyor left Kabul with no return date. He got engaged to his childhood sweetheart and was moving to the other side of Afghanistan to study environmental science, with the hope of focusing on water engineering. For the time being, he had laid aside all plans and hopes he previously had with the community.

Insaan understood that the Stalwarts would not be part of the community forever. But this didn't make it any easier when they grew up and moved on. After a brief period of 'empty nest syndrome', Insaan reaffirmed his commitment to ongoing peace work and began to identify and recruit new leaders from the next generation of volunteers.

THERE IS RECENT demonstrable evidence of calls for peace from within Afghanistan. One of the more incredible movements emerged out of the heartland of the Taliban, in Helmand province, triggered by a car bomb suicide attack that killed over a dozen people in March 2018. Relatives of the victims, women's rights activists, youth activists and other residents from Helmand erected a tent at the scene of the bombing, the Ghazi Ayub Khan Stadium in the city of Lashkargah, and began a sit-in for peace. Solidarity protests, which included hunger strikes, spread to sixteen other provinces and across ethnic divides, and were significant not only for the potential for a nationwide peace movement, but for the unusual and important contribution women made to the political protests in traditionally conservative areas.

From there, the movement gained momentum. On 12 May 2018, eight of the Helmand protesters began a peace march to Kabul. Their 700-kilometre journey lasted thirty-eight days and their demands were clear: they wanted the withdrawal of foreign forces, a ceasefire between the Taliban and government forces and a resumption of peace talks. In Ghazni province Hazara girls joined young Pashtun boys to sing Afghanistan's national anthem as a welcome to the peace-walkers. Often local villagers treated the sandal-wearing peace-walkers for dehydration, exhaustion and damage to their torn and blistered feet. They were greeted in villages and towns throughout their journey, speaking with thousands of Afghans about peace. By the time the walkers arrived in Kabul, their numbers had increased to sixty-five people. Their arrival to Kabul's historic Abdul Rahman mosque was flanked by local supporters, media and politicians.[1]

The Afghan Analysts Network reported the Helmand peace march was 'the first time that people in southern Afghanistan had publicly, and over a sustained period of time, raised their voices against Taliban violence'.[2] During the march, more than 2000 Afghan religious scholars from around the country issued a fatwa, an Islamic directive, to end the war, declaring it as 'unjust and in contradiction to sharia law' and calling upon the warring factions to announce a ceasefire.[3]

Perhaps in response to this pressure, President Ashraf Ghani ordered a temporary ceasefire during Eid. Within those ten days, the Taliban agreed to observe a three-day truce, except against foreign forces. In unprecedented scenes, at least 30,000 Taliban fighters entered cities and provinces all over Afghanistan to take part in the Eid prayers and enjoy the celebrations alongside civilians, government officials and members of the ANSF.[4]

Once the three-day ceasefire was over, the Taliban ordered its militants to resume fighting.[5]

Insaan and the volunteers hope that the Helmand group will stick to nonviolent approaches and share the volunteers' commitment to building peace without weapons, armies and military means. Insaan believes the Afghan people are at a point where they have the potential to say no to war and yes to nonviolent peace, though it may come at a great cost.

APPENDIX A

COMMUNITY'S TIMELINE OF EVENTS

2002 — Insaan begins work with refugees in Pakistan
2004 — Insaan relocates to Afghanistan
2008 — Insaan begins the peace workshop at the university
— Undergraduate multi-ethnic community forms for one semester
2009 — Building of first peace park, inaugurated on 1 October
— Tent vigil at the peace park
— Commencement of World Peace Exchange program
2010 — Volunteers make leather cell phone pouches for Kandahar youth
— Visit to Daykundi province
— Insaan connects with UK activist Mary Smith
2011 — Insaan and the volunteers move their activities to Kabul and start a live-in community
2012 — Paiman, the first Pashtun volunteer, joins the live-in community
— The live-in community moves to the Parliament house
— Horse, Muslimyor and Abdul join
— Street kids school pilot program starts
— Insaan and the live-in community relocate to the Human Rights Commission house
— Hafizullah joins
— Duvet project starts
— Tailoring project begins
2013 — Hojar moves to Kabul and starts university
— Hojar visits India
— Muslimyor and Horse temporarily leave the community
— Peace park created in Kabul

269

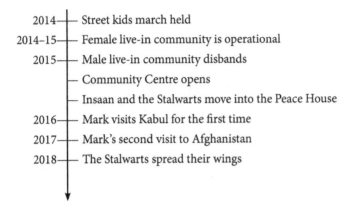

2014 — Street kids march held
2014–15 — Female live-in community is operational
2015 — Male live-in community disbands
— Community Centre opens
— Insaan and the Stalwarts move into the Peace House
2016 — Mark visits Kabul for the first time
2017 — Mark's second visit to Afghanistan
2018 — The Stalwarts spread their wings

APPENDIX B

AFGHANISTAN'S TIMELINE OF EVENTS

Around 330 BCE (Before Common Era)	Alexander the Great defeats the Persian Empire and conquers the region now known as Afghanistan. After his death control swings between the Hindu Maurya Empire, Parthians, Indo-Greek rulers, Persians and Turks.
7th century CE (Common Era)	Arab Islamic conquest of Afghanistan.
1219	Genghis Khan and the Mongols invade Afghanistan.
1405	Herat becomes the capital of the Timurid Empire for the next century.
1504	Babur, a descendant of both Timur and Genghis Khan, establishes what would become the Mughal Empire, with its capital at Kabul. Mughal rule lasts for 200 years.
1747	The modern state of Afghanistan is founded by Ahmad Shah Durrani, with its capital at Kandahar. Branches of the Durrani dynasty rule Afghanistan until 1973.
1838–42	Fearing expansion into British India by Russia, Britain invades Afghanistan, starting the First Anglo-Afghan War. Britain installs King Shah Shuja on the throne in Kabul, but he is assassinated in 1842. The British eventually withdraw from Afghanistan and a combined British-Indian force is massacred after leaving Kabul.
1878–80	Britain starts the Second Anglo-Afghan War after Afghanistan's ruler, Dost Mohammad's son Sher Ali, accepts Russian envoys at his court but refuses to accept a British delegation. A treaty gives Britain control of Afghan foreign affairs.
1880–1901	Britain supports Amir Abdul Rahman's claim to the throne. The Iron Amir massacres non-Pashtuns.

1896 — The Durand Line is established, separating Afghanistan and British India, and dividing Pashtun tribal areas and the Balochistan region.

1919–21 — The British are defeated in the Third Anglo-Afghan War and Afghanistan becomes a fully independent and sovereign nation.

1921–29 — Amir Amanullah Khan declares Afghanistan a kingdom, proclaims himself king and begins a campaign of socioeconomic reform. Domestic critics of Amanullah's policies form an opposition against him and, by 1929, the king abdicates and leaves the country.

1933 — Zahir Shah becomes king of Afghanistan, bringing relative stability to the country for the next forty years.

1947 — Britain withdraws from India. A violent partition of British India creates the Hindu-majority state of India and the Muslim-majority state of Pakistan. Afghanistan lays claim to the Pashtun areas of Pakistan.

1953 — General Mohammed Daoud Khan, cousin of the king, becomes prime minister and introduces social reforms including allowing women a more public presence. As part of Daoud's reforms, women can attend university and enter the workforce. He steps down in 1963.

1964 — King Zahir Shah introduces a new constitution that permits a parliament, elections, freedoms for the press, civil rights, women's rights and universal suffrage. The constitution also prohibits political activity by any members of the royal family other than the monarch.

1973–78 — The former prime minister Mohammed Daoud Khan seizes power in a coup, abolishes the monarchy and declares himself president of the Republic of Afghanistan.

1978 — Mohammed Daoud Khan is killed in a communist coup. Nur Muhammad Taraki, one of the founding members of the Afghan Communist Party, takes control of the country as president.

1979 — A power struggle between Taraki and Deputy Prime Minister Hafizullah Amin begins. Taraki is assassinated at Amin's orders on 14 September. Hafizullah Amin becomes president of Afghanistan.

— The USSR invades Afghanistan to support the faltering communist regime. On 27 December Soviet troops execute Amin and many of his family members and followers. Deputy Prime Minister Babrak Karmal becomes prime minister.

1979–89 — Mujahedin rebels fight against Soviet troops and the USSR-backed Afghan Army. The US, Pakistan, China, Iran and Saudi Arabia supply money and arms to the Mujahedin. By 1989 the Mujahedin triumph and Soviet forces exit Afghanistan.

1989 — While fighting in Afghanistan, Osama bin Laden establishes al-Qaeda, a militant Sunni Islamist organisation, whose combatants were originally trained by US forces and whose weapons were supplied by the US government.

1989–96 — Civil war further develops as the Mujahedin fight President Dr Mohammad Najibullah's Soviet-sponsored regime. The regime is toppled in 1992. Fighting continues between rival militias competing for control. Mohammad Najibullah is eventually killed by Taliban forces in 1996.

1996–2001 — A newly formed Islamic militia group, the Taliban, rises to power promising peace and stability. They introduce strict laws, ban women from work and implement brutal punishments such as stoning to death and amputations.

1996 — Osama bin Laden allies with the Taliban and begins to build a major al-Qaeda presence in Afghanistan, infiltrating the country with foreign fighters. Al-Qaeda quickly becomes a major power in Afghanistan, from which it launches a global jihad against the US and its allies and organises the 9/11 terrorist attacks.

1999 — Jordanian jihadist Abu Musab al-Zarqawi runs an Islamic militant training camp near Herat, supported by Osama bin Laden and al-Qaeda. Al-Zarqawi's militant group, Jama'at al-Tawhid wal-Jihad, would later join with several Iraqi Sunni insurgent groups to become the Islamic State of Iraq and the Levant.

2001 — On 11 September two aeroplanes are deliberately flown into the Twin Towers of the World Trade Center in New York, with another plane hitting the Pentagon in Virginia, and a fourth crashing in Pennsylvania, causing nearly 3000 deaths.

2001 — President George W Bush declares a 'War on Terror' and begins the US and NATO–led military invasion of Afghanistan, demanding the Taliban extradite bin Laden and expel al-Qaeda from Afghanistan. By December 2001 Coalition and Northern Alliance forces capture the Taliban stronghold, Kandahar, and dismantle the Taliban regime. On 5 December Afghan groups agree to a deal in Bonn, Germany, for an interim power-sharing government. Hamid Karzai is sworn in as head of state.

2002 — Despite the Taliban's defeat, fighting persists across the country. The first contingent of foreign peacekeepers – the NATO-led International Security Assistance Force – is deployed, the security organisation's first-ever commitment outside of Europe.

2005 — Afghans vote in their first parliamentary elections in more than thirty years.

2006 — NATO assumes control of security throughout Afghanistan, amidst continued fighting between Taliban and al-Qaeda fighters and the Afghan government forces.

2009 — US President Barack Obama increases US troop numbers in Afghanistan by 30,000, bringing the total to 100,000.

2014 — The validity of the 2014 Afghan presidential election is challenged by accusations of fraud. Former US Secretary of State John Kerry brokers a power-sharing deal and creates the National Unity Government (NUG). Ashraf Ghani becomes president, while runner-up Abdullah Abdullah is appointed as the Chief Executive Officer.

— In December 2014, after thirteen years of military presence, the US and allies withdraw the majority of their combat troops from Afghanistan and transfer full responsibility for security of the country to the Afghan National Security Forces.

2015 — The Islamic State of Iraq and the Levant–Khorasan Province establishes itself in Afghanistan. By the end of 2016 the group has increased its presence in almost all regions of the country.

— The UN reports that more civilians were killed in 2015 than in any of the previous fifteen years.

2017 — US President Donald Trump deploys 3000 more American troops to Afghanistan.

2018 — Helmand Peace March to Kabul passes through six provinces, covering 700 kilometres in thirty-eight days.

— President Ashraf Ghani and the Taliban agree to a temporary, three-day ceasefire for Eid al-Fitr, the holiday celebrating the end of the Muslim holy month of Ramadan.

SOURCES:

ABC. 'Timeline: Afghanistan's Turbulent History'. Updated 16 November 2012. http://www.abc.net.au/news/2009-06-02/timeline-afghanistans-turbulent-history/1702156

BBC. 'Afghanistan Profile'. 31 January 2018. http://www.bbc.com/news/world-south-asia-12024253

PBS. 'A Historical Timeline of Afghanistan'. Updated 31 December 2014. https://www.pbs.org/newshour/politics/asia-jan-june11-timeline-afghanistan

Stanford University. 'The Islamic State'. Updated 23 October 2017. http://web.stanford.edu/group/mappingmilitants/cgi-bin/groups/view/1

APPENDIX C

DEMOGRAPHIC MAP OF AFGHANISTAN

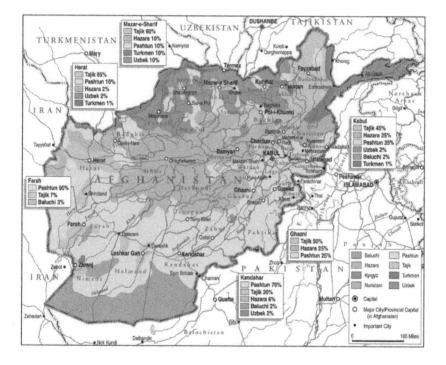

SOURCE:
Institute for the Study of War. 'Map of Afghanistan's Ethno-linguistic groups'.
Institute for the Study of War. 19 May 2009.
http://www.understandingwar.org/map/afghanistans-ethno-linguistic-groups

NOTES

Introduction

1   Researchers from the ERC interviewed close to 300 people in 22 countries including Syria, Iran, Iraq, Afghanistan, Nigeria and Zimbabwe. The team documented their findings in a series of reports titled 'Deported to Danger'.
Of the 179 Afghan returnees in 2001, many of whom had been detained in the offshore detention centre in Nauru, 31 had been killed upon return. Many of those deaths were linked to the Taliban.

Prologue

1   UNAMA. 'Afghanistan Annual Report: Protection of Civilians in Armed Conflict'. 14 February 2016. https://unama.unmissions.org/sites/default/files/poc_annual_report_2015_final_14_feb_2016.pdf
2   Rashid, A. *Taliban: The Power of Militant Islam in Afghanistan and Beyond.* London: I B Tauris and Co Ltd, 2000, 8–13.
3   There has been a naming dispute regarding the Persian language in Afghanistan. Dari became an official language in Afghanistan in the country's 1964 constitution. Two earlier constitutions in the 20th century had labelled it Farsi. Many Persian speakers in Afghanistan prefer and use the name Farsi. They say the term 'Dari' was forced on them by the dominant Pashtun ethnic group.
Mazhar, M. S., Khan, S. O. & Goraya, N. S. 'Ethnic Factor in Afghanistan'. *Journal of Political Studies*, vol. 19 no. 2, 2013, 99–100. http://pu.edu.pk/images/journal/pols/pdf-files/Naheed-winter2012.pdf
Bezhan, F. 'Dari Or Farsi? Afghanistan's Long-Simmering Language Dispute'. Radio Free Europe Radio Liberty. 7 November 2017. https://www.rferl.org/a/afghanistan-dari-farsi-persian-language-dispute/28840560.html
4   Mazhar, M. S., Khan, S. O. & Goraya, N. S. 'Ethnic Factor in Afghanistan'. *Journal of Political Studies*, vol. 19 no. 2 (2013), 99–100. http://pu.edu.pk/images/journal/pols/pdf-files/Naheed-winter2012.pdf

5   Bowley, G. 'Spy Balloons Become Part of the Afghanistan Landscape, Stirring Unease'. *The New York Times*, 12 May 2012. https://www.nytimes.com/2012/05/13/world/asia/in-afghanistan-spy-balloons-now-part-of-landscape.html

6   Rashid, A. *Descent into Chaos: The United States and the Failure of Nation Building in Pakistan, Afghanistan and Central Asia*. New York: Viking Books, 2007, 22.

7   Al Jazeera. 'Afghan Blast Targets Indian Embassy'. 9 October 2009. https://www.aljazeera.com/news/asia/2009/10/2009108531259700.html

8   Sarwan, R. & Zahid, N. 'Taliban Battle Leads to Kabul Blackout'. VOA News, 11 February 2016. http://www.voanews.com/content/taliban-battle-leads-to-kabul-blackout/3187048.html

9   World Bank. 'Afghanistan: Country Snapshot'. March 2014. http://siteresources.worldbank.org/SOUTHASIAEXT/Resources/223546-1398285132254/Afghanistan-Country-Snapshot-Spring-Meetings-2014.pdf

10 I first met Martin when we worked together for the Salvation Army in Australia's immigration detention centre on the Pacific Island republic of Nauru. In 2004–05 Martin worked in Afghanistan with the International Committee of the Red Cross as a translator for eighteen months, inspecting Afghan-run and US-run prisons trying to ensure that the Geneva Conventions were observed. He had returned to Afghanistan almost every year since, assisting the Edmund Rice Centre with its work, documenting the status of Afghan asylum seekers who were returned to Afghanistan by Australian governments.

11 Al Jazeera. 'Suicide Attacks Kill Dozens in Afghanistan'. 28 February 2016. https://www.aljazeera.com/news/2016/02/suicide-bomber-kills-11-eastern-afghanistan-160227062901757.html

12 BBC News. 'Kabul Attack: Taliban Kill 95 with Ambulance Bomb in Afghan Capital'. 28 January 2018. http://www.bbc.com/news/world-asia-42843897

13 UNAMA. *UNAMA Population Movement Bulletin*. Issue 3, 15 May 2016.
    Bengali, S. & Latifi, A. M. 'Talks with Taliban a "Waste of Time" Says Critic of Afghanistan's President'. *LA Times*, 18 February 2016. https://www.latimes.com/world/afghanistan-pakistan/la-fg-afghanistan-taliban-talks-20160218-story.html

14 Overseas Security Advisory Council. 'Afghanistan 2016 Crime & Safety Report'. US Department of State, Washington, DC, 2016. https://www.osac.gov/pages/ContentReportDetails.aspx?cid=19292

15 Oxfam & the Swedish Committee for Afghanistan (SCA). 'Aid Effectiveness in Afghanistan 2011: Progress in Implementing the Paris Declaration'. Vol. II. https://www.oecd.org/dac/effectiveness/Afghanistan%205.pdf

16 Edmund Rice Centre for Justice and Community Education Sydney. 'The Responsibility to Protect: Afghanistan's Current Situation, Drivers of Migration and Returnees Experience'. Sydney, July 2017.

17 Jalali, A. 'Forging Afghanistan's National Unity Government'. US Institute of Peace, January 2015. https://www.usip.org/sites/default/files/PB183-Forging-Afghanistans-National-Unity-Government.pdf

18 Sharan, T. & Bose, S. 'NUG One Year On: Struggling to Govern'. *Foreign Policy*, 29 September 2015. http://foreignpolicy.com/2015/09/29/afghan-national-unity-government-one-year-on-struggling-to-govern/

19 Human Rights Watch. 'Afghanistan: Events of 2015'. https://www.hrw.org/world-report/2016/country-chapters/afghanistan

20 Transparency International. 'Corruption by Country: Afghanistan'. Berlin, Germany, 2016. http://www.transparency.org/country/AFG

Chapter 1

1 ABC News. 'Kabul Bomb: Taliban-claimed Attack in Afghan Capital Leaves at Least 30 Dead, Hundreds Injured', updated 19 April 2016. http://www.abc.net.au/news/2016-04-19/kabul-bomb-blast-several-dead-hundredsinjured/7339716

2 Samuels, G. 'Kabul Suicide Bombing: Taliban Attack Kills Eleven in Afghan Capital During Morning Rush Hour'. *The Independent*, 25 May 2016. http://www.independent.co.uk/news/world/middle-east/talibansuicide-bomber-kills-eleven-commuters-in-kabul-during-morning-rush-hour-a7048211.html

3 Rasmussen, S. 'Isis Claims Responsibility for Kabul Bomb Attack on Hazara Protesters'. *The Guardian*, 24 July 2016. https://www.theguardian.com/world/2016/jul/23/hazara-minority-targeted-by-suicide-bombs-at-kabul-protest

4 BBC News. 'Australian Aid Worker "Kidnapped" in Afghanistan'. 29 April 2016. http://www.bbc.com/news/world-australia-36166800

5 BBC News. 'Indian Woman Kidnapped in Afghanistan'. 10 June 2016. http://www.bbc.com/news/world-asia-india-36496378

6 BBC News. 'US and Australian Professors Kidnapped in Afghanistan'. 8 August 2016. http://www.bbc.com/news/world-asia-37006257

7 Farmer, B. & Yousafazai, S. 'Taliban and US Discuss Prisoner Swap for Two Captive University Professors'. *The Telegraph*, 20 December 2018. https://www.telegraph.co.uk/news/2018/12/20/taliban-us-discuss-prisoner-swap-two-captive-university-professors/

8 Encyclopaedia Iranica. 'Hazara ii. History'. 15 December 2003, last updated 20 March 2012. http://www.iranicaonline.org/articles/hazara-2

9 King Jr, M. L. K. 'Nobel Prize Acceptance Speech'. 11 December 1964. https://www.nobelprize.org/prizes/peace/1964/king/lecture/

Chapter 2

1 NDTV. 'Timeline of Kabul Attacks Since 2016'. Updated 31 May 2017. https://www.ndtv.com/world-news/timeline-of-kabul-attacks-since-2016-1706164

2 Mujahid, A. M. 'Why Do Afghans Have a Life Expectancy of Only 44 Years?' *The Huffington Post*, 18 June 2009, last updated 25 May 2011. https://www.huffingtonpost.com/abdul-malik-mujahid/why-do-afghans-have-a-lif_b_204626.html

The Asia Foundation. 'Afghanistan in 2017: A Survey of the Afghan People'. 14 November 2017. https://reliefweb.int/report/afghanistan/afghanistan-2017-survey-afghan-people

3   Rzehak, L. 'Doing Pashto: Pashtunwali as the Ideal of Honourable Behaviour and Tribal Life among the Pashtuns'. Afghan Analysts Network, January 2011. http://www.afghanistan-analysts.org/wp-content/uploads/downloads/2012/10/20110321LR-Pashtunwali-FINAL.pdf

4   Tolstoy, L. *The Kingdom of God Is Within You*. 1894.

5   Gandhi, M., Merton, T. (ed.). *Gandhi on Non-Violence: Selected Texts from Gandhi's 'Non-violence in Peace and War'*. New York: New Directions Paperbook, 2007.

6   King Jr, M. L. K. 'Nobel Prize Acceptance Speech'. 11 December 1964. https://www.nobelprize.org/prizes/peace/1964/king/lecture/

7   Kurlanksy, M. *Nonviolence: The History of a Dangerous Idea*. New York: Modern Library, 2006.

Chapter 3

1   Nordland, R. 'Saving an Afghan Symbol, With Afghans Only'. *The New York Times*, 5 April 2017. https://www.nytimes.com/2017/04/05/world/asia/saving-an-afghan-symbol-with-afghans-only.html?smid=tw-nytimes&smtyp=cur&_r=0

2   Lawson, A. 'Afghan Gold: How the Country's Heritage Was Saved'. BBC News, 1 March 2011. http://www.bbc.com/news/world-south-asia-12599726
    The Telegraph. 'Taliban Destroyed Museum Exhibits'. 23 November 2001. https://www.telegraph.co.uk/news/worldnews/asia/afghanistan/1363272/Taliban-destroyed-museum-exhibits.html

3   Sobhani, O. 'Afghanistan to Restore Bombed-out "Safe Haven" Palace'. Reuters, 8 June 2016. https://www.reuters.com/article/us-afghanistan-palace/afghanistan-to-restore-bombed-out-safe-haven-palace-idUSKCN0YU118

4   The World Bank. 'Poverty'. Last updated 24 September 2018. http://www.worldbank.org/en/topic/poverty/overview

5   Shah Omid, S. H. '54 Percent of Afghans Live Below Poverty Line: Survey'. *TOLOnews*, 6 May 2018, last updated 7 May 2018. https://www.tolonews.com/business/54-percent-afghans-live-below-poverty-line-survey
    World Bank and Ministry of Economy, Islamic Republic of Afghanistan. 'Afghanistan Poverty Status Update: Progress at Risk'. 2017. http://documents.worldbank.org/curated/en/667181493794491292/pdf/114741-WP-v1-P159553-PUBLIC.pdf

Chapter 4

1   Shogan, R. 'Mankind's Challenge: Living With Terror: The Bomb Is 40'. *LA Times*, 4 August 1985.
    https://www.latimes.com/archives/la-xpm-1985-08-04-mn-4275-story.html

2   King, Jr, M. L. K. 'Beyond Vietnam' speech. Stanford University, 4 April 1967. https://kinginstitute.stanford.edu/king-papers/documents/beyond-vietnam

3   Tamera. 'Peace Community of San Jose de Apartado, Colombia'. https://www.tamera.org/peace-community-colombia/

4   Elliott, L. 'World's Eight Richest People Have Same Wealth as Poorest 50%'. *The Guardian*, 16 January 2017. https://www.theguardian.com/global-development/2017/jan/16/worlds-eight-richest-people-have-same-wealth-as-poorest-50

5   Hagan, S. 'Billionaires Made So Much Money Last Year They Could End Extreme Poverty Seven Times'. *Money*, 22 January 2018. http://time.com/money/5112462/billionaires-made-so-much-money-last-year-they-could-end-extreme-poverty-seven-times/

6   Oppenheim, M. 'Noam Chomsky: Republican Party is the Most Dangerous Organisation in Human History'. *Independent*, 27 April 2017. https://www.independent.co.uk/news/world/americas/noam-chomsky-republican-party-most-dangerous-organisation-human-history-us-politics-mit-linguist-a7706026.html

7   Tian, N., Fleurant, A., Wezeman, P. D. & Wezeman, S. T. 'Trends in Military Expenditure, 2016'. SIPRI Fact Sheet, April 2017. https://www.sipri.org/sites/default/files/Trends-world-military-expenditure-2016.pdf
    According to Amnesty International, in 2016 the world spent $US1.69 trillion on the military and the top 100 arms companies had sold more than $5 trillion worth of arms since 2002; Amnesty International. 'Geneva: As global arms trade surges, states greenlight reckless, harmful deals'. 11 September 2017. https://www.amnesty.org/en/latest/news/2017/09/geneva-as-global-arms-trade-surges-states-greenlight-reckless-harmful-deals/

Chapter 5

1   Official Website of the V20: Vulnerable Twenty Group of Ministers of Finance. http://www.v-20.org/about/

2   The Killid Group. 'Acute Water Shortage in the Near Future'. 6 March 2017. http://tkg.af/english/2017/03/06/acute-water-shortage-near-future/

3   Hassib, S. 'Afghan Capital's Thirsty Residents Dig Deep to Combat Drought, Overuse'. Reuters, 28 February 2017. https://www.reuters.com/article/us-afghanistan-water/afghan-capitals-thirsty-residents-dig-deep-to-combat-drought-overuse-idUSKBN1670FO

4   *TOLOnews*. '21 Provinces Face Drought as Rainfall Reduces'. 27 April 2018. https://www.tolonews.com/business/21-provinces-face-drought-rainfall-reduces

5   World Health Organization, Regional Office for the Eastern Mediterranean. 'Afghanistan: Environmental Health'. www.emro.who.int/afg/programmes/eh.html

6   World Food Programme. 'WFP Afghanistan Country Brief'. February 2018. https://docs.wfp.org/api/documents/766832236a7a4a1cbf8c4d24f87037b7/download/?_ga=2.162410367.2140646168.1527551395-234118770.1527551395

7   Rashid, A. *Descent into Chaos: The United States and the Failure of Nation Building in Pakistan, Afghanistan and Central Asia*. New York: Viking Books, 2007, 6.

8   Samim, M. 'Pakistan: Afghanistan's Unreliable Breadbasket', *The Diplomat*, 1 August 2016. https://thediplomat.com/2016/08/pakistan-afghanistans-unreliable-breadbasket/

9   Suzuki, D. *The Sacred Balance: Rediscovering Our Place in Nature*, updated and expanded. Vancouver: Greystone Books, 1997, 153.

Chapter 6

1　Bradford, A. 'Rebels on Wheels: The Afghan Women's Cycling Team Pedals Past Taboos'. *The Huffington Post*, 18 November 2016. https://www.huffingtonpost.com/entry/afghan-women-cycling-team-misogyny_us_582f1c55e4b030997bbefd26

2　Skateistan. 'This is Our Story'. https://skateistan.org/ourstory/

3　UNAMA. 'Points of View in Afghanistan on Ulema Council's Statement on Women'. 19 March 2012. https://unama.unmissions.org/points-view-afghanistan-ulema-councils-statement-women
The Guardian. 'Hamid Karzai Backs Restrictive Code for Women'. 6 March 2012. https://www.theguardian.com/world/2012/mar/06/hamid-karzai-restricive-code-women-afghanistan

4　BBC News. 'Afghan Woman Farkhunda Lynched in Kabul "for Speaking Out"'. 23 March 2015. https://www.bbc.com/news/world-asia-32014077

5　Goldsmith, B. 'The World's 10 Most Dangerous Countries for Women'. *The Sydney Morning Herald*, 26 June 2018. https://www.smh.com.au/world/asia/the-world-s-10-most-dangerous-countries-for-women-20180626-p4znrs.html

6　Griffiths, J. C. *Afghanistan: A History of Conflict.* London: Andre Deutsch Ltd, 1981, 127.

7　Central Intelligence Agency. 'The World Factbook: Tajikistan'. https://www.cia.gov/library/publications/the-world-factbook/geos/ti.html#People

8　Lamer, K. & Foster, E. 'Afghan Ethnic Groups: A Brief Investigation'. Civil Military Fusion, August 2011. https://reliefweb.int/sites/reliefweb.int/files/resources/CFC_Afg_Monthly_Ethnic_Groups_Aug2011%20v1.pdf

9　Griffiths, J. C. *Afghanistan: A History of Conflict.* London: Andre Deutsch Ltd, 1981, 74, 82.

Chapter 7

1　Barker, P. 'How Obama Came to Plan for "Surge" in Afghanistan', *The New York Times*, 5 December 2009. https://www.nytimes.com/2009/12/06/world/asia/06reconstruct.html

2　Rashid, A. *Taliban: The Power of Militant Islam in Afghanistan and Beyond.* London: I B Tauris and Co Ltd, 2000, 9-12.

3　Lamer, K. & Foster, E. 'Afghan Ethnic Groups: A Brief Investigation'. Civil Military Fusion, August 2011. https://reliefweb.int/sites/reliefweb.int/files/resources/CFC_Afg_Monthly_Ethnic_Groups_Aug2011%20v1.pdf

4　Rashid, A. *Taliban: The Power of Militant Islam in Afghanistan and Beyond.* London: I B Tauris and Co Ltd, 2000, 13.

5　Larson, A. 'Political Parties in Afghanistan'. United States Institute of Peace, Special Report 362, March 2015. https://www.usip.org/sites/default/files/SR362-Political-Parties-in-Afghanistan.pdf

6　Ruttig, T. 'An April Day That Changed Afghanistan 1: Four Decades after the Leftist Takeover'. Afghan Analysts Network, 25 April 2018. https://www.afghanistan-analysts.org/an-april-day-that-changed-afghanistan-four-decades-after-the-leftist-takeover/

7   Clark, K. 'Death List Published: Families of Disappeared End a 30 Year Wait for News'. Afghan Analysts Network, 26 September 2013. https://www.afghanistan-analysts.org/death-list-published-families-of-disappeared-end-a-30-year-wait-for-news/

8   Kaplan, R. D. *Soldiers of God: With Islamic Warriors in Afghanistan and Pakistan.* New York: Vintage Books, 2001, 115.

9   Griffiths, J. C. *Afghanistan: A History of Conflict.* London: Andre Deutsch Ltd, 1981, 173.

10 Gibbs, D. N. 'Reassessing Soviet Motives for Invading Afghanistan: A Declassified History'. *Critical Asian Studies* vol. 38, no. 2, 2006, 239-63.
    Hilali, A. Z. 'The Soviet Decision-Making for Intervention in Afghanistan and its Motives'. *The Journal of Slavic Military Studies* vol. 16 no. 2, 2003, 113-44.

11 Tanner, S. *Afghanistan: A Military History from Alexander the Great to the Fall of the Taliban.* New York: Da Capo Press, 2002, 238.

12 Gopal, A. *No Good Men Among the Living.* New York: Picador, 2015, 56.

13 Gopal, A. *No Good Men Among the Living.* New York: Picador, 2015, 57.

14 Griffiths, J. C. *Afghanistan: A History of Conflict.* London: Andre Deutsch Ltd, 1981, 197.
    Rashid, A. *Taliban: The Power of Militant Islam in Afghanistan and Beyond.* London: I B Tauris and Co Ltd, 2000, 21.

15 Gopal, A. *No Good Men Among the Living.* New York: Picador, 2015, 59.

16 Tanner, S. *Afghanistan: A Military History from Alexander the Great to the Fall of the Taliban.* New York: Da Capo Press, 2002, 276.

17 The first time Pashtuns lost control of Kabul was in January 1929, when Habibullah Kalakani, a Tajik rebel and the son of a water carrier, took control of Kabul and removed King Amanullah Khan from power. The Bandit King, as Habibullah became known, reigned for nine months before Nadir Khan, an exiled member of the royal family, returned from India with an Afghan army to reclaim Kabul and execute Habibullah.

18 Stanford University. 'Mapping Militant Organizations: The Taliban'. Stanford, California: 2016. http://web.stanford.edu/group/mappingmilitants/cgi-bin/groups/view/367

19 The term 'taliban' is derived from the Persian and Pashtun plural of the Arabic word talib ('seeker of knowledge' or 'student').

20 Rashid, A. *Taliban: The Power of Militant Islam in Afghanistan and Beyond.* London: I B Tauris and Co Ltd, 2000, 17-40.

21 Stanford University. 'Mapping Militant Organizations: The Taliban'. Stanford, California, 2016. http://web.stanford.edu/group/mappingmilitants/cgi-bin/groups/view/367

22 Rashid, A. *Taliban: The Power of Militant Islam in Afghanistan and Beyond.* London: I B Tauris and Co Ltd, 2000, 17-40.

23 Gopal, A. *No Good Men Among the Living.* New York: Picador, 2015, 66.

24 Human Rights Watch. 'The Massacre in Mazar-i Sharif'. vol. 10 no. 7, November 1998. https://www.hrw.org/legacy/reports98/afghan/Afrepor0.htm

25 Harding, L. 'Afghan Massacre Haunts Pentagon'. *The Guardian*, 14 September 2002. https://www.theguardian.com/world/2002/sep/14/afghanistan.lukeharding

26 Rashid, A. *Taliban: The Power of Militant Islam in Afghanistan and Beyond.* London: I B Tauris and Co Ltd, 2000, 159–80.

27 Laub, Z. 'The Taliban in Afghanistan'. Council on Foreign Relations, last updated 4 July 2014. http://www.cfr.org/afghanistan/taliban-afghanistan/p10551

Chapter 8

1   Wehelie, B. 'Sacred Ground: Inside the Dakota Pipeline Protests'. CNN, December 2016. https://edition.cnn.com/interactive/2016/12/us/dapl-protests-cnnphotos/

2   Parvaz, D. 'Afghanistan's Internal Refugee Crisis'. Al Jazeera, 11 April 2016. https://www.aljazeera.com/indepth/features/2016/04/afghanistan-internal-refugee-crisis-160411083354489.html

3   US Department of State. '2016 Country Reports on Human Rights Practices—Afghanistan'. 3 March 2017. https://www.refworld.org/docid/58ec8a7fa.html

4   Rashid, A. *Taliban: The Power of Militant Islam in Afghanistan and Beyond.* London: I B Tauris and Co Ltd, 2000, 128–40.

5   BBC. 'The History of the War in Afghanistan'. Last updated 8 March 2012. http://www.bbc.co.uk/history/the_war_in_afghanistan

6   Gillan, A. 'Bin Laden Appears on Video to Threaten US'. *The Guardian*, 9 October 2001. https://www.theguardian.com/world/2001/oct/08/afghanistan.terrorism

7   Australia's thirteen-year involvement in Afghanistan began in 2001, when it joined the US invasion to overthrow the Taliban. It was Australia's longest war, costing more than A$7.5 billion. That same year, in the aftermath of September 11, the John Howard government opened offshore detention centres in Manus Island, Papua New Guinea and Nauru to deter people seeking asylum to Australia by boat, including Afghans fleeing the Taliban regime; Dudgeon, I. 'Increasing Australia's Military Commitment to Afghanistan'. Australian International Institute of Affairs, 16 May 2017. https://www.internationalaffairs.org.au/australianoutlook/australias-commitment-afghanistan/

8   Fields, M. & Ahmed, R. 'A Review of the 2001 Bonn Conference and Application to the Road Ahead in Afghanistan'. Institute for National Strategic Studies Strategic Perspectives, no. 8. Washington, DC: National Defense University Press, November 2011. http://inss.ndu.edu/Portals/68/Documents/stratperspective/inss/Strategic-Perspectives-8.pdf

9   Rashid, A. *Descent into Chaos: The United States and the Failure of Nation Building in Pakistan, Afghanistan and Central Asia.* New York: Viking Books, 2007, 171–95.

10 Human Rights Watch. 'Unwelcome Guests: Iran's Violation of Afghan Refugee and Migrant Rights'. 20 November 2013. https://www.refworld.org/docid/528f27454.html

11 Marai, S. 'When Hope is Gone'. Correspondent, 30 April 2018. https://correspondent.afp.com/when-hope-gone

12 Barlas, M. A. 'Why Afghanistan?' *Daily Times*, 21 May 2018. https://dailytimes.com.pk/242608/why-afghanistan/

13 Rashid, A. *Descent into Chaos: The United States and the Failure of Nation Building in Pakistan, Afghanistan and Central Asia*. New York: Viking Books, 2007, 171–95.

14 Bjelica, J. & Ruttig, T. 'The State of Aid and Poverty in 2018: A New Look at Aid Effectiveness in Afghanistan'. Afghan Analysts Network, 17 May 2018. https://www.afghanistan-analysts.org/the-state-of-aid-and-poverty-in-2018-a-new-look-at-aid-effectiveness-in-afghanistan/

15 Special Inspector General for Afghanistan Reconstruction. 'Afghanistan Reconstruction Trust Fund: The World Bank Needs to Improve How it Monitors Implementation, Shares Information, and Determines the Impact of Donor Contributions'. April 2018. https://www.sigar.mil/pdf/audits/SIGAR-18-42-AR.pdf

16 Rasmussen, S. 'Kabul's Expat Bubble Used to be Like Boogie Nights – Now it's More Like Panic Room'. *The Guardian*, 19 July 2016. https://www.theguardian.com/world/2016/jul/18/kabul-expat-bubble-boogie-nights-panic-room-afghanistan-war

17 Tchalakov, M. 'The Northern Alliance Prepares for Afghan Elections in 2014'. Washington, DC: Institute for the Study of War, 2013, 16–17.

18 Suhrke, A., Harpviken, K. B. & Strand A. 'After Bonn: Conflictual Peace Building'. *Third World Quarterly*, vol. 23 no. 5, 2002, 879.

19 Scahill, J. 'Donald Trump and the Coming fall of the American Empire'. The Intercept, 23 July 2017. https://theintercept.com/2017/07/22/donald-trump-and-the-coming-fall-of-american-empire/

20 Constable, P. 'Opium Use Booms in Afghanistan Creating a Silent Tsunami of Addicted Women'. *The Washington Post*, 19 June 2017. https://www.washingtonpost.com/world/asia_pacific/opium-use-booms-in-afghanistan-creating-a-silent-tsunami-of-addicted-women/2017/06/19/6c5b16f2-3985-11e7-a59b-26e0451a96fd_story.html?noredirect=on&utm_term=.b26b075a5b80

21 Peceny, M. & Bosin, Y. 'Winning with Warlords in Afghanistan'. *Small Wars & Insurgencies*, vol. 22 no. 4, 2011, 604.

22 Coll, S. *Directorate S: The CIA and America's Secret Wars in Afghanistan and Pakistan*. New York: Penguin, 2018.

23 Hersh, S. M. 'The Killing of Osama bin Laden'. *London Review of Books*, vol. 37 no. 10, 21 May 2015, 3–12. https://www.lrb.co.uk/v37/n10/seymour-m-hersh/the-killing-of-osama-bin-laden

24 Healy, J. 'Soldier Sentenced to Life without Parole for Killing 16 Afghans'. *The New York Times*, 23 August 2013. https://www.nytimes.com/2013/08/24/us/soldier-gets-life-without-parole-in-deaths-of-afghan-civilians.html

25 McKenzie, N. & Masters, C. 'Abdul's Brother Went Out to Buy Flour. He Never Came Home'. *The Sydney Morning Herald*, 8 June 2018. https://www.smh.com.au/politics/federal/abdul-s-brother-went-out-to-buy-flour-he-never-came-home-20180607-p4zk38.html

26 McKenzie, N. & Masters, C. 'Special Forces Rookie "Blooded" by Executing an Unarmed Man'. *The Sydney Morning Herald*, 9 June 2018. https://www.smh.com.au/politics/federal/special-forces-rookie-blooded-by-executing-an-unarmed-man-20180605-p4zjmw.html

27 Rashid, A. *Descent into Chaos: The United States and the Failure of Nation Building in Pakistan, Afghanistan and Central Asia.* New York: Viking Books, 2007, 293–316.

28 Mazzetti, M. 'Panel Faults C.I.A. Over Brutality and Deceit in Terrorism Interrogations'. *The New York Times*, 9 December 2014. https://www.nytimes.com/2014/12/10/world/senate-intelligence-committee-cia-torture-report.html

29 Rashid, A. *Descent into Chaos: The United States and the Failure of Nation Building in Pakistan, Afghanistan and Central Asia.* New York: Viking Books, 2007, 293–316.

30 Human Rights Watch. 'Q&A: Guantanamo Bay, US Detentions, and the Trump Administration'. 4 May 2017, last updated 27 June 2018. https://www.hrw.org/news/2018/06/27/qa-guantanamo-bay-us-detentions-and-trump-administration

31 SBS. '2018 Was the Afghan War's Bloodiest Year, According to UN'. 24 February 2019. https://www.sbs.com.au/news/2018-was-the-afghan-war-s-bloodiest-year-according-to-un

32 Hersh, S. M. 'The Killing of Osama bin Laden'. *London Review of Books*, vol. 37 no. 10, 21 May 2015, 3–12. https://www.lrb.co.uk/v37/n10/seymour-m-hersh/the-killing-of-osama-bin-laden

33 North Atlantic Treaty Organization. 'Resolute Support Mission in Afghanistan'. Brussels: 2016. http://www.nato.int/cps/en/natohq/topics_113694.htm

34 The Balance. 'Afghanistan War Cost, Timeline and Economic Impact'. Last updated 15 March 2019. https://www.thebalance.com/cost-of-afghanistan-war-timeline-economic-impact-4122493

Chapter 10

1 Al Jazeera. 'Afghans' Dire Need for Clean Water'. 14 August 2011. https://www.aljazeera.com/video/asia/2011/08/2011814103014219874.html

Chapter 11

1 UNICEF. 'All Children in School and Learning: Global Initiative on Out-of-School Children, Afghanistan Country Study'. 2018, 27. https://www.unicef.org/afghanistan/media/2471/file

2 Guillaume, M. '2017 Afghanistan: Evaluation of Street Working Children's Project'. UNICEF, 2017. https://www.unicef.org/evaldatabase/index_102726.html

3 Harrison, T. 'Chaos and Uncertainty: The FY 2014 Defense Budget and Beyond'. Center for Strategic and Budgetary Assessments, October 2013, 11. https://csbaonline.org/uploads/documents/Analysis-of-the-FY-2014-Defense-Budget.pdf

4 Minority Rights. 'Uzbeks'. Last updated April 2018. http://minorityrights.org/minorities/uzbeks-3/

Chapter 12

1 Meyer, K. 'The Peacemaker of the Pashtun'. *The New York Times*, 7 December 2001. https://www.nytimes.com/2001/12/07/opinion/the-peacemaker-of-the-pashtun-past.html

2 BBC News. 'Afghanistan: Before and after the Taliban'. 2 April 2014. https://www.bbc.com/news/world-asia-26747712

TOLOnews. 'Syria Overtakes Afghanistan With Highest Refugee'. 20 June 2015, last updated 17 October 2016. https://www.tolonews.com/afghanistan/syria-overtakes-afghanistan-highest-refugee-rate

3   Human Rights Watch. 'Unwelcome Guests: Iran's Violation of Afghan Refugee and Migrant Rights'. 20 November 2013. https://www.refworld.org/docid/528f27454.html

4   UNHCR. 'Islamic Republic of Iran'. 2019. https://www.unhcr.org/islamic-republic-of-iran.html
    Plesch, V. & Inayat, N. 'Pakistan Wants Millions of Afghan Refugees Gone. It's a Humanitarian Crisis Waiting to Happen'. PRI, 30 March 2017. https://www.pri.org/stories/2017-03-30/pakistan-wants-millions-afghan-refugees-gone-its-humanitarian-crisis-waiting

5   Rzehak, L. 'Doing Pashto: Pashtunwali as the Ideal of Honourable Behaviour and Tribal Life among the Pashtuns'. Afghan Analysts Network, January 2011. http://www.afghanistan-analysts.org/wp-content/uploads/downloads/2012/10/20110321LR-Pashtunwali-FINAL.pdf

6   Smith, D. J. 'Decisions, Desires and Diversity: Marriage Practices in Afghanistan'. Afghanistan Research and Evaluation Unit, February 2009. https://www.refworld.org/pdfid/4992cc722.pdf

7   Special Inspector General for Afghanistan Reconstruction. 'Afghan Refugees and Returnees: Corruption and Lack of Afghan Ministerial Capacity Have Prevented Implementation of a Long-term Refugee Strategy'. August 2015. https://www.sigar.mil/pdf/audits/SIGAR-15-83-AR.pdf

Chapter 13

1   Edmund Rice Centre for Justice and Community Education Sydney. 'The Responsibility to Protect: Afghanistan's Current Situation, Drivers of Migration and Returnees Experience'. Sydney, July 2017.

2   According to the 2016 census, at least 87 per centof Australia's Afghan population has arrived since 1996 and 61 per cent migrated in the ten-year period between 2006 and 2015. The vast majority of Afghans in this wave of migration have been refugees accepted through Australia's humanitarian program; SBS. 'Cultural Atlas: Afghans in Australia'. https://culturalatlas.sbs.com.au/afghan-culture/afghans-in-australia

3   Nordland, R. & Mashal, M. 'Europe Makes Deal to Send Afghans Home, Where War Awaits Them'. *The New York Times*, 6 October 2016. https://www.nytimes.com/2016/10/06/world/asia/afghanistan-eu-refugees-migrants.html?mcubz=0

4   Deutsche Welle English. 'Afghanistan—There are No Safe Zones'. 11 November 2016. http://www.dw.com/en/afghanistan-there-are-no-safe-zones/a-36365972
    Sennott, C. N. 'Foreverstan: Afghanistan's Ring Road Offers a Look at America's Continuing War'. *The Huffington Post*, 21 April 2015. https://www.huffingtonpost.com/the-groundtruth-project/foreverstan-afghanistans_b_7101308.html

5   Edmund Rice Centre for Justice and Community Education Sydney. 'The Responsibility to Protect: Afghanistan's Current Situation, Drivers of Migration and Returnees Experience'. Sydney, July 2017.

6 Harooni, M. 'Taliban Claim Attacks in Afghan Capital, at Least 15 Dead'. Reuters, 1 March 2017. https://www.reuters.com/article/us-afghanistan-blast/taliban-claim-attacks-in-afghan-capital-at-least-15-dead-idUSKBN1683MR

7 Harooni, M. 'Taliban Claim Attacks in Afghan Capital, at Least 15 Dead'. Reuters, 1 March 2017. https://www.reuters.com/article/us-afghanistan-blast/taliban-claim-attacks-in-afghan-capital-at-least-15-dead-idUSKBN1683MR

8 ESRI Terrorist Attacks 2017. https://storymaps.esri.com/stories/terrorist-attacks/?year=2017

9 BBC News. 'Afghanistan Bombings: Dozens Killed Across the Country'. 10 January 2017. http://www.bbc.com/news/world-asia-38567241

10 Rasmussen, S. 'Dozens Killed in Suicide Blast at Afghanistan's Supreme Court'. *The Guardian*, 8 February 2017. https://www.theguardian.com/world/2017/feb/07/dozens-killed-in-suicide-blast-at-afghanistans-supreme-court

Chapter 14

1 *Afghanistan Times*. 'Illiteracy Rate in Afghanistan Stands at 64 percent'. 14 November 2014. http://www.afghanistantimes.af/illiteracy-rate-in-afghanistan-stands-at-64pc/

Chapter 15

1 Nordland, R. 'Despite Education Advances, a Host of Afghan School Woes'. *The New York Times*, 20 July 2013. https://www.nytimes.com/2013/07/21/world/asia/despite-education-advances-a-host-of-afghan-school-woes.html

Chapter 16

1 Human Rights Watch. 'Stop Reporting or We'll Kill Your Family'. Threats to Media Freedom in Afghanistan. 21 January 2015. https://www.hrw.org/report/2015/01/21/stop-reporting-or-well-kill-your-family/threats-media-freedom-afghanistan
BBC Media Action. 'The Media of Afghanistan: The Challenges of Transition'. Policy Briefing #5, March 2012. http://downloads.bbc.co.uk/mediaaction/policybriefing/bbc_media_action_afghanistan_is_in_transition.pdf

2 Barefoot College. 2019. https://www.barefootcollege.org/

Chapter 17

1 Afghanistan has only one high-security psychiatric facility, the Red Crescent Secure Psychiatric Institution in Herat which houses almost 300 patients, many of whom are chained and sedated. Nationwide, only 320 hospital beds in the public and private sector are available for people suffering from mental health problems. World Health Organization. 'Afghanistan: Mental and Disability Health'. 2019. http://www.emro.who.int/afg/programmes/mental-health.html
Raphelson, S. 'Afghanistan's Lone Psychiatric Hospital Reveals Mental Health Crisis Fueled by War'. NPR, 14 February 2018. https://www.npr.org/2018/02/14/585494599/afghanistans-lone-psychiatric-hospital-reveals-mental-health-crisis-fueled-by-wa

Chapter 18

1 PEN International is a worldwide association of writers which emphasises the role of literature in mutual understanding and world culture; defends freedom of expression; supports persecuted and exiled writers; and promotes linguistic rights. PEN International has 144 centres in 102 countries across the globe, including 3 in Australia (Sydney, Melbourne and Perth).

2 van Linschoten, A. S. & Kuehn, F. (editors). *Poetry of the Taliban*. London: Hurst, October 2013.

3 Mohammadi, R. 'Afghanistan has Poetry in its Soul'. *The Guardian*, 21 May 2012. https://www.theguardian.com/commentisfree/2012/may/21/afghanistan-poetry-in-soul-taliban

4 Excerpt from *I Am the Beggar of the World*, translated by Eliza Griswold, photographs by Seamus Murphy. Text copyright ©2014 by Eliza Griswold. Reprinted with permission of Farrar, Straus and Giroux.
Griswold, E. (translator), Gray Jr E. T. (reviewer). 'I Am the Beggar of the World: Landays from Contemporary Afghanistan'. *Harvard Review*, 17 June 2014. http://www.harvardreview.org/?q=features/book-review/i-am-beggar-world-landays-contemporary-afghanistan

5 Schiffman, R. 'The Islamic Extremist War Against the Sufis'. *The Huffington Post*, 2 October 2012, last updated 2 December 2012. https://www.huffingtonpost.com/richard-schiffman/the-islamic-extremist-war_b_1931979.html

6 Excerpt from *Poetry of the Taliban*, edited by Alex Strick van Linschoten and Felix Kuehn. Text copyright © 2012 Alex Strick van Linschoten and Felix Kuehn. Reprinted with permission of Hurst Publishers, London.

7 Miglani, S. 'Taliban Executions Still Haunt Afghan Soccer Field'. Reuters, 13 September 2008. http://www.reuters.com/article/us-afghan-stadium-idUSSP 12564220080913

8 Gordon, R. 'How Drones Expand the War on Terror'. *The Huffington Post*, 25 May 2018. https://www.huffingtonpost.com/entry/recognizing-the-camels-nose_us_5b06c516e4b01a19d2c96bc5
The Bureau of Investigative Journalism. 'Drone Warfare'. https://www.thebureauinvestigates.com/projects/drone-war/

9 Liebelson, D. 'Ex-Drone Operator Says Program Is "Good at Killing People, Just Not the Right Ones"'. *The Huffington Post*, 20 November 2015. https://www.huffingtonpost.com.au/entry/drones-isis-terrorism-barack-obama_us_564e03d6e4b00b7997f99af0

10 The Bureau of Investigative Journalism. 'Obama's Covert Drone War in Numbers: Ten Times More Strikes than Bush'. 17 January 2017. https://www.thebureauinvestigates.com/stories/2017-01-17/obamas-covert-drone-war-in-numbers-ten-times-more-strikes-than-bush

11 The Bureau of Investigative Journalism. 'Drone Warfare'. https://www.thebureauinvestigates.com/projects/drone-war/

12 Kenny, S. 'Instability in Afghanistan: Why Afghanistan Matters and What Australia Can Do to Address the Causes of Instability'. Canberra: Centre for

Defence and Strategic Studies, 2016, 6–8. http://www.defence.gov.au/ADC/Publications/IndoPac/Kenny%20Afghanistan%20IPSP.pdf

13 Kenny, S. 'Instability in Afghanistan: Why Afghanistan Matters and What Australia Can Do to Address the Causes of Instability'. Canberra: Centre for Defence and Strategic Studies, 2016, 6–8. http://www.defence.gov.au/ADC/Publications/IndoPac/Kenny%20Afghanistan%20IPSP.pdf

14 Kenny, S. 'Instability in Afghanistan: Why Afghanistan Matters and What Australia Can Do to Address the Causes of Instability'. Canberra: Centre for Defence and Strategic Studies, 2016, 6–8. http://www.defence.gov.au/ADC/Publications/IndoPac/Kenny%20Afghanistan%20IPSP.pdf

15 Afghan Analysts Network. 'Afghan Taliban Contain Islamic State's Regional Reach'. 17 November 2015. https://www.afghanistan-analysts.org/wp-content/uploads/2016/02/oxford-analytica-afghan-taliban-contain-islamic-states-regional-reach.pdf

16 Osman, B. 'Descent into Chaos: Why did Nangarhar Turn into an IS Hub?'. Afghan Analysts Network, 27 September 2016. https://www.afghanistan-analysts.org/descent-into-chaos-why-did-nangarhar-turn-into-an-is-hub/

17 Kenny, S. 'Instability in Afghanistan: Why Afghanistan Matters and What Australia Can Do to Address the Causes of Instability'. Canberra: Centre for Defence and Strategic Studies, 2016, 6–8. http://www.defence.gov.au/ADC/Publications/IndoPac/Kenny%20Afghanistan%20IPSP.pdf

18 Osman, B. 'ISKP's Battle for Minds: What Are its Main Messages and Who Do They Attract?'. Afghan Analysts Network, 12 December 2016. https://www.afghanistan-analysts.org/iskps-battle-for-minds-what-are-their-main-messages-and-who-do-they-attract/

19 Rubin, Dr B. 'Opinion: An Open Letter to the Taliban'. *TOLOnews*, 28 February 2018, last updated 8 March 2018. https://www.tolonews.com/opinion/opinion-open-letter-taliban

20 Yusupov, A. 'Every War Has to End'. Friedrich-Ebert-Stiftung, 26 February 2017. https://www.fes-connect.org/trending/every-war-has-to-end/

21 Gibbons-Neff, T. 'How Obama's Afghanistan Plan is Forcing the Army to Replace Soldiers with Contractors'. *The Washington Post*, 1 June 2016. https://www.washingtonpost.com/news/checkpoint/wp/2016/06/01/how-obamas-afghanistan-plan-is-forcing-the-army-to-replace-soldiers-with-contractors/?noredirect=on&utm_term=.96aeafefa2d4

22 CBS News. 'Kabul Under Siege While America's Longest War Rages On'. 3 June 2018. https://www.cbsnews.com/news/kabul-afghanistan-capital-under-siege-while-americas-longest-war-rages-on-60-minutes/

23 Ward, A. 'Trump is Sending More than 3,000 troops to Afghanistan'. *Vox*, 19 September 2017. https://www.vox.com/world/2017/9/19/16227730/trump-afghanistan-3000-troops-mattis

24 Woody, C. 'The US is on Pace to Bomb Afghanistan More Than Ever This Year, But the Nominee to be US Commander There "Can't Guarantee … an End Date"'. *Business Insider*, 21 June 2018. https://www.businessinsider.

com.au/us-bombing-afghanistan-at-record-pace-but-no-end-date-in-sight-2018-6?r=US&IR=T

25 Osman, B. Clark, K. & van Bijlert, M. '"Mother of All Bombs" Dropped on ISKP: Assessing the Aftermath'. Afghan Analysts Network, 15 April 2017. https://www.afghanistan-analysts.org/mother-of-all-bombs-dropped-on-iskp-assessing-the-aftermath/

26 Loewenstein, A. 'Natural Resources Were Supposed to Make Afghanistan Rich. Here's What's Happening to Them'. *The Nation*, 14 December 2015. https://www.thenation.com/article/resources-were-supposed-to-make-afghanistan-rich/

27 Loewenstein, A. 'Afghan Minerals in the Crosshairs of Blackwater's Erik Prince'. *TRT World*, 14 November 2018. https://www.trtworld.com/magazine/afghan-minerals-in-the-crosshairs-of-blackwater-s-erik-prince-21655

28 Nakamura, D. & Phillip, A. 'Trump Announces New Strategy for Afghanistan that Calls for a Troop Increase'. *The Washington Post*, 21 August 2017. https://www.washingtonpost.com/politics/trump-expected-to-announce-small-troop-increase-in-afghanistan-in-prime-time-address/2017/08/21/eb3a513e-868a-11e7-a94f-3139abce39f5_story.html?utm_term=.9b3001272a75

Chapter 20

1 Roosevelt, F. D. 'Franklin D. Roosevelt's Last Message to the American People'. US Library of Congress, 1945. https://www.loc.gov/resource/rbpe.24204300/?st=text

Epilogue

1 Sabawoon, A. M. 'Going Nationwide: The Helmand Peace March Initiative'. Afghan Analysts Network, 23 April 2018. https://www.afghanistan-analysts.org/going-nationwide-the-helmand-peace-march-initiative/

2 Sabawoon, A. M. 'Going Nationwide: The Helmand Peace March Initiative'. Afghan Analysts Network, 23 April 2018. https://www.afghanistan-analysts.org/going-nationwide-the-helmand-peace-march-initiative/

3 Amiri, S. 'Afghan Clerics Declare Current War Un-Islamic'. *TOLOnews*, 4 June 2018. https://www.tolonews.com/afghanistan/afghan-clerics-issue-joint-fatwa-call-ongoing-war-illegal

4 Smith-Spark, L. & Popalzai, E. 'Eid Celebrations in Afghanistan Marred by Deadly Bombing'. CNN, 16 June 2018. https://edition.cnn.com/2018/06/16/asia/afghanistan-taliban-ceasefire-eid-intl/index.html

5 BBC News. 'Taliban Rules Out Extension of Afghanistan Eid Festival Ceasefire'. 17 June 2018. https://www.bbc.com/news/world-asia-44513657

ACKNOWLEDGEMENTS

THIS BOOK IS dedicated to all the human rights defenders, community workers, social workers, health workers, advocates, activists and volunteers who are working to make this world a better place. Your efforts don't go unnoticed. Keep fighting the good fight.

To Insaan and the community, thank you for being a beacon of hope in the gloom of global political pessimism; for showing us there are real and pragmatic alternatives to violence that everyone can adopt and implement in their own lives. Thank you for your bravery in the face of life-threatening dangers. Thank you for trusting me with your story.

To Martin Reusch and Donna Mulhearn, dear friends and mentors, without whom I may never have travelled to Afghanistan and learned about the community. I am forever grateful for your guidance, support and affection. I can't wait for my next writer's retreat in the Blue Labyrinth Bush Retreat (shameless plug).

To Phil Glendenning and the Edmund Rice Centre for sending me on my initial adventure to Afghanistan and for your ongoing support of the community. All donations for the community can be directed towards the Edmund Rice Centre's 'Afghan Project' https://www.erc.org.au/make_a_donation

I also invite readers to join the #lettersforpeace campaign and send letters and postcards of hope and support to the peace community in Afghanistan. If readers post correspondence to the following address, we will ensure it arrives in Afghanistan: Letters For Peace, Edmund Rice Centre, 15 Henley Road, Homebush West, NSW, Australia 2140.

To Kate Daniel, my superstar editor. Thank you for performing wonders with this book. It would've been twice as long and half as good without you. You are phenomenal!

And to my unofficial editors David and Tom Isaacs, Tim Knapp and Lucy Fiske; you performed the most laborious (but least recognised) part of the book-writing process. Your hard work and attention to detail were invaluable. Your insights no doubt resulted in a better book, but, most importantly, made me look smarter than I really am.

I am in the fortunate position where my father is also my friend, my writing partner and my fellow advocate. Davey, I couldn't be happier to be sharing this journey with you. Here's to working on more books and campaigns with you.

To Fran Berry, Arwen Summers, Anna Collett and the team at Hardie Grant, for being brave enough to invest in this story of hope, love and peace. Thank you for believing in me and giving me the opportunity to live my dream.

To Lyn Tranter and Australian Literary Management, who gave me a shot all those years ago. Lyn, you continue to be a powerful advocate on my behalf. I hope I'm repaying your faith in me.

In order to write this book I relied upon the expert advice of many people. Thanks must go to Niamatullah Ibrahimi and Linda Briskman, for providing invaluable commentary on Afghan and Iranian history and culture. To Ro Morrow, for your tireless work in communities all over the world. Our planet needs more people like you. And to Antony Lowenstein, for your years of generous expertise and advice.

I'm also grateful to Tom Keneally, Debra Adelaide, Behrouz Boochani and Robin de Crespigny. You offered your services, without question, at the last hour.

This book was written in many cafes, but Bondi Surfish allowed me to occupy a seat in the sun for months on end, buying nothing more than a tea or a juice.

I have been blessed with a multitude of loving friends and family who support me in big and little ways. Without you I'm nothing. While there isn't space to list you all, one family deserve a special mention.

The Sarmeds, my dearest friends, my second family. You introduced me to Afghanistan all those years ago; nobody could have predicted how much that would shape my life. May we enjoy many more years together.

These acknowledgements wouldn't be complete without mentioning the two most important women in my life.

Mum, the older I get the more I understand just how wonderful you are. You're the glue that keeps us all together. I'm proud to call you my mother.

Tika, you are my everything.